GLOBAL RISK MANAGEMENT: FINANCIAL, OPERATIONAL, AND INSURANCE STRATEGIES

INTERNATIONAL FINANCE REVIEW

Series Editor: J. Jay Choi

International Finance Review is an annual book series in the international finance area (broadly defined). The IFR will publish theoretical, empirical, institutional or policy-oriented articles on multinational business finance and strategies, global capital markets and investments, global risk management, global corporate finance and institutions, currency markets and international financial economics, emerging market finance, or related regional or country-specific issues. Each volume generally will have a particular theme. Those interested in contributing an article or editing a volume should contact the series editor or members of the editorial advisory board.

Volume 1: *Asian Financial Crisis: Financial, Structural and International Dimensions*, Editor: J. Choi, Elsevier Science, 2000.

Volume 2: *European Monetary Union and Capital Markets*, Editors: J. Choi and J. Wrase, Elsevier Science, 2001.

EDITORIAL ADVISORY BOARD

INTERNATIONAL FINANCE REVIEW   VOLUME 3

GLOBAL RISK MANAGEMENT: FINANCIAL, OPERATIONAL, AND INSURANCE STRATEGIES

EDITED BY

J. JAY CHOI AND MICHAEL R. POWERS

Temple University, Fox School of Business and Management, Philadelphia, USA

2002

JAI
An Imprint of Elsevier Science

Amsterdam – Boston – London – New York – Oxford – Paris
San Diego – San Francisco – Singapore – Sydney – Tokyo

ELSEVIER SCIENCE Ltd
The Boulevard, Langford Lane
Kidlington, Oxford OX5 1GB, UK

First edition 2002

Library of Congress Cataloging in Publication Data
A catalog record from the Library of Congress has been applied for.

British Library Cataloguing in Publication Data
A catalogue record from the British Library has been applied for.

ISBN: 0-7623-0982-2
ISSN: 1569-3767 (Series)

♾ The paper used in this publication meets the requirements of ANSI/NISO Z39.48-1992 (Permanence of Paper).
Printed in The Netherlands.

CONTENTS

LIST OF CONTRIBUTORS

George Allayannis	Darden Graduate School of Business, University of Virginia, USA
Jean-Pierre Berliet	Actuarial Service Group, Ernst & Young LLP, Hartford, USA
Gordon M. Bodnar	The Paul H. Nitze School of Advanced International Studies, Johns Hopkins University, Washington, D.C., USA
J. Jay Choi	Series Editor, *International Finance Review* and The Fox School, Temple University, Philadelphia, USA
Bhagwan Chowdhry	Center for International Business Education and Research (CIBER), The Anderson School at UCLA, USA
Joon-Hai Chung	Department of Risk, Insurance, and Healthcare Management, The Fox School, Temple University, Philadelphia, USA
E. K. Gatzonas	Department of Economics and Finance, School of Business and Global Studies, La Verne University, Athens, Greece
Llewellyn D. Howell	College of Business Administration, University of Hawaii at Manoa, Honolulu, USA
Joan Lamm-Tennant	General Cologne Re Capital Consultants, Stamford, USA
Richard C. Marston	The Wharton School, University of Pennsylvania, Philadelphia, USA

vii

Michael G. Papaioannou   International Monetary Fund, Washington
                            D.C., USA

Neil D. Pearson   University of Illinois at Urbana-Champaign,
                            USA

Michael R. Powers   The Fox School, Temple University,
                            Philadelphia, USA

David M. Schizer   Columbia University School of Law, New
                            York, USA

Martin Shubik   Cowles Foundation and School of
                            Management, Yale University, New Haven,
                            USA

Mary A. Weiss   The Fox School, Temple University,
                            Philadelphia, USA

James P. Weston   Jones Graduate School of Management, Rice
                            University, Houston, USA

FOREWORD

Risk management has become a wider-ranging and more vital concept as the events of September 11, 2001 have brought the risk of terrorism to the forefront of corporate decisions worldwide. The safety and security of people and physical assets, and the risk of legal liability as a result of acts of terrorism, have come to dominate capital markets as well as insurance and reinsurance markets.

Additionally, the plights of Enron, Andersen, and WorldCom have brought to light other major risk topics formerly placed on the back burner: the accuracy of financial statements, the responsibility of corporate executives, and the broader issue of business ethics that affect the viability of corporations, and more importantly, the entire capitalist system.

Global risk management thus faces both new and not-so-new challenges when such issues become front-page news and affect the entire economy. This volume, although largely written prior to these recent events, provides a major contribution to the ever-evolving concepts of risk and its measurement and management, both in the U.S. and abroad.

I am very pleased that the Institute of Global Management Studies and the Advanta Center for Financial Services Studies, both at the Fox School of Business, held this important conference and brought forth the subsequent proceedings on these critical topics.

My congratulations and thanks to Professors Jay Choi and Michael Powers for their leadership and hard work in bringing the scholars and practitioners together. I have great respect for their scholarship. Their individual and collective contributions have added immensely to this volume and to the discipline of financial risk management.

M. Moshe Porat
Dean and Boettner Professor of Risk Management and Insurance
The Fox School, Temple University

PREFACE

Often viewed as a narrow field focusing on derivatives or insurance, risk management is in fact a much broader discipline, encompassing operational strategies as well as the financial and/or insurance decisions of the firm. This is particularly true for complex business enterprises operating in the international market.

In view of the importance of risk management in practice as well as in the academic literature, the Fox School of Business and Management at Temple University invited leading scholars of finance, risk management, and international business to examine the current status and future direction of global risk management as a discipline.

The conference was held on April 20, 2001 at the Fox School under the auspices of the Institute of Global Management Studies (IGMS) and the Advanta Center for Financial Services Studies, as the *Second Annual International Business Forum* sponsored by the IGMS.

The conference was designed to be international in perspective and comprehensive in coverage. It included discussions of concepts, measurement, and management of various types of risk. Each speaker was asked to make a presentation on one topic within the broad theme that not only would address the state of the art but would also provide insights into specific emerging issues within the chosen topic. Much of this volume is a collection of articles presented at that conference. Because of time restrictions or prior commitments, we regret that original presentations by William Curt Hunter (Federal Reserve Bank, Chicago), Marti Subrahmanyam (New York University), Shaheryar Azhar (Salomon Smith Barney), Mark Carey (Federal Reserve Board), and Cheryl J. Rathbun (Citicorp) were not able to be included. Still, this volume gathers together twelve significant papers, including the keynote presentation of distinguished economist and game-theorist Martin Shubik (Yale University). It is hoped that this collection will provide a new research agenda for the risk management discipline, as well as a source of reference for scholars, practitioners, and graduate students.

We would like to thank a number of people who were instrumental in the success of the conference and this book. We thank Dean M. Moshe Porat and Senior Associate Dean Rajan Chandran for their strong support of the conference as well as the IGMS and Advanta Center at the Fox School. We appreciate the leadership and support of Arvind Phatak, the Executive Director of IGMS and now also the Director of the Center for International Business Education and Research (CIBER). The conference and book are part of the efforts of the IGMS that brought the CIBER to the Fox School, and resulted in the recognition of Dean Porat as "Dean of the Year" by the Academy of International Business. We also thank Melissa Wieczorek and Amanda Brennan of the IGMS, and Piyawadee Khovidhunkit of the Advanta Center, for their highly effective organizational assistance. Finally, we thank Trudy McGinley and Piyawadee Khovidhunkit for their assistance with the preparation of the manuscript, and Wencke Boerrigter and Monique Wilbers of the Elsevier editorial staff for their continued support.

J. Jay Choi
Michael R. Powers
Editors

PART I:
CONCEPTS, MEASUREMENT, AND MANAGEMENT OF RISK

1. GLOBAL RISK MANAGEMENT: CONCEPTS AND STRATEGIES

J. Jay Choi and Michael R. Powers

The term "global risk management" is something of a verbal hologram. Tilt it to one side, and it can be read as "*international* risk management"; tilt it to the other side, and it reads "*comprehensive* risk management." While this semantic duality may be a hindrance in business – e.g. one can imagine a high-priced consultant wincing at the uncomfortable question: "What exactly do you mean by *global* risk management services?" – it is precisely the kind of ambiguity beloved of academic researchers striving for the highest degree of scholarly generality. That is why we chose it for the title of this volume.

By employing the term "global risk management," we clearly desire to capture both obvious meanings: (1) the management of corporate risks in an international setting – i.e. for multinational corporations operating potentially far-flung enterprises; and (2) the management of all corporate risks – financial, property-liability, personnel, political, etc. – in one comprehensive program. However, we also propose to take things one step further, by distilling out the essential abstract concept common to both connotations – i.e. the "breaking down of barriers" that characterizes both international business and comprehensive approaches to business operations.

Over the past fifteen to twenty years, business enterprises (as well as societies in general) around the world have experienced a number of dramatic trends involving the breaking down of barriers. The fall of the Berlin Wall in 1989 provides the most salient physical metaphor for a period that has witnessed massive political, economic, social, and technological change. The democratization of nations throughout the Soviet Bloc and the developing

Global Risk Management: Financial, Operational, and Insurance Strategies,
Volume 3, pages 3–5.
ISBN: 0-7623-0982-2

world, the rise of market-driven economies in China and Eastern Europe, and the ascendancy of free trade worldwide (e.g. NAFTA, the introduction of the Euro, China's entry into the WTO, etc.) have been accompanied by vastly greater access to powerful computers and statistical data, as well as the enhanced personal and business communication made possible by the Internet and wireless technology. With the dramatic events of September 11, 2001, the world saw a further barrier fall: the presumed immunity of the U.S. and other western business communities to terrorist attacks on their home turf.

With these political, economic, social, and technological changes in mind, we therefore use the term "global risk management" to refer to the identification, assessment, accounting, control, financing, and management of risks in a manner necessitated and/or facilitated by any aspect of the dynamic – even volatile – world of the early twenty-first century.

The present volume is divided into four parts, each containing several thought-provoking essays. While most of the pieces were presented in an earlier form at a conference held at Temple University's Fox School in April of 2001, all of the final articles drew inspiration from the cutting-edge work presented at that conference.

Part I of the book is entitled *Concepts, Measurements, and Management of Risk*, and serves as an introduction to the topics of risk and risk management, as well as their broader implications. Immediately following the present chapter, we begin with a "big picture" analysis by **Martin Shubik** (Yale University) of the role of risk in human experience and perception from ancient societies to the modern world. This is followed by an overview of the current use of Value-at-Risk (VaR) techniques, provided by **Neil D. Pearson** (University of Illinois). Finally, **Michael R. Powers** (Temple University) offers a new paradigm for assessing and managing "extreme-event" risk in light of the events of September 11, 2001 and subsequent developments.

Part II addresses various specific issues of *Market, Credit, and Financial Risk*. In the first piece, **Michael G. Papaioannou** (International Monetary Fund) and **E. K. Gatzonas** (La Verne University) provide a VaR assessment of market and credit risks associated with country-specific investment funds. In the second piece, **David M. Schizer** (Columbia University) addresses the impact of legal frictions on hedge fund returns. Lastly, **Bhagwan Chowdhry** (UCLA) discusses the relative advantages and disadvantages of financial vs. operational hedging.

With Part III, we turn to a number of general issues of *International Risk*. First, **Gordon M. Bodnar** (Johns Hopkins University) and **Richard C. Marston** (University of Pennsylvania) provide a "simple" model of foreign-exchange risk. Next, **George Allayannis** (University of Virginia) and **James P.**

Weston (Rice University) discuss the impact of the Asian financial crisis on multinational corporations. Finally, **Llewellyn D. Howell** (University of Hawaii) confronts the problem of managing political risk in a world of international terrorism.

Part IV addresses several general issues associated with *Insuring Risk*. It begins with a presentation by **Jean-Pierre Berliet** (Ernst & Young; formerly with Tillinghast-Towers Perrin) on security measures and their use in determining the capital requirements of insurers. This is followed by a study by **Joan Lamm-Tennant** (GeneralCologne Re) on integrating reinsurance and asset strategies to achieve capital efficiency. The final piece, by **Mary A. Weiss** (Temple University) and **Joon-Hai Chung** (Temple University), discusses issues of quality, capacity, and price in reinsurance markets.

In this age of international terrorism and international economic contagion, it is clear that "globalization" in its broadest sense – i.e. the "breaking down of barriers" – is often a double-edged sword. The world economy of the early twenty-first century offers substantial growth potential and strategic benefits for firms, but it also entails much risk, which must be measured and managed effectively. Consequently, businesses in today's world must constantly be alert to opportunities afforded by improving technology and financial market integration as they seek to develop successful risk management programs.

$G\partial\partial \ D8l$

2. RISK, PUBLIC PERCEPTION, AND EDUCATION: QUANTITATIVE AND QUALITATIVE RISK

Martin Shubik

ABSTRACT

A brief survey of the development of the study of risk and probability is given together with some basic observations on their application to insurance. This is followed with observations on the lack of appreciation of probability studies and an elementary feeling for probability by the public at large and a suggestion that the time is ripe for a new science museum involving basic economics and the exposition of the role of probability in finance.

It is my pleasure to accept the invitation of Professor Michael Powers to address the 2nd annual business research forum. I have divided my discussion into two parts. The first consists of four brief observations, which if fully considered, go a long way towards the appreciation of the study of risk. I then have some remarks on the history of the study of risk and some observations on the state of public perceptions concerning risk and what we might do about them.

My first observation is made at the risk of sounding like Pangloss. The amazing thing about the world we live in is not how bad matters are, but how good they happen to be. When we consider the potential for disaster of almost every variety it seems to me to be a miracle that the world has not destroyed itself. Given the lethality of terrorist groups such as the *Aum Shinrikyo*, why is it that

Global Risk Management: Financial, Operational, and Insurance Strategies,
Volume 3, pages 7–13.
© 2002 Published by Elsevier Science Ltd.
ISBN: 0-7623-0982-2

the largest size of casualties by a terrorist action is still around 300 to 400?[1] Floods, famines, earthquakes, volcanic action, political instability, revolutions, pillage, and plague notwithstanding, we are still here and are even insuring many phenomena. Given the potentials for disaster, why are things so good?

My second observation is at the heart of understanding the evolutionary development of new insurance. The big arbitrages are in concepts not in calculations. The sensible institutionalized incremental improvements involve computations. We do not know how to teach how to re-conceptualize the roles of current practices and procedures and the potential for basically new approaches. But that is where the biggest challenges happen to be.

Third, in a world being more and more buried in statistics and in the speed-of-light transmission of vast data sets it is more and more important that we remind ourselves that it is not what the numbers are, but what the numbers mean that count. Statistical manipulation has its virtue, but basic data conceptualization, gathering and clean up are at least as important as any statistical technique.

My last comment concerns the role of expertise. The trite platitude, "There is no substitute for knowing your business," is by no means a platitude. In teaching mathematical economics, finance and probability, decisions involving risk are treated as though they were lottery tickets. But such a treatment abstracts away the importance of perception, experience and special knowledge which are called for in understanding the important differences in the quality and quantity of risk which exist when dealing with fire or life or marine or other forms of insurance. The imponderables differ, the dimensions of risk differ and are more or less difficult to quantify. The data are of varying difficulty to obtain. The financial system in general is, in part, a perception device and the assessment of risk in particular is highly dependent on the skills in evaluation. There is no substitute for knowing your business.

These four simple points are well known to the perceptive practitioner, but they merit our reminding ourselves of the role they play in framing our perception of risk.

Now we turn to some comments on history.[2] A somewhat surprising aspect of the study of risk is that there do not appear to be any clear references to the concept of probability in China, Egypt, India or Greece yet evidence on gambling abounds. In spite of the long history and evidence of an early form of dice playing (astragals or knucklebones) on Egyptian wall paintings no clear information on odds-making has been found.

In spite of the lack of clear references to probability, the Code of Hammurabi in Mesopotamia of 1800 BC contains references to bottomry or ship insurance and Rome of around 200 A.D. (Ulpian, 225 A.D.) had trade in life insurance policies. It appears that the premia may have been set using some form of life tables. But I am unable to find any evidence on the production or accuracy of such tables. Perhaps one way a seller can insure in a little understood new policy is to err by grossly overcharging thereby losing potential market size but also cutting down on the danger of exposure. Michael Powers (1999) in his encyclopedia article on insurance refers to Vaughan (1997) who notes that Chinese merchants as far back as around 3000 B.C. engaged in splitting cargoes as an elementary way of utilizing the law of large numbers.[3]

A reasonable conjecture as to why we find no probability calculations in early civilizations with gambling is that such calculations require easy arithmetic and algebraic operations and these in turn require a decent arithmetic notation at least advanced enough to have the concept of zero well established. It took until 1202 in Europe where the publication by Fibonacci of *Liber Abaci* introduced arabic numerals into Europe. But it required several centuries before this superior notation took over in Europe.

In 1494 Fra Luca Pacioli published his great *Summa de Arithmetica* in which the first formal scholarly description of double entry bookkeeping was given. It also contained a nicely posed probabilistic problem in Balla that remained an open problem for many years. Individuals A and B are playing a game where the first to win 6 times wins. They quit after the score is 5–3. They decide to split the stakes. How should the stakes be split?

In 1525 Cardano in *Liber de Ludo Alea* provided a publication of gambling probabilities and was the first to raise the idea of degrees of belief. Over a hundred years later, in 1657 Huygens published his book on probability and the interchanges between Pascal, Chevalier de Mere and Fermat provided much of the basis for the modern calculation of probabilities and with it a suggested just division for the *balla* problem.

Two developments which are of considerable importance to modern risk assessment and to economics were provided in 1703 and 1708. The first was by Jacob Bernouilli with his concern for the "Quality of Probability". He considered the difference between the view of the odds concerning the playing of dice vs. the odds involving life expectancy, thus formulating the key problem in the use of probability calculations which links to applications in the study of risk and insurance today. This is possibly nicely posed in considering the difference between making a choice between guessing the color of a ball selected from an urn where you are told there are 50 red balls and 50 black and another urn where all that you know are that there is an unknown mix of red and black.

"How can I be lost if I do not care where I am going?" This phrase reminds us that it not merely uncertainty but the importance (or lack of importance) of the uncertainty that must be taken into account when considering insurance. The Saint Petersburg paradox posed in 1738 by Daniel Bernouilli provided an explicit link between probability and utility. Even recently there have been open questions on Bernouilli's model and on the measurement of the utility of wealth (Menger, 1967).

In 1764 there was a posthumous publication of Thomas Bayes *Essay towards solving a problem in the doctrine of chances* which contributed the logical structure to the problem of updating contingent probabilities as new information is received.

Probability theory is an elegant part of mathematics. But insurance requires not merely the computation and the logical understanding of well-defined chance events, but the evaluation of risk. Thus, a critical role is played in the evolution of sampling and statistical considerations for life, fire and other tables. Before the Romans there appears to be little evidence of life tables, and after the Romans a considerable time elapsed until formal tables were constructed.

The modern approach began in 1662 with the publication by John Graunt of *Natural and Political Observations made upon the Bills of Mortality:* Births and deaths in London 1604–1661. The great English economist Petty in 1674 provided an estimate of life expectancy at birth in London of 18. In 1693 Halley provided life tables based on population of Breslau for which there were particularly good statistics and in 1725 De Moivre *Annuities upon lives* was published.

In 1661 an event in accounting took place that cannot be ignored in risk assessment. The East India Company which before this date had distributed any returns from an individual ship voyage to the owners, switched to paying dividends out of retained earning and thus opened the era of accrual accounting together with its attendant judgment calls and risk assessments.

Post 1700 it is customary to talk about the industrial revolution. It is possibly more accurate to talk about the financial and industrial revolutions. Events crowded upon events. A few are noted. In 1687 Lloyds was founded. In 1696 Lloyds shipping list was published. The Bank of England and stock markets appeared around 1700. By 1720 the Royal Exchange Assurance and London Assurance were formed. In North America in 1751 the Ben Franklin Fire Assurance Company was formed and in 1759 Presbyterian Ministers Fund was opened in Philadelphia.

This brief sketch is provided in a compact form not merely to save time, but to give a feeling for the twin evolution of probability theory and the application of risk management. They are allied but different activities. The science of probability has developed impressively, but the art of odds estimation in many areas is still an art dependent on conceptualization and aided by measurement. In the modern world more and more random or uncertain events are under consideration for risk assessment ranging from insurance for snow on the ski slopes to sickness caused by radon, or problems with the disposal of nuclear waste or "what are the real odds" in the dangers from asbestos or smoking (see Shubik, 1991).

When we turn to some of the problems in the conceptualization of risk, at the least we need to distinguish exogenous risk, risk generated by natural phenomena such as weather, from strategic risk, which is the risk generated by the actions of others in a situation which may be modeled as a game of strategy.

We also need to distinguish between risk taking by individuals acting for their own accounts from risk taking by fiduciaries, frequently acting for aggregates of individuals with varying risk preferences. Much of economic life and many military actions involve making risk decisions involving other peoples' money and lives.

Perhaps one of the central concepts in the understanding of probability is the state space or the set of all possible outcomes. Although it is elementary and basic it is not intuitively grasped by most individuals The debate between objective and subjective probability involves an understanding of the nature of the observations and perceptions made in the construction of the state space.

Risk assessment is an integral part of forecasting and the key to forecasting involves the specifying the dimensions of risk and the empirical problem of selecting the right subset of variables to study. We may teach elementary economics or probability theory regarding risky choices as abstract lottery tickets but if our concern is with application we soon realize that the reason why there are divisions in insurance such as: Fire, Marine, Casualty, Life, Health, Automobile, . . . etc., is because each requires a different body of substantive knowledge. Tasks such as attempting to insure political risk or country risk still require a high mix of art with science. The development of new financial derivatives calls not merely for advanced probability calculations but for an understanding and skill in cutting up the carcass of risk much in the way a good butcher knows how to carve out the different cuts of beef. Expertise, special data and finer perceptions than the average are called for.

I have suggested that special skills are required in risk assessment. But it is also important to note that the professions who offer our society their skills in risk assessment owe it to themselves and the society to help to educate the public at large concerning the many existing misperceptions. A few are noted:

The odds are 50:1 or 2%?

You meet a boy who tells you that he has a sibling. What is the probability his sibling is male or female? Is it 50% as many individuals would guess?

What is the probability of tossing a Heads after four Heads have been tossed in sequence?

Does the contextual framing of the odds make any difference? If you are told that there will be 10 deaths out of 100 will you make the same decision if you are briefed that 90 out of 100 will survive?

Are losses treated as the negative of gains or are they qualitatively different?

You are told that after a large number of tosses of a fair coin Heads has appeared 10 more times than Tails; what is the expected number of tosses required for the number of Tails to equal Heads?

It would appear that most individuals have little intuition concerning small probability events. Furthermore probability, social psychology and game theory all come together in trying to understand crowd or herd behavior. This includes the existence of stock market and other panics.

Another critical problem which remains a mystery to all of us concerns the role of hope and morale. How do they influence the odds?

We have much to learn ourselves about the subtleties of risk assessment, but we also have much to teach. Finance in general and insurance in particular are critical aspects of every day modern life. Although we have science museums and educational programs of every variety in the physical sciences, in economics, finance and risk assessment we have no major science museum and few public educational programs on topics which influence virtually everyone in everyday life. It is my belief that the professionals, educational and financial institutions of our society owe it to themselves and the society to narrow the gap between public perception and professional understanding. The time is ripe for a new science museum and we should be building it.

NOTES

1. Since this talk the number has gone to 4,000, which is still low by what I had expected in my study of terrorism (Shubik, 1997).

2. A well-written and popular overview of the history of risk by Bernstein (1996) provides an overall coverage up to current times, but I find that the description of the many highly technical developments in the 20th century somewhat problematical. Hald (1990) and Stigler (1986) provide good, less popular treatments.

3. I note that Vaughan (1997) does not provide a source for the original research.

REFERENCES

Bernstein, P. L. (1996). *Against the Gods.* New York: Wiley.

Hald, A. (1990). *A History of Probability and Statistics and Their Applications Before 1750.* New York: Wiley.

Menger, K. (1967). Essays in Mathematical Economics in Honor of Oskar Morgenstern. In: M. Shubik (Ed.). Princeton: Princeton University Press.

Powers, M. R. (1999). Insurance. *Encyclopedia of Electrical and Electronics Engineering, 10,* 340–351.

Shubik, M. (1997). Terrorism, Technology and the Socioeconomics of Death. *Comparative Strategy, 16*(4), October–December, 399–414.

Shubik, M. (Ed.) (1995). Proceedings of the Conference: Accounting and Economics in honor of the 500th Anniversary of the Publication of Luca Pacioli's Summa de Arithmetica, Geometria, Proportioni et Proportionalita, Siena, 18th-19th, 1992. New York: Garland Publishing.

Shubik, M. (Ed.) (1991). *Risk, Organizations, and Society: Studies in Risk and Uncertainty.* Norwell, MA: Kluwer Academic Publishers.

Stigler, S. M. (1986). *The History of Statistics: The Measurement of Uncertainty Before 1900.* Cambridge, MA: Belknap Press.

Vaughan, E. J. (1997). *Risk Management.* New York: Wiley.

3. WHAT'S NEW IN VALUE-AT-RISK? A SELECTIVE SURVEY

Neil D. Pearson

1. INTRODUCTION

The risk measurement techniques of value-at-risk and stress testing are by now well established. Even though the phrase "value-at-risk" was almost unknown outside the large derivatives dealers until its appearance in the Group of Thirty report published in July 1993 (Group of Thirty, 1993), and the release of the first version of RiskMetrics in October 1994 (Morgan Guaranty Trust Company, 1994), by now it is difficult to find financial professionals unfamiliar with value-at-risk. Currently banks of all types and sizes, brokerage firms, fund managers, pension plans and other institutional investors, insurance companies, other financial institutions, non-financial corporations, and even regulators use value-at-risk. The complementary risk measurement methodology of stress testing used in conjunction with value-at-risk is almost equally well accepted.

At the outset, three approaches to computing value-at-risk were proposed: the delta-Normal or variance-covariance method; historical simulation; and (full) Monte Carlo simulation, which requires repricing the entire portfolio for each factor realization.[1] While these three techniques remain the workhorses of value-at-risk computations, the years since the initial release of RiskMetrics have witnessed the development of significant refinements of and elaborations upon these approaches, as well as a few alternatives to them. This paper provides a selective survey of recent developments in the methodologies for computing value-at-risk and selecting scenarios for stress testing. The next section briefly reviews some new computational approaches to overcome some

Global Risk Management: Financial, Operational, and Insurance Strategies,
Volume 3, pages 15–37.
Copyright © 2002 by Elsevier Science Ltd.
ISBN: 0-7623-0982-2

of the limitations of the original three methodologies, and then Section 3 turns to the issue of evaluating the performance of a value-at-risk model, i.e. "backtesting." Section 4 describes a new approach for selecting stress scenarios, while Sections 5 and 6 discuss elaborations of value-at-risk, namely adjusting VaR for liquidity and decomposing a VaR estimate to measure the contributions of the various positions or components of a portfolio. Section 7 briefly describes an alternative approach to computing value-at-risk using extreme value theory, while Section 8 concludes by discussing some conceptual problems with value-at-risk and a new class of risk measures which has been proposed as an alternative.

2. IMPROVEMENT IN SPEED AND ACCURACY

From the outset Monte Carlo simulation has been the preferred approach for computing value-at-risk, due to its ability (in contrast to the delta-Normal method) to measure accurately the risk of portfolios with significant options content and the lack of any need for the large historical samples (and attendant assumption of stable volatilities) required by historical simulation. In addition, stress testing and sensitivity analysis fit naturally within the framework of the Monte Carlo method. However, a significant drawback is that, for real-world portfolios, implementation of the Monte Carlo simulation method can be complex and often requires significant computer resources. As a result, researchers have focused attention on approximation methods to compute the VaR of options portfolios without simulation and ways to increase the speed of Monte Carlo simulations.

A limitation of the delta-Normal method is that it amounts to replacing the portfolio by a linear approximation, and then computing the value-at-risk of the linear approximation. Thus, use of the delta-Normal method leads to significant errors in the value-at-risk estimate when the portfolio value is a highly nonlinear function of the underlying market factors, because in such cases a linear approximation will not adequately capture the risks of the portfolio. The delta-gamma-Normal and delta-gamma-theta-Normal methods originally due to Zangari (1996a, b) represent a natural next step in that they use second-order or quadratic approximations of the portfolio value function.[2] This approach involves computing the first four moments (mean, variance, skewness, and kurtosis) of the second-order approximation to the value of the portfolio, and then finding another a flexible distribution that matches these four moments. Once this has been done, the value-at-risk is then computed from that flexible distribution.[3]

The delta-gamma and delta-gamma-theta Monte Carlo methods described in Duffie and Pan (1997) also use second order approximations, but in a different way. Specifically, they begin by computing a delta-gamma or delta-gamma-theta approximation of the portfolio value. Then, the approximation is used to revalue the portfolio for each "draw" of the market factors in the simulation. Using the approximation to revalue the portfolio avoids valuing each of the instruments for each of the thousands of draws in the simulation. Even though computing the derivatives in the second order approximation may be of equal or greater difficulty than computing the portfolio value, the approach saves greatly on computation because the derivatives need only be computed once. Through this mechanism, the method breaks the link between the number of draws in the Monte Carlo and the number of times the portfolio must be revalued.

A limitation of the preceding methods is their dependence on local approximations (i.e. Taylor series), the errors of which typically increase with the size of the realizations of the changes in the risk factors. An alternative approach is a grid Monte Carlo method. In this approach, market factor changes are generated as in the full and delta-gamma Monte-Carlo approaches. The difference is that the portfolio is revalued only on the nodes of a grid of factor value realizations, with linear interpolation used to revalue the portfolio for factor realizations that fall between the nodes. Unfortunately, a naive grid approach that reflected changes in all of the market factors would be of very high dimension. For example, a grid constructed for 9 possible values of 20 market factors results in $9^{20} = 1.218 \times 10^{19}$ nodes. While this breaks the link between the number of draws in the Monte Carlo simulation and the number of times the portfolio must be revalued is broken, it does so in the wrong way: the number of times the portfolio must be revalued exceeds the number of draws.

Modified grid Monte Carlo described in Pritsker (1997) addresses this problem by limiting the factors to be modeled on the grid to those factors involving the most severe nonlinearities, with the effect of the other factors on portfolio value captured by a first (or higher) order Taylor series. The gains from this are large if nonlinearities are important for only a small number of factors, but not otherwise. Principal components grid Monte Carlo due to Frye (1998) addresses this issue by using the method of principal components to reduce the number of factors. For example, the first three principal components, often interpreted as level, slope, and curvature, explain most of the risk of changes in interest rate term structures. By using only the first few principal components as factors, the number of nodes on the grid is reduced – e.g. using 9 possible changes in the term structure level, 5 possible changes in slope, and 3 possible changes in curvature,[4] there would be only $9 \times 5 \times 3 = 135$ nodes.

These grid Monte Carlo methods are satisfactory if the approximate portfolio values computed by linear interpolation from the grid are adequate. However, they are less useful for portfolios of instruments such as options on individual common stocks, for which the residual risk not explained by factor models can be important.

Scenario simulation due to Jamshidian and Zhu (1997) takes a slightly different approach. It breaks the link between the number of Monte Carlo draws and number of portfolio repricings by approximating the distributions of changes in the factors rather than by approximating the portfolio value. First, principal components analysis is used to reduce the number of factors. Each risk factor is then assumed to take only a small number of distinct values, leading to a small (or, at least manageable) number of possible scenarios, each corresponding to a portfolio value that needs to be computed only once. Monte Carlo simulation is then used to sample among these scenarios, reducing the number of portfolio revaluations required.

These approaches described above are meant to capture nonlinearity in the portfolio value without incurring the computational burden of the full Monte Carlo method. For the historical simulation method the issue is not the computational burden but rather accuracy. While the historical simulation method is well suited to portfolios that include options and does not require the specification of a particular distribution, standard historical simulation is subject to purely statistical errors or sampling variation because the location of the $1 - a$ percent VaR is determined by where the worst a percent of the outcomes fall. Because this depends on the random past realizations of the market factors, reasonable accuracy can be obtained only by using very large samples of past historical changes. As a result, historical simulation does not do a good job of tracking changes in market volatilities.

Boudoukh, Richardson and Whitelaw (1998) proposed overcoming this drawback by combining historical simulation with exponentially weighted past returns. In particular, the portfolio return n periods in the past is weighted by $c\lambda^{n-1}$, where $\lambda < 1$, the coefficient $c = (1 - \lambda)/(1 - \lambda^N)$ is chosen to make the sum of the weights equal one, and N is the total number of past observations. The weights $c, c\lambda, \ldots c\lambda^{n-1}, \ldots c\lambda^{N-1}$ are used to construct the empirical distribution (histogram) of the returns by acting as if a proportion $c\lambda^{n-1}$ of the observations had profit or loss X_{t-n}, and the VaR estimate is then read off the empirical distribution. While this allows the VaR estimate to reflect recent volatility, it can exacerbate the estimation error, because "deweighting" the past observations using the weights $c\lambda^{n-1}$ is similar to using a smaller sample.

Duffie and Pan (1997) and Hull and White (1998) propose a method to overcome this drawback while still reflecting recent volatility by scaling the past changes in market factors using estimates of current volatilities. This is done by computing daily volatility estimates for every market factor for both the current date and every day during the period covered by the historical data, scaling the historical changes in market factors by the ratios of current to past volatilities, and then using these scaled changes in place of the original ones. Specifically, let t denote the current date, $x_{i,t-n}$ the change in the i-th market factor n days in the past, $\sigma_{i,t-n}$ the estimate of the volatility of the change $x_{i,t-n}$, and $\sigma_{i,t}$ the estimate of the current volatility of the i-th factor. These volatilities may be estimated using either exponentially weighted moving averages of squared returns or GARCH models. The approach is to compute the hypothetical changes in the portfolio value using the scaled changes in market factors $(\sigma_{i,t}/\sigma_{i,t-n})x_{i,t-n}$ (or $\sigma_{i,t}/\sigma_{i,t-n})[(x_{i,t-n}) - E(x_{i,t-n})])$ instead of the (unscaled) changes $x_{i,t-n}$ (or $x_{i,t-n} - E(x_{i,t-n})$), form the empirical distribution (histogram) from the profits and losses computed using the rescaled changes in market factors, and then obtain the VaR estimate from this distribution. The advantage of this approach is that it reflects current estimates of market volatility through the rescaled changes in the market factors, while still using a long historical sample to provide information about the "fatness" of the tails.

3. REFINEMENTS IN BACKTESTING

Value-at-risk estimates are just that: estimates. Errors occur because the distributional assumptions used to compute them may not correspond to the actual distribution of changes in the market factors (and will never correspond *exactly* to the actual distribution of changes in the market factors), because some of the methods are based on approximations to the value of the portfolio, because the estimates are based on past data which need not reflect current market conditions, because some value-at-risk systems will embody logical or computer coding errors of varying degrees of severity, and because it is conceivable that in some situations users will have incentives to introduce biases or errors into value-at-risk estimates. As a result, "backtesting" is crucial to verify model accuracy and identify areas in which improvement is needed.

Underlying the simplest backtesting framework is the idea that, for a $1 - a$ confidence VaR model, one expects to observe "exceptions," i.e. losses greater than the VaR estimate, on a fraction a of the days. For example, if $a = 0.05$ and the model is backtested using the last 250 daily P/L's, the expected number of exceptions is $0.05 \times 250 = 12.5$. Of course, the actual number of exceptions depends on the random outcomes of the underlying market factors in addition to the quality of the VaR model. Even if the VaR model is "correct," the actual number typically will differ from the expected number. This leads to a rule based on a range, determined by the willingness to reject a correct VaR model. For example, if $a = 0.05$ and the model is backtested using the last 250 daily P/L's, there is a probability of 5.85% that the number of exceptions e is outside the range $7 \le e \le 19$. If a probability of rejecting a correct VaR model of 5.85% is tolerable, then the model should be rejected if the number of exceptions is outside this range, and not rejected otherwise.

This simple approach is widely used and is enshrined in Basle framework allowing banks to use internal risk models to determine capital requirements. However, a crucial limitation should be clear – many incorrect VaR models will generate between 7 and 19 exceptions out of 250 returns. For example, for a biased VaR model for which the probability of an exception is actually 7.5%, the probability that the number of exceptions is between 7 and 19 is 58.4%; even the expected number of exceptions, 18.75, is within the range $7 \le e \le 19$. If each day the probability of an exception is 10%, the probability that the total number of exceptions out of 250 returns is between 7 and 19 is 12.1%.[5]

In short, this approach is just not very powerful: a range wide enough that a correct model is rejected with only low probability is so wide that many incorrect models are also rejected with only low probability, while a range narrow enough that most incorrect models are rejected with high probability results in a high probability of rejecting correct models. The situation is even worse if one wants to backtest 99% confidence VaR models.

One way of stating the problem with backtests based on exceptions is that by considering only the exceptions, they ignore much of the information in the sample of returns, i.e. they focus on only one quantile of the distribution, the VaR. As a result, they are inherently not very powerful. However, most value-at-risk models produce an estimate (perhaps implicit) of the entire probability distribution as an intermediate step in computing the value-at-risk. The trick is to exploit this information. The estimated distributions are conditional distributions, which change each day as both the portfolio and volatility estimates change. From each distribution one observes only one realization, the portfolio profit or loss for that day. While at first glance this might not seem like sufficient information to evaluate the VaR model, it is.

If X is a random variable, then knowing its distribution function F amounts to knowing all of its quantiles, e.g. to knowing the quantile x such that $0.01 = P(X \le x)$, the quantile y such that $0.02 = P(X \le y)$, etc. Of course, when using a VaR model the estimates of these quantiles change every day as the estimate of the distribution function changes. Imagine collecting a sample of, say, 500 portfolio returns, computing the (estimates of the) quantiles for each of the 500 days, and then comparing the returns to the estimated quantiles. One expects $5 = 0.01 \times 500$ of the returns to be less than or equal to the 1% quantiles, another 5 to be between the 1% and 2% quantiles, another 5 to be between the 2 and 3% quantiles, etc. It is not necessary that these intervals all contain the same probability; in general, a fraction $F(x) - F(y)$ of the P/L's X should satisfy $y < X \le x$. After picking a set of intervals, one can evaluate the VaR model by comparing the observed proportion of the sample falling into each interval to the proportion that would be expected if the VaR model were correct. This is the same idea that underlies the simple backtests, except that now one looks at many intervals instead of simply the losses that exceed the value-at-risk.

The statement that a fraction $F(x) - F(y)$ of the P/L's X should satisfy $y < X \le x$ is equivalent to the statement that a fraction $F(x)$ should satisfy $X \le x$. But if a fraction $F(x)$ satisfies $X \le x$, then the transformed variable $u = F(X)$ is uniformly distributed on the interval [0,1]. Crnkovic and Drachman (1996) and Diebold, Gunther and Tay (1998) point out that this leads immediately to statistical tests: if the estimate of the distribution function F actually is the distribution function of the P/L X, then the transformed random variable $u = F(X)$ should be distributed uniformly on the interval [0,1]. This can be examined using standard tests of goodness of fit such as the Kolmogorov-Smirnov test.

Berkowitz (1999) suggests extending this approach by introducing another transformation to create Normal random variables. If F is the distribution function of a random variable z, and the transformed random variable $u = F(z)$ is uniformly distributed on [0,1], then the random variable $z = F^{-1}(u)$ has the distribution F, where F^{-1} is the inverse of F. Applying this idea to the standard Normal distribution function N, the random variable $z = N^{-1}(u)$ has a standard Normal distribution. This observation, together with the earlier one that $u = F(X)$ is uniformly distributed if F is the distribution function of X, implies that if F is the distribution function of X then the transformed random variable

$$z = N^{-1}(u) = N^{-1}(F(X)) \tag{1}$$

has a standard Normal distribution. Also, the z's from different dates should be independent, i.e. z_{t+j} should be independent of z_t for $j > 0$.

The transformation in Eq. (2) is convenient, because it sets the problem in the standard Gaussian likelihood-based testing framework. Whether F correctly describes the location and dispersion of the P/L X can be evaluated by testing whether the mean and variance of z are zero and one, respectively, while whether it captures the "fatness" of the tails of the distribution of returns can be tested by nesting the Normal distribution within a fat-tailed family such as the t-distribution that includes the Normal as a special case. Results in

Berkowitz (1999) indicate that these tests have reasonable power to detect biased VaR models with as few as 100 observations.

A second problem with simple backtests is that to pass them a VaR model need only be correct "on average."[6] For example, consider a model that generates a VaR of $100 billion on every day but the 100th day when it generates a VaR of $0. Since this model would at most generate an exception on every 100th day and on only 2 or 3 days out of every 250 it would pass simple backtests, even though it provides no useful risk information. A more realistic example is a VaR model that does not fully respond to changes in market volatility, thereby producing downward-biased estimates during high volatility periods and upward-biased estimates during low volatility periods.

A nice feature of Berkowitz's approach described above is that it can also identify model failures of this kind. Specifically, if the VaR model correctly captures the conditional distribution of profit and loss on each date, the z's for different dates defined in Eq. (2) should be independent. Time-series dependence among the z's for different dates can be evaluated by testing that the autocorrelation coefficient is zero. If one is interested exclusively in a certain part of the distribution such as one tail, it is possible to base tests on the truncated Normal distribution.

4. LIQUIDITY-ADJUSTED VALUE-AT-RISK AND OTHER DYNAMIC TRADING STRATEGIES

Standard VaR measures the risk of a portfolio over a fixed, usually short, holding period. Inherent in it is the implicit assumption that the risk can be eliminated by the end of the holding period, by either liquidating or hedging the portfolio. In periods of market illiquidity, this implicit assumption may not be valid. Even in normal periods it is unlikely to be valid for all assets. Dembo, Aziz, Rosen and Zerbs (2000) point out that in the Monte Carlo framework this issue can be addressed through the computation of Liquidity-adjusted VaR (LaVaR).

LaVaR recognizes that there are limits to the rate at which a portfolio can be liquidated. To illustrate its computation, consider a portfolio of only a single asset and assume that only b units of the asset can be sold each day; e.g. a 100-unit portfolio requires $n = 100/b$ days to liquidate. If liquidation of the portfolio becomes necessary, a possible strategy would be to liquidate b units each day and invest the proceeds at the risk-free rate r. The proceeds from selling the b units are thus no longer exposed to market risk, while the positions that have not yet been liquidated remain so exposed. Under this liquidation strategy, b units are exposed to market risk for one day and then invested at the risk-free rate r for the remaining $n - 1$ days; another b units would be exposed to market risk for two days and then invested at r for $n - 2$ days; another b units would be exposed to market risk for three days and then invested at r for $n - 3$ days; etc. If the initial price per unit is S_0 and the return on the i-th day is r_i at the end of n days this strategy results in a liquidated value of

$$bS_0\left[(1+r_1)(1+r)^{n-1} + (1+r_1)(1+r_2)(1+r)^{n-2} + (1+r_1)(1+r_2)(1+r_3)^{n-3} \right.$$

$$\left. + \ldots + \prod_{i=1}^{n}(1+r_i) \right].$$

LaVaR is then obtained by estimating the distribution of this liquidated value, similar to the way standard VaR is obtained by estimating the distribution of the mark-to-market portfolio value. Since LaVaR measures portfolio risk over an n-day horizon, it follows that LaVaR will exceed a standard VaR over a one-day horizon whenever $n > 1$ but will be less than standard VaR over an n-day horizon.

Realistic implementations of LaVaR will allow for different liquidation rates for different securities, and can incorporate the fact that illiquidity is correlated with extreme market movements by making the liquidation rates depend on the outcomes for the market factors. A few seconds of thought lead to the insight that liquidating a portfolio is only one possible dynamic trading strategy. An approach that allows for gradual portfolio liquidation can also handle other dynamic trading strategies, for example reinvesting coupons or dividends or rebalancing hedges. Thus, it becomes possible to overcome the limitation that value-at-risk measures the risk of the *current* portfolio, and does not reflect any changes to the portfolio that might be made during the holding period. An issue is that doing this requires that the dynamic trading strategy be specified, which may be difficult or impossible. A further drawback is that LaVaR and similar calculations require simulation of the entire sample path of each of the market factors, increasing the computational burden of the calculation.

5. RISK DECOMPOSITION

Meaningful use of value-at-risk almost requires risk decomposition.[7] Value-at-risk, or any other risk measure, is useful only to the extent that one understands the sources of risk. For example, how much of the total firm or portfolio risk is due to each position, trading desk, or asset class? If one reduces a position or puts on a hedge, what will be the effect on risk? In fund management, what fraction of the risk is due to tracking error? How much is due to each portfolio manager? These questions can be answered by risk decomposition. To explain it, we require a bit of notation.

Let $w = (w_1, w_2, \ldots w_N)'$ denote the vector of portfolio weights in N instruments or positions, asset classes, trading desks, or portfolio managers, let r_i denote the return on the i-th such instrument or position, and let VaR(w) denote the value at risk, which depends on the positions or weights w_i. Imagine multiplying all of the portfolio weights by the same constant k, i.e. consider the portfolio $kw = (kw_1, kw_2, \ldots kw_N)'$, and the associated value-at-risk measure VaR(kw). A key property of value-at-risk is that scaling all positions by the common factor k scales the value at risk by the same factor, i.e. VaR(kw) = kVaR(w). This is almost obvious, because scaling every position by k clearly scales every profit or loss by k, and thus scales the value at risk by k.

An implication of this scaling property is that value at risk can be decomposed as

$$VaR(w) = \frac{\partial VaR(w)}{\partial w_1} w_1 + \frac{\partial VaR(w)}{\partial w_2} w_2 + \ldots + \frac{\partial VaR(w)}{\partial w_N} w_N, \qquad (2)$$

where the i-th partial derivative $\dfrac{\partial VaR(w)}{\partial w_i}$ is interpreted as the effect on risk of increasing w_i by one unit.[8] Specifically, changing the i-th weight by a small amount from w_i to $w_i{}^*$ changes the risk by approximately $\dfrac{\partial VaR(w)}{\partial w_i} (w_i{}^* - w_i)$.

The i-th term $\dfrac{\partial VaR(w)}{\partial w_i} w_i$ is called the risk contribution of the i-th position, and can be interpreted as measuring the effect of percentage changes in the portfolio weight w_i. For example, the change from w_i to $w_i{}^*$ is a percentage change of $(w_i{}^* - w_i)/w_i$, and the change in the value at risk resulting from this change in the portfolio weight is $\dfrac{\partial VaR(w)}{\partial w_i} (w_i{}^* - w_i) = \dfrac{\partial VaR(w)}{\partial w_i} w_i \times \dfrac{w_i{}^* - w_i}{w_i}$, the product of the risk contribution and the percentage change in the portfolio weight.

A key feature of the risk contributions is that they sum to the portfolio risk, permitting the portfolio risk to be decomposed into the risk contributions of the N positions w_i as in Eq. (2). It is straightforward to compute these risk contributions for delta-Normal VaR given by

$$VaR(w) = -\left[\sum_{i=1}^{N} w_i E[r_i] - c\sigma(w) \right],$$

where the constant c (e.g. $c = 1.645$) is a quantile of the standard Normal distribution.[9] Computing the derivative with respect to the position in the i-th market, we find

$$\frac{\partial VaR(w)}{\partial w_i} = -E[r_i] + c \frac{\partial \sigma(w)}{\partial w_i},$$

where

$$\frac{\partial \sigma(w)}{\partial w_i} = \frac{\sum_{j=1}^{N} w_j \, \text{cov}(r_i, r_j)}{\sigma(w)}$$

and the numerator $\sum_{j=1}^{N} w_j \, \text{cov}(r_i, r_j)$ is the covariance between the return r_i and the portfolio return $\sum_{j=1}^{N} w_j \, r_j$. This implies that the risk contribution of the i-th position is

$$\frac{\partial VaR(w)}{\partial w_i} w_i = -E[r_i] w_i + c \frac{\sum_{j=1}^{N} w_j \, \text{cov}(r_i, r_j)}{\sigma w}$$

$$= -E[r_i] w_i + c\sigma(w)\beta_i,$$

where $\beta_i \equiv \sum_{j=1}^{N} w_j \, \text{cov}(r_i, r_j)/\sigma^2(w)$ is the regression coefficient or beta of the return on the i-th position on the return of the portfolio. The key insight from this is that the risk contribution of the position in the i-th market depends on that position's contribution to the expected return $E[r_i] w_i$, together with the covariance between the return on the i-th position and the portfolio. This second component is zero either when the return on the i-th position is uncorrelated with the portfolio, or when the weight $w_i = 0$.

Computing these risk contributions for the various positions, trading desks, or asset classes allows one to determine the extent to which various positions contribute to the overall portfolio risk. This identifies the portfolio's "hot spots" or areas of particular concern to the risk or portfolio manger, and will help him or her decide what positions to reduce (or increase) if the risk of the portfolio is above (or below) the desired level. Combined with information about expected returns, the risk decomposition can also help optimize the risk-return tradeoff. For example, it can also help the portfolio manager decide if the benefits of altering a position are large enough to justify the transactions costs of trading.

In interpreting the risk decomposition, it is crucial to keep in mind that it is a marginal analysis: a small change in the portfolio weight from w_i to w_i^* changes the risk by approximately $\dfrac{\partial VaR(w)}{\partial w_i}(w_i^* - w_i)$. Alternatively, if the risk decomposition indicates that the i-th position accounts for one-half of the risk, increasing that position by a small percentage will increase risk as much as increasing all other positions by the same percentage. The marginal effects cannot be extrapolated to large changes, because the partial derivatives $\dfrac{\partial VaR(w)}{\partial w_i}$ change as the position sizes change. In terms of correlations, a large change in a position in a market changes the correlation between the portfolio and that market. For example, if the i-th market is uncorrelated with the current portfolio, the risk contribution of a small change in the allocation to the i-th market is zero. However, as the allocation to the i-th market increases, that market comprises a larger fraction of the portfolio, and the portfolio is no longer uncorrelated with the ith market. Thus, the risk contribution of the i-th market increases as the position in that market is increased.

6. IMPROVEMENTS IN STRESS TESTING

At first glance the selection of stress scenarios might seem immune to formal statistical modeling. This is true when selecting scenarios for the core, key risk factors such as the levels of benchmark interest rates or the returns on broad stock market indexes. But once the stress scenarios for these have been specified, recent work has pointed out that statistical tools can be used to determine the scenarios for other factors.

In particular, the predictive stress test described by Kupiec (1998) generates scenarios by combining assumed changes in the core risk factors with the covariance matrix of changes in the market factors to compute the changes in the peripheral market factors. For example, suppose the stress scenario is a U.S. stock market crash, defined as a 20% decline in the S&P 500. Rather than set the changes in the other market factors equal to zero or specify them in an ad hoc fashion, the predictive stress test would use the covariance matrix (and expected changes, if these are non-zero) of the market factors to compute the conditional expectations of the peripheral market factors, and then set them equal to their conditional expectations.

Doing this requires a fact about conditional expectations. Suppose there are K market factors taking values $x = (x_1, x_2, \ldots, x_K)'$, with a $K \times K$ covariance matrix Σ and means given by a $K \times 1$ vector μ. The first $H < K$ market factors are the core factors which will be specified directly in the stress test, while the other $H - K$ are the peripheral factors which will be computed-based on the assumed changes in the first H.

Partition the vector x into the core and peripheral market factors $x^{core} = (x_1, x_2, \ldots, x_H)'$ and $x^{periph} = (x_{H+1}, x_{H+2}, \ldots, x_K)'$ with expected values μ^{core} and μ^{periph}, respectively. Similarly, partition the covariance matrix Σ as

$$\Sigma = \begin{bmatrix} A & B \\ B' & D \end{bmatrix},$$

where A is the $H \times H$ covariance matrix of the core market factors, D is the $(K - H) \times (K - H)$ covariance matrix of the peripheral market factors, and B is the $H \times (K - H)$ matrix formed from the covariances between the core and peripheral factors. Given the outcomes for the core market factors x^{core}, the conditional expected values of the peripheral market factors are given by

$$E[x^{periph} \mid x^{core}] = \mu^{periph} + B'A^{-1}(x^{core} - \mu^{core})$$
$$= \mu^{periph} - B'A^{-1}\mu^{core} + B'A^{-1}x^{core} \qquad (3)$$

If the unconditional expected changes μ^{core} and μ^{periph} are treated as zero this simplifies to

$$E[x^{periph} \mid x^{core}] = B'A^{-1}x^{core}.$$

Equation (3) has a nice intuitive interpretation. Consider $E[x_{h+j} \mid x^{core}]$, *the j*-th element of the vector of conditional expectations $E[x^{periph} \mid x^{core}]$. Equation (3) says that

$$E[x_{H+j} \mid x^{core}] = E[x_{H+j}] - [\sigma_{1,H+j} \cdots \sigma_{H,H+j}]A^{-1}E[x^{core}]$$
$$+ [\sigma_{1,H+j} \, \sigma_{2,H+j} \cdots \sigma_{H,H+j}]A^{-1}x^{core}$$
$$= \beta_{H+j,0} + \sum_{i=1}^{H} \beta_{H+j,i}x_i$$

where the intercept

$$\beta_{H+j,0} = E[x_{H+j}] - [\sigma_{1,H+j} \, \sigma_{2,H+j} \cdots \sigma_{H,H+j}]A^{-1}E[x^{core}]$$

and each coefficient $\beta_{H+j,i}$ is the i-th element of the vector

$$[\sigma_{1,H+j} \, \sigma_{2,H+j} \cdots \sigma_{H,H+j}]A^{-1}.$$

Examination of virtually any econometrics or multivariate statistics book (and recognition that $b'A^{-1}x^{core} = (x^{core})A^{-1}b$ for all vectors b) reveals that $\beta_{H+j,i}$ is the i-th slope coefficient in the regression of the j-th peripheral factor x_{H+j} on the core market factors, and $\beta_{H+j,0}$ is the intercept. Thus, the values of the peripheral factors in the predictive stress tests are the forecasts of these market factors that would be obtained by regressing each of the peripheral market factors on the core market factors.

The principal advantage of this approach is that it results in generally sensible stress scenarios that are consistent with the volatilities and correlations used in the value-at-risk calculation. The disadvantage, aside from the additional complexity of using the covariance matrix, is that the covariance matrix may change during periods of market stress. If this is the case, then the changes in the peripheral market factors are computed using the "wrong" covariance matrix. This last drawback can be addressed by combining the predictive stress test with a separate estimate of the covariance matrix that applies during periods of market stress.

This seems straightforward, but where does one obtain the estimates of correlations during stress scenarios? The broken arrow stress test recently proposed by Kim and Finger (2000) involves assuming that the available data on factor changes represent a mixture of realizations from stressed and non-stressed market environments, and estimating a statistical model that allows for different covariance matrices in the different market environments. This approach results in generally sensible stress scenarios that are consistent with the data from past periods of market stress, and thus defensible. However, the complexity of the procedure is a drawback.

7. ANOTHER FRAMEWORK FOR COMPUTING VaR: EXTREME VALUE THEORY

It is well known that the actual distributions of changes in market rates and prices have "fat tails" relative to the Normal distribution, implying that an appropriately fat-tailed distribution would provide better value-at-risk estimates for high confidence levels. However, since by definition the data contain relatively few extreme observations, we have little information about the tails. As a result, selecting a reasonable fat-tailed parametric distribution and estimating the parameters that determine the thickness of the tails are inherently difficult tasks.

Extreme value theory (EVT) has recently attracted a great deal of attention because it offers a potential solution to the problem of estimating the tails. Loosely, EVT tells us that the behavior of certain extreme values is the same (i.e. described by a particular parametric family of distributions), regardless of the distribution that generates the data.[10]

One important class of models in EVT are known as *peaks over threshold* (POT) models.[11] These are based on a mathematical result that, for a large class of distributions, extreme realizations above a high (or below a low) threshold are described by a particular distribution, the generalized Pareto distribution. Thus, EVT solves the problem of how to model the tails: they are described by the generalized Pareto distribution, regardless of the distribution that generates the data. Since knowing the tail of the distribution is exactly what is required for value-at-risk estimates at high confidence levels, the applicability of this result to value-at-risk calculations is clear.

To describe the use of EVT in computing value-at-risk we first need to introduce a bit of notation. Let X be the random variable under consideration (e.g. a mark-to-market loss), and use F to denote its distribution function. Consider a threshold u, and define $X - u$ to be the excess loss over the threshold. The conditional distribution function $F(x \mid X > u)$ gives the conditional probability that the excess loss $X - u$ is less than x, given that the loss exceeds u. It follows that $1 - F(x \mid X > u)$ is the conditional probability that the excess $X - u$ exceeds x.

The key result underlying POT models is that in the limit as the threshold $u \rightarrow \infty$ the conditional distribution function $F(x \mid X > u)$ approaches the generalized Pareto distribution (GPD) given by

$$
G(x) = \begin{cases} 1 - \left(1 + \xi \dfrac{x}{\beta}\right)^{-1/\xi} & \text{if } \xi \neq 0, \\[3mm] 1 - \exp\left(-\dfrac{x}{\beta}\right) & \text{if } \xi = 0, \end{cases}
$$

where $x \geq 0$ if $\xi \geq 0$ and $0 \leq x < -\beta/\xi$ if $\xi < 0$. The parameter ξ is a shape parameter that determines the fatness of the tail, while β is an additional scaling parameter. The GPD is generalized in that it subsumes three distributions as special cases: if the shape parameter $\xi > 0$, it is equivalent to the ordinary Pareto distribution, used in insurance as a model for large losses; if $\xi = 0$, it is the exponential distribution; and if $\xi < 0$, it is the Pareto type II distribution.

The case $\xi > 0$ is the one most relevant for financial data, as it corresponds to heavy tails. Considering this case, the preceding equation implies that the conditional probability that the excess loss $X - u$ is greater than x is approximated by

$$P(X - u > x \mid X > u) \approx 1 - G(x) = \left(1 + \xi \frac{x}{\beta}\right)^{-1/\xi}, \tag{4}$$

where $P(A)$ is the probability of the event A. Of course in applications one cannot actually let the threshold $u \to \infty$. Instead, one picks a threshold high enough to "approximate" infinity, and above that threshold treats Eq. (4) as though it holds exactly. Doing this, the unconditional probability that the excess loss is greater than a number x, depends on the probability that the random variable X exceeds u, and is given by

$$P(X - u > x) = P(X > u)P(X - u > x \mid X > u)$$

$$\approx P(X > u)\left(1 + \xi \frac{x}{\beta}\right)^{-1/\xi} \tag{5}$$

Thus, provided u is chosen to be large enough that the approximation in Eqs (4) and (5) is sufficiently accurate, it is possible to compute value-at-risk without knowledge of the distribution that describes the data.

It turns out that it is reasonably straightforward to estimate the threshold u above which the GPD provides a good approximation, and also straightforward to estimate the parameters β and ξ. Then, using the obvious fact that $P(X - u > x) = P(X > u + x)$, the $1 - a$ percent confidence value-at-risk is the number $VaR = u + x$ such that

$$a = P(X > VaR)$$

$$= P(X > u + x)$$

$$= P(X > u)\left(1 + \xi \frac{x}{\beta}\right)^{-1/\xi}$$

$$= P(X > u)\left(1 + \xi \frac{VaR - u}{\beta}\right)^{-1/\xi},$$

implying that

$$VaR = u + \frac{\beta}{\xi}\left[\left(\frac{a}{P(X > u)}\right)^{-\xi} - 1\right].$$

Typically it is straightforward to estimate the probability of exceeding the threshold $P(X > u)$, allowing the value-at-risk to be computed from this formula.

Evidence in Neftci (2000) and McNeil and Frey (2000) suggests that the GPD provides a good fit to the tails of the distributions of changes in individual market factors, and EVT appears to be useful in measuring credit risk when there is a single important factor (Parisi, 2000). However, the available empirical evidence does not bear directly on the question of whether EVT is useful for measuring the VaR of portfolios that depend (perhaps non-linearly) on multiple sources of risk. Classical EVT is "univariate," i.e. it does not characterize the joint distribution of multiple risk factors. To apply EVT to portfolios that depend on multiple sources of risk, one must estimate the distribution of profit and loss by historical simulation, and then fit the GPD to the tail of the distribution of profit and loss. This is straightforward, but requires that one accept most of the limitations of the historical simulation method. Also, the available empirical evidence does not bear directly on the question of whether EVT is useful for measuring the VaR of portfolios that depend (perhaps non-linearly) on multiple sources of risk.

8. COHERENT RISK MEASURES

Value-at-risk was criticized from the outset because it says nothing about the magnitude of losses greater than the value-at-risk estimate. Artzner, Delbaen, Eber and Heath (hereafter, ADEH) (1997, 1999) have recently offered a subtler, and much deeper, criticism: value-at-risk does not correctly aggregate risk across portfolios. Combined with another property that ADEH argue any reasonable risk measure must possess, this implies that value-at-risk does not correctly capture the effect of diversification. Ironically, aggregating risk across portfolios and capturing the benefits of diversification are two of the commonly cited advantages of value-at-risk.

As a substitute for value at risk, ADEH propose a new class of risk measures that they call *coherent*. They argue that one should restrict attention to coherent risk measures because only such measures are consistent with certain basic properties that any reasonable risk measure must have. Value-at-risk is a coherent risk measure if the possible changes in portfolio value are described by the Normal distribution, but not generally.

To see the problems with value-at-risk, consider two portfolios of digital puts and calls on the same underlying asset, price, or rate. Portfolio A consists of $400,000 in cash and a short digital put with a notional amount of $10 million, a 4% probability of being exercised, and time to expiration equal to the time

horizon of the value at risk estimate. Portfolio B consists of $400,000 in cash
together with a short digital call with a notional amount of $10 million, a 4%
probability of being exercised, and a time to expiration equal to the time
horizon of the value at risk estimate. Assume for simplicity that the interest rate
is zero, and that the risk-neutral probabilities of exercise of both options are
also 4%. These assumptions imply that the current mark-to-market values of
the two portfolios are both $400,000 − 0.04($10,000,000) = $0.

For both portfolios, the probability distribution of possible profits and losses
over the time horizon of the value-at-risk estimate is

$$\text{profit} = \begin{cases} \$400,000 & \text{with probability } 0.96, \\ -\$10,000,000 & \text{with probability } 0.04. \end{cases}$$

Because the probability of a loss is only 4%, 95% value-at-risk measures would
indicate that the two portfolios have no risk. To see a less obvious problem,
consider the aggregate portfolio consisting of the sum of portfolios A and B,
and the diversified portfolio consisting of one half of portfolio A and one half
of portfolio B. Because the digital put and call will not both be exercised, the
distribution of profit and loss for the aggregate portfolio is

$$\text{profit of aggregate portfolio} = \begin{cases} \$800,000 & \text{with probability } 0.92, \\ -\$10,000,000 & \text{with probability } 0.08. \end{cases}$$

and the distribution of profit and loss for the diversified portfolio is

$$\text{profit of diversified portfolio} = \begin{cases} \$400,000 & \text{with probability } 0.92, \\ -\$5,000,000 & \text{with probability } 0.08. \end{cases}$$

Thus, the 95% confidence value-at-risk measures of the aggregate and
diversified portfolios are $10 million and $5 million, respectively. The problem
is that the value-at-risk of the aggregate portfolio exceeds the sum of the value-
at-risk measures of portfolios A and B (which are both zero), and the
value-at-risk estimate of the diversified portfolio exceeds the average of
the value-at-risk estimates of portfolios A and B. ADEH argue that no
reasonable risk measure can have these properties, implying that value-at-risk
cannot be a reasonable risk measure.

To replace value at risk, ADEH propose a new class of risk measures they
call "coherent." The setup in ADEH (1997, 1999) is a capital market with
a finite number K of outcomes or "states of the world." Let x and y be

K-dimensional vectors representing the possible state-contingent payoffs of two different portfolios, $p(x)$ and $p(y)$ the portfolios' risk measures, a and b arbitrary constants (with $a > 0$), and r the risk-free interest rate. ADEH argue that any reasonable risk measure should satisfy the following four properties:

(i) $p(x + y) \leq p(x) + p(y)$;   (sub-additivity)
(ii) $p(aX) = ap(X)$;   (homogeneity)
(iii) $p(X) \geq p(Y)$, if $X \leq Y$ (monotonicity)
(iv) $p(x + b(1 + r)) = p(x) - b$ (risk-free condition)

Property (i) says that the risk measure of an aggregate portfolio must be less than or equal to the sum of the risk measures of the smaller portfolios which comprise it, and ensures that the risk measure should reflect the impact of hedges or offsets.

Property (ii) says that the risk measure is proportional to the scale of the portfolio, e.g. halving the portfolio halves the risk measure. Properties (i) and (ii) together imply that the risk of a diversified portfolio must be less than or equal to the appropriate weighted average of the risks of the instruments or sub-portfolios that comprise the diversified portfolio. For example, if the payoff of a diversified portfolio is $z = wx + (1 - w)y$, where w and $1 - w$ are the weights on two sub-portfolios with payoffs x and y, then properties (i) and (ii) require that $p(z) \leq wp(x) + (1 - w)p(y)$. Risk measures that do not satisfy these conditions fail to capture the benefits of diversification.

Property (iii) says it is good to receive cash. Specifically, if the portfolio with payoffs y dominates that with payoffs x in the sense that each element of y is at least as large as the corresponding element of x (i.e. $x \leq y$), then the portfolio with payoffs y must be of lesser or equal risk. Property (iv) says that adding a risk-free instrument to a portfolio decreases the risk by the size of the investment in the risk-free instrument. This property ensures that coherent risk measures can be interpreted as the amount of capital needed to support a position or portfolio.

Value-at-risk satisfies (ii), (iii), and (iv), but is not a coherent risk measure because it fails to satisfy (i). For example, the aggregate portfolio of the digital put and call discussed above fails to satisfy (i), while the diversified portfolio fails to satisfy the combination of (i) and (ii) with $a = 1/2$. However, value-at-risk satisfies property (i) if the price changes of all instruments are described by a multivariate Normal distribution. Under this assumption it correctly aggregates risk and reflects the benefit of diversification.

A key result in ADEH (1999) is that all coherent risk measures can be represented in terms of "generalized scenarios." To construct a generalized scenario risk measure, first construct a list of N scenarios of future market factors and portfolio values, as might be done in Monte Carlo simulation or deterministic scenario analysis. Second, assign probabilities to the N scenarios. These probabilities determine how the different scenarios are weighted in the risk measure, and need not reflect the likelihood of the scenarios; they are probabilities in the sense that they are numbers between zero and one whose sum (over the N scenarios) is one.

Third, repeat the assignment of probabilities M times to construct a set of M probability measures on the N scenarios; these are the M generalized scenarios. For example, one measure might say that the N scenarios are equally likely, while another might say that the n-th scenario occurs with probability one while the other scenarios have probability zero. At most, one of the probability measures will correspond to the likelihoods of events, so unless $M = 1$ (and sometimes even in that case) the probability measures will not be based on the risk manager's assessment of the likelihood of the scenarios. Fourth, for each of the M probability measures, calculate the expected loss. Finally, the risk measure is the largest of the M expected losses.

This seemingly abstract procedure corresponds to two widely-used risk measures, the expected shortfall measure defined by $E[\text{loss} \mid \text{loss} < \text{cutoff}]$ and the measure produced by Standard Portfolio Analysis of Risk® (SPAN®) system developed by the Chicago Mercantile Exchange and used by many others. Nonetheless, coherent risk measures do not appear to be making inroads on VaR among banks and their regulators. A drawback of explicitly scenario-based approaches is that it is unclear how reasonably to select scenarios and probability measures on scenarios in situations in which portfolio values depend on dozens or even hundreds of risk factors. This requires significant thought, and probably knowledge of the portfolio.[12] In situations with many market factors, scenario-based approaches lose intuitive appeal and can be difficult to explain to senior management, boards of directors, regulators, and other constituencies.

NOTES

1. These methods are described in Linsmeier and Pearson (2000).

2. The delta-gamma-theta-Normal method uses the first two derivatives with respect to the market factors/underlying assets (the delta's and gamma's), and the time derivative (theta). If the time derivative is not used, the method is referred to as the delta-gamma method.

3. Limitations of the delta-gamma and delta-gamma-theta approaches are discussed in Mina and Ulmer (1999) and Pichler and Selitsch (2000). El-Jahel, Perraudin and Sellin (1999) describe a more sophisticated delta-gamma approach that allows for stochastic volatility, so that changes in the market factors are no longer multivariate normal. Cardenás, Fruchard, Koehler, Michel and Thomazeu (1997) and Rouvinez

(1997) also describe approaches based on the characteristic function of the delta-gamma approximation of the change in portfolio value. However, rather than match moments, they invert the characteristic function to obtain either the density or distribution of the change in portfolio value, and then read off the VaR estimate. Duffie and Pan (1999) use a similar approach in a more general framework that allows for jumps and credit risk. Feuerverger and Wong (2000) describe an alternative approach based on the moment generating function and saddlepoint approximations, while Britten-Jones and Schaeffer (1998) express the distribution of a delta-gamma approximation in terms of a sum of non-central chi-square random variables.

4. Frye (1998) suggests using fewer grid points for the second and third factors because the principal components analysis has identified them as making a smaller contribution to the risk than the first factor, so that the error from using a crude approximation is smaller.

5. These problems with simple backtests are discussed in Kupiec (1995), while Lopez (1999) analyzes other backtesting methods.

6. In statistical jargon, simple backtests consider only the marginal distribution of the exceptions.

7. The approach to risk decomposition described here is that of Litterman (1996), which has become standard. An alternative approach is described in Golub and Tilman (2000).

8. This decomposition is an application of Euler's law, which says that any function satisfying $f(kw) = kf(w)$ (i.e. any function that is homogeneous of degree 1) can be decomposed as in Eq. (3). This is discussed further in Chapter 10 of Pearson (2002).

9. A technique for computing these risk contributions for historical and Monte Carlo simulation is described in Sections 6.2–6.3 of Mina and Xiao (2001).

10. Embrechts, Resnick and Samorodnitsky (1998) and McNeil (1999) provide overviews of the use of extreme value theory in risk measurement, while Diebold, Schuermann and Stroughair (1998) provide a critical review of the use of extreme value theory in risk measurement, focusing on issues of estimation.

11. Classical extreme value theory gives us *block maxima* models, which are models for the maxima out of large samples of (identically distributed) observations. These are based on a long-standing result that, for large blocks, the maxima satisfy the generalized extreme value (GEV) distribution. For example, if the observations are daily interest rate changes and the blocks are years, a block maxima model using the GEV distribution might be used to estimate the distribution of the maximum one-day interest rate change within the year. Such models can offer guidance regarding the scenarios that should be considered in stress testing.

12. However, ADEH (1997) argue that an approach that "requires thinking before computation . . . can only improve risk management."

REFERENCES

Abken, P. A. (2000). An Empirical Evaluation of Value at Risk By Scenario Simulation. *Journal of Derivatives*, 12–30.

Artzner, P., Delbaen, F., Eber, J., & Heath, D. (1997). Thinking Coherently. *Risk*, *10*(11), 68–71.

Artzner, P., Delbaen, F., Eber, J., & Heath, D. (1999). Coherent Measures of Risk. *Mathematical Finance*, *9*(3), 203–228.

Berkowitz, J. (1999). Evaluating the Forecasts of Risk Models. *Federal Reserve Board Working Paper* (March).

Boudoukh, J., Richardson, M., & Whitelaw, R. (1998). The Best of Both Worlds. *Risk, 11*(5), 64–66.

Britten-Jones, M., & Schaeffer, S. M. (1998). Non-Linear Value at Risk. *European Finance Review, 2*(2), 161–187.

Cardenás, J., Fruchard, E., Koehler, E., Thomazeau, C., & Thomazeau, I. (1997). VaR: One Step Beyond. *Risk, 10*(10), 72–75.

Crnkovic, C., & Drachman, J. (1996). Quality Control. *Risk, 9*(9), 138–143.

Dembo, R. S., Aziz, A. R., Rosen, D., & Zerbs, M. (2000). *Mark to Future A Framework for Measuring Risk and Reward.* Toronto: Algorithmics Publications.

Diebold, F. X., Gunther, T. A., & Tay, A. S. (1998). Evaluating Density Forecasts. *International Economic Review, 39*(4), 863–906.

Diebold, F. X., Schuermann, T., & Stroughair, J. D. (1998). Pitfalls and Opportunities in the Use of Extreme Value Theory in Risk Management. In: A. N. Refenes, A. N. Burgess & J. E. Moody (Eds), *Decision Technologies for Computational Finance* (pp. 3–12). Boston: Kluwer Academic Publishers.

Duffie, D., & Pan, J. (1997). An Overview of Value at Risk. *Journal of Derivatives, 4*(3), 7–49.

Duffie, D., & Pan, J. (1999). Analytical Value at Risk with Jumps and Credit Risk. Working Paper, Graduate School of Business Stanford University (November).

El-Jahel, L., Perraudin, W., & Sellin, P. (1999). Value at Risk for Derivatives. *Journal of Derivatives*, Spring, 7–26.

Embrechts, P., Resnick, S., & Samorodnitsky, G. (1998). Living on the Edge. *Risk, 11*(1), 96–100.

Feuerverger, A., & Wong, A. C. M. (2000). Computation of Value-at-Risk for Nonlinear Portfolios. *Journal of Risk, 3*(1), 37–56.

Frye, J. (1988). Monte Carlo by Day. *Risk, 11*(11), 66–71.

Gibson, M. S., & Pritsker, M. (2000). Improving Grid-Based Methods for Estimating Value at Risk of Fixed-Income Portfolios. *Federal Reserve Board Finance and Economics Discussion Series*, 2000–2025.

Golub, B. W., & Tilman, L. M. (2000). *Risk Management: Approaches for Fixed Income Markets.* New York: John Wiley & Sons.

Group of Thirty (1993). *Derivatives: Practices and Principles.* New York: Group of Thirty.

Hull, J., & White, A. (1998). Incorporating Volatility Up-dating Into the Historical Simulation Method for Value at Risk. *Journal of Risk, 1*(1), 5–19.

Jamshidian, F., & Zhu, Y. (1997). Scenario Simulation: Theory and Methodology. *Finance and Stochastics, 1*(1), 43–67.

Kim, J., & Finger, C. C. (2000). A Stress Test to Incorporate Correlation Breakdown. *Journal of Risk, 2*(3), 5–19.

Kupiec, P. H. (1998). Stress Testing in a Value at Risk Framework. *Journal of Derivatives, 6*, 7–24.

Linsmeier, T. J., & Pearson, N. D. (2000). Value at Risk. *Financial Analysts Journal, 56*(2), 47–67.

McNeil, A. J. (1999). Extreme Value Theory for Risk Managers. *Internal Modeling and CAD II. Risk Books.* London, 93–113.

McNeil, A. J., & Frey, R. (2000). Estimation of Tail-related Risk Measures for Heteroscedastic Financial Time Series: An Extreme Value Approach. *Journal of Empirical Finance, 7*(3–4), 271–300.

Mina, J., & Yi Xiao, J. (2001). Return to RiskMetrics: *The Evolution of a Standard*. New York: RiskMetrics Group.

Neftci, S. N. (2000). Value at Risk Calculations, Extreme Events, and Tail Estimation. *Journal of Derivatives, 5*, 23–37.

Pearson, N. D. (2002). *Risk Budgeting: Using Value-at-Risk in Portfolio Problem Solving*. New York: John Wiley & Sons.

Pritsker, M. (1997). Evaluating Value at Risk Methodologies: Accuracy vs. Computational Time. *Journal of Financial Services Research, 12*(2/3), 201–242.

Rouvinez, C. (1997). Going Greek with VAR. *Risk, 10*(2), 57–65.

Zangari, P. (1996a). A VaR Methodology for Portfolios that Include Options. *RiskMetrics Monitor*, First Quarter, 4–12.

Zangari, P. (1996b). How Accurate is the Delta-Gamma Methodology? *RiskMetrics Monitor*, Third Quarter, 12–29.

4. "LEAPFROGGING" THE VARIANCE: THE FINANCIAL MANAGEMENT OF EXTREME-EVENT RISK

Michael R. Powers

ABSTRACT

The events of September 11, 2001 have triggered great interest in the identification, assessment, and management of "extreme events." In this article, we offer a new mathematical framework for the development of financial risk management techniques to address these exposures. Based upon our analysis, we argue that: (1) the decreasing marginal utility of net wealth does not adequately explain the economics of insurance/ reinsurance; and (2) our proposed apprehended value criterion provides approximate justification of mean-third central moment-fourth central moment (M-T-F) decision making, thereby "leapfrogging" (skipping over) the variance. Appropriate extensions of traditional financial risk management concepts are then considered, along with their implications for insurer/reinsurer underwriting and investment activity.

1. INTRODUCTION

The weeks and months following September 11, 2001 saw primary insurers, reinsurers, and other financial institutions scrambling to identify, assess, and manage their exposures to various types of "extreme events." The problem of risk identification and assessment has been well stated and elucidated

Global Risk Management: Financial, Operational, and Insurance Strategies,
Volume 3, pages 39–58.
Copyright © 2002 by Elsevier Science Ltd.
All rights of reproduction in any form reserved.
ISBN: 0-7623-0982-2

elsewhere (see, e.g. Powers & DeMartini, 2002). In this article, we offer a new mathematical framework for the development of suitable financial risk management techniques to address these potentially devastating exposures.

We begin by delimiting the class of exposures under discussion. By an "extreme event," we mean a well-defined "sudden" occurrence that falls into one of three distinct categories: (1) natural catastrophes, (2) accidental man-made catastrophes, or (3) intentional man-made catastrophes.[1] The second column in Table 1 provides historical examples of some of the largest and most widely publicized extreme events for each of these categories. Given the incidents listed in the second column, several questions come to mind:

- Are severe storms becoming more frequent, perhaps as a result of climatic changes such as "global warming"?
- Are man-made accidents becoming less common and/or less costly, perhaps because of improving risk-management efforts?
- Are intentional man-made disasters becoming more frequent, and is there an upper bound on their severity? and

Table 1.   Extreme Events, Examples by Category.

Category	Recent Historical Events	Potential (?) Future Events
Natural Catastrophes	Hurricane Hugo (1989) Mount Pinatubo volcanic eruption (1991) Oakland wildfires (1991) Hurricane Andrew (1992) Northridge Earthquake (1994) Kobe Earthquake (1995) Winter Storm Lothar (1999) Mad Cow Disease (2001)	"The Big One" (CA earthquake) Drug-resistant plague Asteroid/comet impact Demise of nearby star
Accidental Man-Made Catastrophes	Bhopal gas leak (1984) Chernobyl nuclear accident (1986) Piper Alpha oil rig fire (1988) Exxon Valdez oil spill (1989)	Liquefied natural gas disaster Nuclear plant meltdown
Intentional Man-Made Catastrophes	Tylenol tampering (1982) IRA Harrods bombing (1983) World Trade Center bombing (1993) Tokyo Subway nerve gas attack (1995) Oklahoma City bombing (1995) "I Love You" e-mail virus (2000) September 11 attacks (2001)	"Dirty" bombs More ambitious suicide attacks Nuclear weapons Chemical weapons Biological weapons

- Is it meaningful – or even possible – to discern trends in such volatile events, given the limited historical database?

In a similar vein, Professor Martin Shubik of Yale University posed the following questions in April 2001:[2]

> Given the lethality of terrorist groups such as the *Aum Shinrikyo*,[3] why is it that the largest size of casualties by a terrorist action is still around 300 to 400? Floods, famines, earthquakes, volcanic action, political instability, revolutions, pillage, and plague notwithstanding, we are still here and are even insuring many phenomena. Given the potentials for disaster, why are things so good?

Professor Shubik's comments – made less than five months prior to the September 11 attacks – were not only prescient, but remain disquietingly relevant today. Surely, one can imagine replacing the name *Aum Shinrikyo* with that of *Al Qaeda*, increasing the casualty figures by a factor of 10 (i.e. from 300–400 to 3000–4000), and then asking the same questions over again.

In short, extreme events, with their low (but unpredictable) frequencies and high (but unpredictable) severities, embody a tremendous potential to surprise us in the months and years ahead. A brief review of the hypothetical incidents in the third column of Table 1 provides some idea of the possible magnitudes of such future events. It is quite sobering to recognize that even if we, as a global society, are able to find a way to avoid the use of weapons of mass destruction, we will still be confronted with the dismal inevitability of naturally occurring catastrophes: perhaps a magnitude 7 + earthquake in Los Angeles or San Francisco; a drug-resistant plague on the scale of Europe's Black Death; or an asteroid impact on a densely populated area with a force comparable to that of the Tunguska fireball of 1908.

Given these extremely volatile hazards, two fundamental problems arise for insurers, reinsurers, and other market makers (including government): (1) how to provide appropriate economic incentives to allocate the capital necessary to support meaningful levels of coverage for these risks; and (2) given the availability of capital, how to price these types of coverage. To understand and address these problems, practitioners need an appropriate mathematical theory of the underlying sources of uncertainty.

Clearly, traditional mean-variance (M-V) optimization does not provide an adequate framework for dealing with the highly negatively skewed distributions of extreme-event losses. However, M-V optimization may be augmented by adding higher-order moments (the third central moment, fourth central moment, etc.); moreover, one can also employ the more comprehensive expected utility (EU) paradigm. Interestingly, insurers and reinsurers often omit all considerations of variance (or standard deviation) from their analyses of catastrophe loss data, focusing instead on the mean and various percentiles of the loss distribution,[4] which serve as a measure of skewness. This "leapfrogging" (i.e. skipping over) of the variance is a phenomenon that requires further explanation.

In this article, we explore the relationship between EU optimization and moment-based preference orderings, and then propose an alternative mathematical framework for the analysis of extreme-event risk. Our study leads to two thought-provoking conclusions regarding decision making in the context of catastrophe losses:

1. The decreasing marginal utility of net wealth does not adequately explain the economics of insurance/reinsurance; and
2. Our proposed *apprehended value* (AV) criterion provides approximate justification of mean-third central moment-fourth central moment (M-T-F) decision making, thereby "leapfrogging" the variance.

Finally, we consider appropriate extensions of traditional financial risk management concepts, along with their implications for insurer underwriting and investment activity.

2. QUANTIFYING UTILITY

Conventional EU optimization traces its development to the "classical" solution of Nicholas Bernoulli's "St. Petersburg Paradox" – a solution based upon the observation that the decreasing marginal utility of wealth imparts an increasing, concave downward utility function to decision makers. Although modern derivations of the EU principle generally begin with a formal axiomatization of the fundamental behavior of rational decision makers (such as that given by von Neumann & Morgenstern, 1934), for our purposes, the axiomatic treatment is less instructive than a simple analysis of Bernoulli's problem.

2.1. The St. Petersburg Paradox

The St. Petersburg problem, originally posed in 1713, consists of the following game:

A fair coin is tossed until it comes up "heads". You are told you will receive a prize of:

$X = \$1$ if "heads" occurs on the first toss;[5]
$X = \$2$ if "heads" occurs on the second toss;
$X = \$4$ if "heads" occurs on the third toss;
$X = \$8$ if "heads" occurs on the fourth toss;
etc.

The mathematical problem is: Assuming that you are permitted one turn at the game, what is the smallest number of dollars, D, that you would be willing to accept to give up this privilege?

At Bernoulli's time, as today, most people would be willing to relinquish a turn at the above game for only a very few dollars (see, e.g. Machina, 1987). This effect was seen as paradoxical by mathematicians of the early eighteenth century, because they were accustomed to using expected value (EV) as the basic measurement of value in decisions involving uncertainty. For a prospective player with initial wealth w_0, the EV criterion implies the following equation (expressed in dollars):

$$w_0 + D = E_f[w_0 + X] = w_0 + \sum_{i=1}^{\infty} x_i f(x_i)$$

$$\Leftrightarrow D = 1\left(\frac{1}{2}\right) + 2\left(\frac{1}{4}\right) + 4\left(\frac{1}{8}\right) + \ldots = \frac{1}{2} + \frac{1}{2} + \frac{1}{2} + \ldots = \infty.$$

Clearly, there was something puzzling about a game whose expected value was infinite, but which most people would be willing to surrender in return for a small amount of money.

The "classical" solution to the St. Petersburg puzzle was provided by the work of Gabriel Cramer in 1728 and Daniel Bernoulli (a cousin of Nicholas) in 1738. The Cramer/Bernoulli solution is based upon the observation that most decision makers are characterized by decreasing marginal utility of wealth – that is, a decision-maker's utility (happiness) will typically increase with each dollar of net wealth gained, but the incremental increases in utility will become progressively smaller as wealth increases.

To determine the true value of the proposed game, one therefore must transform the random outcome, $w_0 + X$, by an increasing and concave downward utility function – i.e. $u(w)$ such that $u'(w) > 0$ and $u''(w) < 0$ – before computing the expected utility. The EU criterion then yields the following equation (expressed in "happiness units" or "utiles"):

$$u(w_0 + D) = E_f[u(w_0 + X)] = \sum_{i=1}^{\infty} u(w_0 + x_i) f(x_i). \tag{1}$$

D. Bernoulli suggested using the utility function $u(w) = \ln(w)$. Inserting this function into Eq. (1), and assuming (for example) that $w_0 = 10,000$, one finds that

$$D = 7.62.$$

This small value is consistent with the observation that most people would be willing to give up a turn at the game for only a few dollars.

A second, and very important, explanation for the unattractiveness of the St. Petersburg game is that human concepts of value are bounded above, and thus it is meaningless to speak of a game offering an "infinite expected payoff," or "infinite expected utility," for that matter. In fact, Menger (1934) showed that the Cramer/Bernoulli solution must be modified by restricting $u(w)$ to the set of bounded functions, or else the paradox can be made to reappear for certain payoff schemes.

A third explanation for the St. Petersburg game's limited desirability is that the game lacks credibility – and is in fact unplayable – because no individual or organizational entity is able to fund the arbitrarily large prizes X associated with arbitrarily long streaks of "tails" in the coin-tossing sequence. While this objection is indeed valid, we note that it easily can be sidestepped simply by truncating the game so that if no "heads" appears in the first n tosses, then the $n+1$ toss will be defined as "heads", and the player will receive a prize of $X = \$2^n$, where 2^n is the largest credible payoff amount – i.e. the largest dollar value that a player could reasonably expect to be paid by the game's sponsor.

A fourth explanation for the unattractiveness of the St. Petersburg game is that decreasing marginal utility, while a thoroughly reasonable hypothesis that illuminates certain aspects of the paradox, addresses only the impact of the payoff amounts, and not the impact of the payoff probabilities. As has been noted by Kahneman and Tversky (1979) in their development of "prospect theory," decision makers often misestimate the probabilities of low-frequency events. Clearly, this type of effect could substantially lower the perceived expected value of N. Bernoulli's game.[6]

The phenomenon of misestimating the probabilities of low-frequency events is especially significant in the context of highly skewed payoff distributions, such as those encountered with extreme-event risks. Consequently, we will return to this criticism of the Cramer/Bernoulli solution in Section 3, where we will argue more broadly that decision makers tend to be rather pessimistic about random outcomes, behaving as though large positive outcomes are less likely to occur, and large negative outcomes are more likely to occur, than they do in actual practice.

2.2. Expected Utility and Moment-Based Preference Orderings

EU optimization may be approximated by M-V optimization as well as by more general moment-based preference orderings. The nature of these approximations can best be seen by considering the Taylor series expansion of expected utility:

$$E_f[u(w_0+X)] = E_f\left[\sum_{j=0}^{\infty}\frac{1}{j!}u^{(j)}(w_0+\mu)(X-\mu)^j\right]$$

$$= u(w_0+\mu) + \frac{1}{2}u''(w_0+\mu)Var_f[X] + \frac{1}{6}u'''(w_0+\mu)CM_f^{(3)}[X]$$

$$+ \frac{1}{24}u^{(4)}(w_0+\mu)CM_f^{(4)}[X] + \dots,$$

where μ denotes the mean of X, and $CM_f^{(j)}[X]$ denotes the j-th central moment.

Obviously, if one can justify setting the sum of the third- and higher-order terms of the above series equal to zero, i.e.

$$\sum_{j=3}^{\infty}\frac{1}{j!}u^{(j)}(w_0+\mu)CM_f^{(j)}[X] = 0, \tag{2}$$

then one can write the expected utility explicitly in terms of the mean and the variance alone. One way to ensure Eq. (2) is to assume that the utility function is well-approximated by a quadratic polynomial, as in the following formal statement of the mean-variance principle.

Theorem 1: Consider a risk averse decision maker with initial wealth w_0, random payoff $X \sim f(x)$ on sample space (a, b), and final net wealth w_0+X. If the decision-maker's utility function is a quadratic polynomial on $(a+w_0, b+w_0)$, then his/her expected utility, $E_f[u(w_0+X)]$, is:

(i) increasing in the mean payoff (i.e. $\dfrac{\partial E_f[u(w_0+X)]}{\partial\mu} > 0$);

(ii) decreasing in the variance of the payoff (i.e. $\dfrac{\partial E_f[u(w_0+X)]}{\partial Var_f[X]} < 0$); and

(iii) unaffected by all higher-order central moments of the payoff (i.e. $\dfrac{\partial E_f[u(w_0+X)]}{\partial CM_f^{(j)}[X]} = 0$ for $j \geq 3$).

Proof: Since $u^{(j)}(x) = 0\ \forall x, \forall j \geq 3$, it follows that

$$E_f[u(w_0+X)] = u(w_0+\mu) + \frac{1}{2}u''(w_0+\mu)Var_f[X],$$

and so:

(i) $\dfrac{\partial E_f[u(w_0+X)]}{\partial \mu} = u'(w_0+\mu) + \dfrac{1}{2}\, u'''(w_0+\mu)Var_f[X] > 0;$

(ii) $\dfrac{\partial E_f[u(w_0+X)]}{\partial Var_f[X]} = \dfrac{1}{2}\, u''(w_0+\mu) < 0;$ and

(iii) $\dfrac{\partial E_f[u(w_0+X)]}{\partial CM_f^{(j)}[X]} = 0\ \forall j \geq 3.$

Naturally, Theorem 1 relies heavily on the assumption of quadratic utility, which is often considered unrealistic. (Specifically, the quadratic utility function fails to satisfy the common assumption of prudence – i.e. that $u'''(w) > 0$ – and therefore implies increasing absolute risk aversion – i.e. that the risk aversion coefficient $-\dfrac{u''(w)}{u'(w)}$ increases with increasing wealth.) However, one can overcome this problem by raising the order of the polynomial used to approximate the utility function, so that the third and higher derivatives of $u(w)$ satisfy all desired properties.

This technique is illustrated by the next result, in which we show that a cubic polynomial for $u(w)$ allows us to incorporate prudence into the model.

Theorem 2: Consider a risk averse decision maker characterized by prudence, with initial wealth w_0, random payoff $X \sim f(x)$ on sample space (a, b), and final net wealth $w_0 + X$. If the decision-maker's utility function is a cubic polynomial on $(a+w_0, b+w_0)$, then his/her expected utility, $E_f[u(w_0+X)]$, is:

(i) increasing in the mean payoff (i.e. $\dfrac{\partial E_f[u(w_0+X)]}{\partial \mu} > 0$);

(ii) decreasing in the variance of the payoff (i.e. $\dfrac{\partial E_f[u(w_0+X)]}{\partial Var_f[X]} < 0$);

(iii) increasing in the third central moment of the payoff (i.e. $\dfrac{\partial E_f[u(w_0+X)]}{\partial CM_f^{(3)}[X]} > 0$); and

(iv) unaffected by all higher-order central moments of the payoff (i.e. $\dfrac{\partial E_f[u(w_0+X)]}{\partial CM_f^{(j)}[X]} = 0$ for $j \geq 4$).

Proof: The proof is analogous to that of Theorem 1, with the addition of one term involving the third central moment in the expression for expected utility.

Obviously, each increase in the order of the polynomial used for $u(w)$ introduces one additional term into the truncated Taylor series for expected utility, so that a polynomial of order m yields an expression for expected utility that depends on the mean, variance, and all central moments up through $CM_f^{(m)}[x]$. However, in order to determine the direction of the comparative static

associated with $CM_f^{(m)}[x]$ – i.e. $sgn\left(\dfrac{\partial E_f[u(w_0+X)]}{\partial CM_f^{(m)}[X]}\right)$ – one needs to specify

$sgn(u^{(m)}(w_0+\mu))$, which is rarely known explicitly for values of $m \geq 4$. Consequently, mean-variance-third central moment (M-V-T) optimization may be the best approximation to EU optimization that is generally practicable.

While both EU and M-V-T optimization appear to provide reasonable formulations for the analysis of extreme-event risks, we are still left with two unanswered questions: (1) How can we model the phenomenon of decision makers misestimating the probabilities of low-frequency events? and (2) Why do practitioners often "leapfrog" the variance in their analyses of catastrophe loss data? In the next section, we will demonstrate that the answers to these two questions are closely intertwined.

3. QUANTIFYING APPREHENSION

We address the issue of misestimating the probabilities of low-frequency events by positing a simple mathematical model to describe this effect. Specifically, we assume that every decision maker is characterized by an "apprehension function," $\alpha(x)$, which reflects the decision-maker's subjective probability distribution over X by modifying the true underlying probability mass (density) function, $f(x)$. This is accomplished by constructing the subjective probability mass (density) function $A(x) \cdot f(x)$, where

$$A(x) = \frac{\alpha(x)}{E_f[\alpha(X)]}.$$

We further assume that most decision makers are "risk pessimistic" in the sense that they tend to underestimate the probabilities of large positive outcomes, and to overestimate the probabilities of large negative outcomes. This behavior is modeled by letting $\alpha(x)$ be any positively valued decreasing function – i.e. $\alpha(x)>0$ and $\alpha'(x)<0$ – such that $\alpha'(\mu)=0$. In other words, the smaller the payoff, the greater the decision-maker's apprehension concerning that payoff; however, in a neighborhood of the mean payoff – i.e. for "typical" values of X – there is very little discernable change in the relative weights applied to the probability function.

In addition to risk pessimism, it seems reasonable to assume that many decision makers are characterized by what might be called "impatience": the

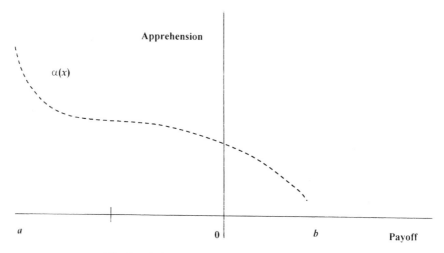

Fig. 1. A Hypothetical Apprehension Function.

property of increasing marginal apprehension below the mean, and decreasing marginal apprehension above the mean; i.e. $\alpha''(x) > 0$ for $x < \mu$ and $\alpha''(x) < 0$ for $x > \mu$ (which implies both $\alpha''(\mu) = 0$ and $\alpha'''(\mu) < 0$). Figure 1 provides a sketch of a hypothetical apprehension function for a decision maker manifesting both risk pessimism and impatience.

3.1. St. Petersburg Revisited

As shown in Table 2, our development of the apprehension concept is somewhat parallel to the development of utility described in Section 2. Returning to the context of the St. Petersburg problem, we can now employ this new concept to resolve the paradox from the perspective of the payoff probabilities rather than the payoff amounts. This alternative approach, based upon apprehended value (AV) optimization rather than EU optimization, is especially significant in the context of highly skewed payoff distributions.

To apply the AV principle to N. Bernoulli's game, first note that the expected payoff amount is given by $\mu = \infty$, which suggests that a risk pessimistic decision maker with impatience would have an apprehension function resembling only the left-hand portion of the curve in Fig. 1; that is, $\alpha(x)$ would be a decreasing, concave upward function. Essentially, this means that the smaller payoffs would be given substantially more weight relative to the larger

Table 2. Parallel Development of EU and AV Principles.

Utility Function $u(w)$	Apprehension Function $\alpha(w)$
Risk Aversion:	*Risk Pessimism*:
Increasing Utility, $u'(w) > 0 \ \forall w$	Positive Apprehension, $\alpha(x) > 0 \ \forall x$
Decreasing Marginal Utility, $u''(w) < 0 \ \forall w$	Decreasing Apprehension,
	$\alpha'(x) < 0 \ \forall x \neq \mu, \ \alpha'(\mu) = 0$
Prudence, $u'''(w) > 0 \ \forall w$	Impatience, $\alpha''(x) > 0 \ \forall x < \mu, \ \alpha''(x) < 0 \ \forall x > \mu$
	$\Rightarrow \alpha''(\mu) = 0, \ \alpha'''(\mu) < 0$
Expected Utility Principle,	Apprehended Value Principle,
$Max\{E_f[u(w_0 + X)]\}$	$Max\{E_{A \cdot f}[w_0 + X]\}$

payoffs, and, for an appropriate selection of $\alpha(x)$, the perceived expected value of the St. Petersburg game could be made arbitrarily close to zero.

3.2. Apprehended Value and Moment-Based Preference Orderings

AV optimization, like EU optimization, may be approximated by moment-based preference orderings. The nature of these approximations can be seen by considering the Taylor series expansion of apprehended value:

$$E_{A \cdot f}[w_0 + X] = w_0 + \sum_{j=0}^{\infty} \frac{1}{j!} E_f[A^{(j)}(\mu)X(X - \mu)^j]$$

$$= w_0 + A(\mu)\mu + \left[A'(\mu) + \frac{1}{2}A''(\mu)\mu \right] Var_f[X]$$

$$+ \left[\frac{1}{2}A''(\mu) + \frac{1}{6}A'''(\mu)\mu \right] CM_f^{(3)}[X]$$

$$+ \left[\frac{1}{6}A'''(\mu) + \frac{1}{24}A^{(4)}(\mu)\mu \right] CM_f^{(4)}[X] + \ldots .$$

The following theorem, which is somewhat analogous to Theorem 2, provides the central mathematical result of this article. We show that if $\alpha(x)$ can be approximated by a cubic polynomial, then AV optimization can be approximated by mean-third central moment-fourth central moment (M-T-F) optimization.

Theorem 3: Consider a risk pessimistic decision maker characterized by impatience, with initial wealth w_0, random payoff $X \sim f(x)$ on support (a, b), and final net wealth $w_0 + X$. If the decision-maker's apprehension function is a cubic polynomial on (a, b), then his/her apprehended value, $E_{A \bullet f}[w_0 + X]$, is:

(i) increasing in the mean payoff (i.e. $\dfrac{\partial E_{A \bullet f}[w_0 + X]}{\partial \mu} > 0$) as long as

$CM_f^{(3)}[X] \leq 0$ and $\dfrac{(Sk_f[X])^2}{Ku_f[X]} \geq \dfrac{3}{4}$;[7]

(ii) unaffected by the variance of the payoff (i.e. $\dfrac{\partial E_{A \bullet f}[w_0 + X]}{\partial Var_f[X]} = 0$);

(iii) increasing in the third central moment of the payoff (i.e. $\dfrac{\partial E_{A \bullet f}[w_0 + X]}{\partial CM_f^{(3)}[X]} > 0$)

as long as $\mu < 0$;

(iv) decreasing in the fourth central moment of the payoff (i.e. $\dfrac{\partial E_{A \bullet f}[w_0 + X]}{\partial CM_f^{(4)}[X]} < 0$); and

(v) unaffected by all higher-order central moments of the payoff (i.e. $\dfrac{\partial E_{A \bullet f}[w_0 + X]}{\partial CM_f^{(j)}[X]} = 0$ for $j > 5$).

Proof: See the Appendix.

From this result, we see that if one uses the AV principle, then there is an approximate moment-based preference ordering that: (1) applies specifically to highly negatively skewed pure risks (i.e. to losses for which $\mu < 0$, $CM_f^{(3)}[X] \leq 0$, and $\dfrac{(Sk_f[X])^2}{Ku_f[X]} \geq \dfrac{3}{4}$); and (2) employs only the mean, third central moment, and fourth central moment, thereby "leapfrogging" the variance.

The following theorem shows that the condition $\dfrac{(Sk_f[X])^2}{Ku_f[X]} \geq \dfrac{3}{4}$ should not, in general, be difficult to satisfy for extreme-event loss distributions.

Theorem 4: Consider the random loss amount

$$X = I \times L,$$

where $I \sim Bernoulli(p)$, $L \sim N(\lambda, \sigma^2)$, and I and L are statistically independent. Let X be termed an "extreme-event" loss in the limit as $p \to 0$, $\lambda \to -\infty$,

$p\lambda \to \mu \in (-\infty, 0)$, and $\dfrac{\sigma}{\lambda} \to 0$. It then follows that any extreme-event loss amount X must satisfy the condition

$$\lim_{p \to 0, \lambda \to -\infty} \frac{(Sk_f[X])^2}{Ku_f[X]} = 1.$$

Proof: First, note that

$$\frac{(Sk_f[X])^2}{Ku_f[X]} = \frac{\{E_f[(X - p\lambda)^3]\}^2}{E_f[(X - p\lambda)^2]E_f[(X - p\lambda)^4]}$$

$$= \frac{\{E_f[I^3L^3 - 3I^2L^2p\lambda + 3ILp^2\lambda^2 - p^3\lambda^3]\}^2}{E_f[I^2L^2 - 2ILp\lambda + p^2\lambda^2]E_f[I^4L^4 - 4I^3L^3p\lambda + 6I^2L^2p^2\lambda^2 - 4ILp^3\lambda^3 + p^4L^4]}$$

$$= \frac{(pE[L^3] - 3p^2E[L^2]\lambda + 2p^3\lambda^3)^2}{(pE[L^2] - p^2\lambda^2)(pE[L^4] - 4p^2E[L^3]\lambda + 6p^3E[L^2]\lambda^2 - 3p^4\lambda^4)}$$

$$= \frac{[p(\lambda^3 + 3\lambda\sigma^2) - 3p^2(\lambda^2 + \sigma^2)\lambda + 2p^3\lambda^3]^2}{[p(\lambda^2 + \sigma^2) - p^2\lambda^2][p(\lambda^4 + 6\lambda^2\sigma^2 + 3\sigma^4) - 4p^2(\lambda^3 + 3\lambda\sigma^2)\lambda + 6p^3(\lambda^2 + \sigma^2)\lambda^2 - 3p^4\lambda^4]}$$

$$= \frac{\left[p\left(1 + 3\dfrac{\sigma^2}{\lambda^2}\right) - 3p^2\left(1 + \dfrac{\sigma^2}{\lambda^2}\right) + 2p^3\right]^2}{\left[p\left(1 + \dfrac{\sigma^2}{\lambda^2}\right) - p^2\right]\left[p\left(1 + 6\dfrac{\sigma^2}{\lambda^2} + 3\dfrac{\sigma^4}{\lambda^4}\right) - 4p^2\left(1 + 3\dfrac{\sigma^2}{\lambda^2}\right) + 6p^3\left(1 + \dfrac{\sigma^2}{\lambda^2}\right) - 3p^4\right]}.$$

Taking limits as $p \to 0$ and $\lambda \to -\infty$, we find that

$$\frac{(Sk_f[X])^2}{Ku_f[X]} \sim \frac{(p)^2}{(p)(p)} \to 1.$$

4. FINANCIAL RISK MANAGEMENT UNDER THE M-T-F PARADIGM

Two commonly used financial risk management techniques are motivated by the traditional M-V principle: *diversification* and *hedging*. Both of these techniques exploit basic statistical properties of random variables to reduce the variance. In the case of diversification, it is the fact that

$$\lim_{n \to \infty} Var[\overline{X}_n] = 0 \tag{3}$$

that inspires an insurer/reinsurer to partition its loss portfolio into a larger number of small, uncorrelated exposures. In the case of hedging, it is the fact that

$$Var[X + Y] = Var[X] + 2E[(X - \mu_X)(Y - \mu_Y)] + Var[Y] \tag{4}$$

that provides the incentive for an insurer/reinsurer to seek out negatively correlated exposures to offset each other's variances.

Within the framework of M-T-F optimization for negatively skewed pure risks, variance-minimization is no longer relevant. However, the risk management technique of diversification is still extremely useful, as is a generalized form of hedging. In addition, a new risk management technique, which we call "balanced speculation," emerges as a means of reducing the skewness of an insurer's/reinsurer's risk portfolio.

4.1. Ordinary Diversification

Just as Eq. (3) provides the statistical rationale for ordinary diversification under M-V optimization, the following two results show how the same type of diversification behavior can increase the third central moment (which is negative) and decrease the fourth central moment (which, like the variance, is always positive):

$$\lim_{n \to \infty} CM^{(3)}[\overline{X}_n] = 0; \text{ and}$$
$$\lim_{n \to \infty} CM^{(4)}[\overline{X}_n] = 0$$

Consequently, in the context of portfolio-diversification, insurers/reinsurers facing extreme-event risks should continue to do exactly the same things that they would under an M-V framework.

4.2. Generalized Hedging

With respect to hedging, the third and fourth central moment analogues of Eq. (4) are respectively:

$$CM^{(3)}[X+Y] = CM^{(3)}[X] + 3E[(X-\mu_X)^2(Y-\mu_Y)]$$
$$+ 3E[(X-\mu_X)(Y-\mu_Y)^2] + CM^{(3)}[Y] \qquad (5)$$

and

$$CM^{(4)}[X+Y] = CM^{(4)}[X] + 4E[(X-\mu_X)^3(Y-\mu_Y)] + 6E[(X-\mu_X)^2(Y-\mu_Y)^2]$$
$$+ 4E[(X-\mu_X)(Y-\mu_Y)^3] + CM^{(4)}[Y]. \qquad (6)$$

Given that both X and Y are negatively skewed pure risks, Eq. (5) shows that the negative third central moment of the insurer's/reinsurer's overall portfolio may be increased by finding individual exposures for which the higher-order "covariance" terms, $E[(X-\mu_X)^2(Y-\mu_Y)]$ and $E[(X-\mu_X)(Y-\mu_Y)^2]$, are positive. Conceptually, this is comparable to seeking negatively correlated random variables, but the verification of the conditions $E[(X - \mu_X)^2(Y - \mu_Y)] > 0$ and $E[(X - \mu_X)(Y - \mu_Y)^2] > 0$, is likely to be somewhat more difficult in practice.

The same sorts of observations can be made with respect to Eq. (6), which shows that the insurer's/reinsurer's positive fourth central moment may be reduced by finding individual exposures for which the higher-order "covariance" terms $E[(X - \mu_X)^3(Y - \mu_Y)]$ and $E[(X - \mu_X)(Y - \mu_Y)^3]$ are negative, and for which the other higher-order term, $E[(X - \mu_X)^2(Y - \mu_Y)^2]$ is as small as possible. Again, while this procedure is conceptually straightforward, it is probably more easily said that done.

4.3. Balanced Speculation

We finally come to a financial risk management technique that is qualitatively different from both diversification and hedging. Returning to Eq. (5), we observe that if the two random variables, X and Y, are statistically independent and of opposite skew, then they may be able to offset each other's third central moments completely. Specifically, if we think of X as a highly negatively skewed extreme-event risk, and of Y as the return form a highly positively skewed speculative investment that is independent of X, then it is possible for the third central moment of the insurer's/reinsurer's overall portfolio to be arbitrarily close to zero. In short, one way to encourage insurers and reinsurers to write more extreme-event risks is to relax regulatory requirements so that they are better able to coordinate more volatile speculative investments with their underwriting objectives.

5. CONCLUSIONS

The study of extreme-event risks is of growing importance to insurers and reinsurers in the post-September 11 environment. In this article, we have presented an alternative mathematical theory for understanding and managing these highly volatile exposures. Our analysis has shown that traditional EU optimization and associated moment-based preference orderings – based upon the concept of decreasing marginal utility of net wealth – are unsatisfactory for two reasons: (1) they fail to recognize that decision makers often misestimate the probabilities of low-frequency events; and (2) they fail to explain why insurers and reinsurers often "leapfrog" the variance in the analysis of catastrophe losses.

Our AV criterion, based upon a model of apprehension functions, risk pessimism, and impatience, addresses both of these problems. The apprehension function permits the explicit modeling of disparities between underlying loss probabilities and the subjective probabilities used by decision makers. The AV approach then provides approximate justification of an M-T-F framework, thereby showing why decision makers are willing to "leapfrog" the variance.

In considering appropriate financial risk management concepts for extreme-event risks, we find that ordinary diversification and a generalized form of hedging remain important components of an insurer's/reinsurer's risk management program. In addition, we find that balanced speculation, consisting of the offsetting of negatively skewed pure risks by positively skewed speculative risks, offers a promising additional risk management tool.

One fertile area of future research is to provide empirical analysis of the extent to which insurers and reinsurers currently employ strategies of balanced speculation within regulatory constraints on investments. On the more theoretical side, research to incorporate the principle of decreasing marginal utility of net wealth into the AV paradigm – although technically difficult – is likely to offer additional insights into the problem of extreme-event risks.

NOTES

1. For the definition of "catastrophe", we accept the commonly used criterion of a single event generating at least \$25 million in insured property losses. Without affecting our analysis or conclusions, we could alternatively refer to any single event that causes at least one primary insurer to exhaust its property catastrophe retention.

2. See Shubik (2002), from the keynote address at Temple University's conference on Global Risk Management, April 20, 2001.

3. The *Aum Shinrikyo* is the Japanese cult responsible for the Tokyo Subway nerve gas attack.

4. One of these percentiles is typically identified as the "probable maximum loss." (See, e.g. Zeng, 2001.)

5. In the original statement of the problem, the unit of currency was "ducats" rather than "dollars".

6. This is consistent with a view advanced by many of the author's own actuarial science students: that a principal – if not *the* principal – reason why the St. Petersburg game seems unappealing, is that it is very difficult to believe that any of the larger values will ever be achieved, given that their probabilities are so low.

7. $Sk_f[X]$ denotes the coefficient of skewness, $\dfrac{CM_f^{(3)}[X]}{(Var_f[X])^{3/2}}$, and $Ku_f[X]$ denotes the coefficient of kurtosis, $\dfrac{CM_f^{(4)}[X]}{(Var[X])^2}$.

ACKNOWLEDGMENTS

This article is based upon work presented at the EURANDOM Reinsurance Workshop held at Eindhoven University of Technology (The Netherlands), and the J. R. Cox/ACE Ltd. Symposium on Extreme Risk held at Bermuda College (Bermuda), both in May 2002. The author thanks the other presenters and participants at these seminars for their helpful comments.

An earlier version of this work is forthcoming in *The Journal of Risk Finance* (Institutional Investor Journals, New York), 2003.

REFERENCES

Kahneman, D., & Tversky, A. (1979). Prospect Theory: An Analysis of Decision under Risk. *Econometrica, 47*(2), 263–291.

Machina, M. (1987). Choice under Uncertainty: Problems Solved and Unsolved. *Journal of Economic Perspectives, 1*(1), 121–154.

Menger, K. (1934). The Role of Uncertainty in Economics. *Zeitschrift für Nationalökonomie* (*Journal of Economics*), *5*, as translated in Shubik, M., 1967, *Essays in Mathematical Economics.* Princeton University Press, Princeton, NJ.

Powers, I. Y., & DeMartini, J. (2002). Managing Extreme-Event Exposures, *Emphasis, 3*, 2–5.

Shubik, M. (2002). Risk, Public Perception, and Education: Quantitative and Qualitative Risk. In: J. Choi & M. R. Powers (Eds), *Global Risk Management: Financial, Operational, and Insurance Strategies.* Amsterdam: Elsevier Science.

von Neumann, J., & Morgenstern, O. (1944). *Theory of Games and Economic Behavior.* Princeton, NJ: Princeton University Press.

Zeng, L. (2001). Using Cat Models for Optimal Risk Allocation of P&C Liability Portfolios. *Journal of Risk Finance, 2*(2), 29–35.

APPENDIX

Proof of Theorem 3: Since $\alpha^{(j)}(x) = 0 \ \forall x, \ \forall j \geq 4$, it follows that

$$E_{A \cdot f}[w_0 + X] = w_0 + A(\mu)\mu + \left[A'(\mu) + \frac{1}{2}A''(\mu)\mu \right] Var_f[X]$$

$$+ \left[\frac{1}{2}A''(\mu) + \frac{1}{6}A'''(\mu)\mu \right] CM_f^{(3)}[X] + \frac{1}{6}A'''(\mu)CM_f^{(4)}[X],$$

and so:

(i)
$$\frac{\partial E_{A \cdot f}[w_0 + X]}{\partial \mu} = A(\mu) + \left[A'(\mu) + \left. \frac{\partial A(x)}{\partial \mu} \right|_{x=\mu} \right] \mu$$

$$+ \left\{ \left[A''(\mu) + \left. \frac{\partial A'(x)}{\partial \mu} \right|_{x=\mu} \right] + \frac{1}{2} A''(\mu) + \frac{1}{2} \left[A'''(\mu) + \left. \frac{\partial A''(x)}{\partial \mu} \right|_{x=\mu} \right] \mu \right\} Var_f[X]$$

$$+ \left\{ \frac{1}{2} \left[A'''(\mu) + \left. \frac{\partial A''(x)}{\partial \mu} \right|_{x=\mu} \right] + \frac{1}{6} A'''(\mu) + \frac{1}{6} \left[A^{(4)}(\mu) + \left. \frac{\partial A'''(x)}{\partial \mu} \right|_{x=\mu} \right] \mu \right\} CM_f^{(3)}[X]$$

$$+ \frac{1}{6} \left[A^{(4)}(\mu) + \left. \frac{\partial A'''(x)}{\partial \mu} \right|_{x=\mu} \right] CM_f^{(4)}[X]$$

$$= \frac{\alpha(\mu)}{E_f[\alpha(X)]} + \left[\frac{\alpha'(\mu)}{E_f[\alpha(X)]} - \frac{\alpha(\mu) \dfrac{\partial E_f[\alpha(X)]}{\partial \mu}}{(E_f[\alpha(X)])^2} \right] \mu$$

$$+ \left\{ \frac{\dfrac{3}{2} \alpha''(\mu)}{E_f[\alpha(X)]} - \frac{\alpha'(\mu) \dfrac{\partial E_f[\alpha(X)]}{\partial \mu}}{(E_f[\alpha(X)])^2} + \frac{1}{2} \left[\frac{\alpha'''(\mu)}{E_f[\alpha(X)]} - \frac{\alpha''(\mu) \dfrac{\partial E_f[\alpha(X)]}{\partial \mu}}{(E_f[\alpha(X)])^2} \right] \mu \right\} Var_f[X]$$

$$+ \left\{ \frac{\dfrac{2}{3} \alpha'''(\mu)}{E_f[\alpha(X)]} - \frac{\dfrac{1}{2} \alpha''(\mu) \dfrac{\partial E_f[\alpha(X)]}{\partial \mu}}{(E_f[\alpha(X)])^2} + \frac{1}{6} \left[\frac{\alpha^{(4)}(\mu)}{E_f[\alpha(X)]} - \frac{\alpha'''(\mu) \dfrac{\partial E_f[\alpha(X)]}{\partial \mu}}{(E_f[\alpha(X)])^2} \right] \mu \right\} CM_f^{(3)}[X]$$

$$+ \frac{1}{6} \left[\frac{\alpha^{(4)}(\mu)}{E_f[\alpha(X)]} - \frac{\alpha'''(\mu) \dfrac{\partial E_f[\alpha(X)]}{\partial \mu}}{(E_f[\alpha(X)])^2} \right] CM_f^{(4)}[X] > 0$$

$$= \frac{1}{E_f[\alpha(X)]} \left\{ \alpha(\mu) - \alpha(\mu)\mu \frac{\partial E_f[\alpha(X)]/\partial \mu}{E_f[\alpha(X)]} + \frac{1}{2} \alpha'''(\mu)\mu Var_f[X] + \frac{2}{3} \alpha'''(\mu) CM_f^{(3)}[X] \right.$$

$$\left. - \frac{1}{6} \alpha'''(\mu)\mu CM_f^{(3)}[X] \frac{\partial E_f[\alpha(X)]/\partial \mu}{E_f[\alpha(X)]} - \frac{1}{6} \alpha'''(\mu) CM_f^{(4)}[X] \frac{\partial E_f[\alpha(X)]/\partial \mu}{E_f[\alpha(X)]} \right\}$$

$$= \frac{1}{E_f[\alpha(X)]\left[\alpha(\mu) + \frac{1}{6}\alpha'''(\mu)CM_f^{(3)}[X]\right]}$$

$$\times \left\{ [\alpha(\mu)]^2 + \frac{1}{6}\alpha(\mu)\alpha'''(\mu)CM_f^{(3)}[X] - \frac{1}{2}\alpha(\mu)\alpha'''(\mu)\mu Var_f[X] \right.$$

$$+ \frac{1}{2}\alpha(\mu)\alpha'''(\mu)\mu Var_f[X] + \frac{1}{12}[\alpha'''(\mu)]^2\mu Var_f[X]CM_f^{(3)}[X]$$

$$+ \frac{2}{3}\alpha(\mu)\alpha'''(m)CM_f^{(3)}[X] + \frac{1}{9}[\alpha'''(\mu)]^2(CM_f^{(3)}[X])^2$$

$$\left. - \frac{1}{12}[\alpha'''(\mu)]^2\mu Var_f[X]CM_f^{(3)}[X] - \frac{1}{12}[\alpha'''(\mu)]^2 Var_f[X]CM_f^{(4)}[X] \right\}$$

$$= \frac{1}{E_f[\alpha(X)]\left[\alpha(\mu) + \frac{1}{6}\alpha'''(\mu)CM_f^{(3)}[X]\right]}$$

$$\times \left\{ [\alpha(\mu)]^2 + \frac{5}{6}\alpha(\mu)\alpha'''(\mu)CM_f^{(3)}[X] \right.$$

$$\left. + [\alpha'''(\mu)]^2(Var_f[X])^3\left[\frac{1}{9}(Sk_f[X])^2 - \frac{1}{12}Ku_f[X]\right] \right\} > 0$$

if $CM_f^{(3)}[X] \le 0$ and $\frac{(Sk_f[X])^2}{Ku_f[X]} \ge \frac{3}{4}$, where we have used the facts that

$$E_f[\alpha(X)] = \alpha(\mu) + \frac{1}{2}\alpha''(\mu)Var_f[X] + \frac{1}{6}\alpha'''(\mu)CM_f^{(3)}[X],$$

$$\frac{\partial E_f[\alpha(X)]}{\partial \mu} = \alpha'(\mu) + \frac{1}{2}\alpha'''(\mu)Var_f[X] + \frac{1}{6}\alpha^{(4)}(\mu)CM_f^{(3)}[X], \text{ and so}$$

$$\frac{\partial E_f[\alpha(X)]/\partial \mu}{E_f[\alpha(X)]} = \frac{\frac{1}{2}\alpha'''(\mu)Var_f[X]}{\alpha(\mu) + \frac{1}{6}\alpha'''(\mu)CM_f^{(3)}[X]};$$

(ii) $\dfrac{\partial E_{A \cdot f}[w_0 + X]}{\partial Var_f[X]} = A'(\mu) + \dfrac{1}{2} A''(\mu)\mu = \dfrac{\alpha'(\mu) + \dfrac{1}{2}\alpha''(\mu)\mu}{E_f[\alpha(X)]} = 0;$

(iii) $\dfrac{\partial E_{A \cdot f}[w_0 + X]}{\partial CM_f^{(3)}[X]} = \dfrac{1}{2} A''(\mu) + \dfrac{1}{6} A'''(\mu)\mu = \dfrac{\dfrac{1}{2}\alpha''(\mu) + \dfrac{1}{6}\alpha'''(\mu)\mu}{E_f[\alpha(X)]} > 0 \text{ if } \mu < 0;$

(iv) $\dfrac{\partial E_{A \cdot f}[w_0 + X]}{\partial CM_f^{(4)}[X]} = \dfrac{1}{6} A'''(\mu) = \dfrac{\dfrac{1}{6}\alpha'''(\mu)}{E_f[\alpha(X)]} < 0; \text{ and}$

(v) $\dfrac{\partial E_{A \cdot f}[w_0 + X]}{\partial CM_f^{(j)}[X]} = 0 \ \forall j \geq 5.$

PART II:
MARKET, CREDIT, AND
FINANCIAL RISK

(v5)   G23

5. ASSESSING MARKET AND CREDIT RISK OF COUNTRY FUNDS: A VALUE-AT-RISK ANALYSIS

Michael G. Papaioannou and E. K. Gatzonas

ABSTRACT

The paper presents a treatment for the measurement and disclosure of market and credit risks in the context of capital adequacy regulation. The proposed approach is in conformity with the Basle Committee's latest proposal on risk measurement, and is based on the Value-at-Risk (VaR) methodology. This approach is applied to investments in close-end country funds of emerging markets. For 13 such funds listed in the New York Stock Exchange during the period October 1994 to December 1997, the average VaR estimate is found to be well above the capital adequacy ratio of 8% required by most regulatory authorities and to be sensitive to the emergence of increased financial turbulence.

1. INTRODUCTION

Inadequate risk measurement and management systems have been blamed for contributing to the exacerbation of the global financial turmoil during the last few years. In retrospect, the build-up of large portfolio positions, often highly leveraged, by a number of home national financial institutions has been considered excessively risky and the structure of such on-balance and off-balance sheet positions has been proven unsustainable. Faulty internal methods

Global Risk Management: Financial, Operational, and Insurance Strategies,
Volume 3, pages 61–79.

of risk assessment used by financial institutions and asset managers, and inappropriate market supervision are held responsible for the emergence of these adverse financial developments. Private sector institutions seem to have miscalculated the extend of their risk undertakings owing to the use of models that assume stable processes of market generating prices and do not take into consideration extreme events. On the other hand, regulators and supervisory agencies failed to diagnose the intensity of the emerging distresses in their countries' financial systems owing to the lack of timely and adequate information about the risk profile of the different asset classes in their financial institutions' portfolios, primarily as a result of the lack of standardized risk-assessment models.

For prudential reasons, financial institutions and investors need to know the risk profile of their portfolios at any point in time and thus to engage in regular assessment and pricing of the financial risks associated with the aggregate amount, as well as with the distribution, of their portfolios. Depending on the outcome of such risk assessments, rebalancing of portfolios may take place if the resulting risk profile deviates significantly from pre-established criteria of risk-taking. In case that the suggested rebalancing is sizeable and in one direction, sharp price movements of the underlying assets may not be avoided, especially in the presence of a market illiquidity. Consequently, frequent risk assessments of portfolios will reduce the possibilities of excessive risk-taking by financial entities and ameliorate systemic risk.

Financial institutions and other market participants use different systems for assessing the risk embodied in their portfolios. The adequacy of existing risk measurement and management methods has been questioned especially after their apparent failing in a number of financial entities during the Asian crisis in 1997–1998. Assessment of the riskiness of the individual assets in their portfolios, including off-balance sheet exposures, is inherently difficult since it depends on the underlying assumptions about market conditions. At turbulent times, assessment of a portfolio's risk exposure might be impossible since settlement of a transaction could trigger the unsettling of markets. In practice, financial institutions employ some generic method of assessing the market risk and credit risk of default for assets in their portfolios, in addition to assessing other risks such as the liquidity risk.

International supervisory authorities have proposed some structured approaches to risk measurement and management so that they can be uniformly applied by the various national financial institutions. These approaches started with the Building Block Approach (BBA) of the Basle proposal on the market risk in 1993 and the European Union's Capital Adequacy Directive. Recently, the inclination of these supranational regulatory authorities is toward using the

Value-at-Risk (VaR) approach (Basle Committee on Banking Supervision, 1996, 1999, 2001). Adaptation of any particular approach of risk assessment of financial entities' portfolios, however, has systemic implications. For example, in the context of the solvency ratio of the EEC, which is aligned to the BIS Basle Accord of 1988, the capital adequacy treatment of all collective investment undertakings (CIU) envisages assignment of a weighting equal to 100% of their book value, which is equivalent to a capital charge of credit risk of 8%. Clearly, such an approach that does not take into consideration the quality (riskiness) of the composition of the underlying portfolio, or the behavior of a CIU itself, allows for systemic inefficiency. The problem is magnified when CIUs are part of the trading book of a financial institution subject to capital charges for market risk. Furthermore, the Basle risk-weights utilized in calculating regulatory capital requirements cannot accurately reflect the various risks in financial institutions' and market participants' portfolios or changes in risk during periods of market turbulence.

For evaluating banks' capital adequacy, the Basle framework for capital adequacy (Basle Accord) has been endorsed by most industrialized countries' central banks, where banks are expected to maintain risk-based capital ratios above Basle minimums. The Basle Accord applies to internationally active banks, where the common shareholders' equity is the key element of capital. In addition to the Basle capital standard, banks may calculate capital ratios on other bases, depending on a bank's policies and practices. However, these ratios may only provide partial evidence of a bank's capitalization, since they mostly assess on-balance sheet activities and not leverage involved in off-balance sheet (e.g. derivative) and proprietary trading activities. Consequently, maintaining these ratios above the Basle minimum adequacy levels may not be sufficient evidence that a bank is sound.

The Basle Committee proposed the Market Risk Amendment to the Basle Accord in 1996, which permitted banks to use their internal VaR models as an alternative to the standardized approach for calculating capital requirements for market risk, subject to regulatory approval of these models. In its efforts to institute a capital adequacy standard that incorporates modern risk management practice while maintaining a regulatory minimum capital requirement, the Basle Committee issued a consultative document that considered various options for reform of the Accord in July 1999. This document proposed three pillars which aimed at the improvement of the framework for the calculation of banks' capital adequacy, the development of a process of supervisory review, and the strengthening of market discipline. The Basel Committee's latest capital framework proposals (January 2001) intend to extend the use of the internal VaR models to also calculate capital requirements for credit risk. As a result, credit risk models, which use similar statistical techniques as VaR models, have recently received wide acceptance in risk management practice.

In this study, we present the broad arguments for the implementation of the Basle proposals for market and credit risks, and outline the potential benefits from the extension of such supervisory standards to most emerging market economies. Our main emphasis is on the capital adequacy of banks' portfolios that include CIUs, defined for our purposes as joint investments, such as mutual funds. In addition, we propose a VaR measurement of the associated credit and market risks from investing in CIUs in the form of close-end emerging market country funds that maintain publicly available net asset values. Our methodology can effectively be used to assess the degree of the potential portfolio loss from investing in similar instruments. When measured in currency units other than the currency of the home country, reasonable assessment of the market and credit risks of emerging market country close-end funds can serve as a basis for imposing appropriate capital charges.

The proposed methodology conforms with the Basle Committee's "internal models approach" by employing a Value-at-Risk (VaR) framework, which is now anticipated to be the universal regulatory standard of banks' capital adequacy requirement. Using daily prices of 13 close-end emerging market country funds listed in the New York Stock Exchange for the period October 1994 to December 1997, the overall sample VaR figure reaches 11.5% which is well above the Basle capital adequacy ratio of 8%. The resulting excess average of 3.5%, justified perhaps by the excess volatility observed in emerging markets, indicates the degree of banks' possible undercapitalization if they maintain a similar mix of close-end country funds in their portfolios and adhere by the 8% capital adequacy ratio pursued by most regulatory authorities. Note that undercapitalization has often been blamed as one of the main causes of the Asian financial crisis. In addition, it is shown that the overall VaR figure tends to be higher during periods of increased financial turbulence, suggesting the possible imposition of varying capital charges according to the prevailing market conditions. Such flexibility in imposing capital charges by regulatory authorities may also enhance the overall efficiency and effectiveness of the international financial system.

This paper is organized as follows: Section 2 discusses the importance of market risk and outlines the treatment of market risk in the context of capital adequacy regulation. Section 3 gives the arguments for EU regulatory authorities' focus on capital adequacy in CIUs and presents a proposal for emerging market closed-end funds. Section 4 concludes.

2. MARKET RISK AND CAPITAL ADEQUACY

Market risk is just one of the fundamental risk components for all financial intermediaries, along with credit risk, operational risk, liquidity risk, compliance risk, and legal risk. It arises from the inherent difficulty in predicting the future values of fundamental market variables, which in turn may lead to losses in the marked-to-market positions of banks, securities, houses, and institutional investors. These positions include trading accounts of varying maturities for fixed income securities, short and long positions in foreign exchange, trading accounts for derivatives, as well as equity and commodity market positions.

Despite the fact that risk is a concept that most decision makers recognize, a precise definition that covers all possible circumstances is not always easy. According to the Organization of Economic Cooperation and Development, market risk is defined as the potential variation in the cash flows of a financial instrument resulting from changes in the market rate of interest for instruments of the same general credit quality, or from foreign exchange rates, or other market prices to which the financial instrument is linked (OECD, 1996). While this definition might be acceptable for many applications, a structured approach to risk measurement and management requires also judgment on a number of interrelated risk types. This last requirement, however, makes the overall risk assessment for a financial entity neither straightforward nor even attainable sometimes.

To avoid the potential plethora of risk measurement approaches by the various national supervisory authorities, international regulatory authorities have proposed certain methodological adjustments to be uniformly applied by financial institutions. These methodologies started with the Building Block Approach (BBA) of the Basle proposal on market risk in 1993 and the European Union's Capital Adequacy Directive (Bank of International Settlements, 1993; Council of European Communities, 1993). Nowadays, despite a lack of implementation experience of the BBA methodology, the entire methodological framework is being revisited by the same regulatory authorities with an inclination towards the Value-at-Risk approach (Hendricks & Hirtle, 1997; Lopez, 1997, 1999; Berkowitz & O'Brien, 2001).

The increasing involvement of depository intermediaries in trading financial instruments, along with the substantial building up of their trading-book positions, has made market risk the center of attention of the latest regulatory developments in the United States and Europe.[1] These developments have also been influenced by the heavily publicized losses from trading practices of highly influential market makers during the last few years. The issue of market risk measurement is increasingly involved owing to new and sophisticated financial instruments and processes that are widely used in forming their trading-book positions and managing market risk.

In response to the increasing exposure of financial institutions to fluctuating interest rates, exchange rates, and other market risk factors, national authorities in the United States and Europe have been working toward harmonizing standards relating to market risk in an effort to enhance preventive supervision. The United States Securities and Exchange Commission's efforts toward facilitating international cooperation in the securities area have been intensified recently, while new initiatives in global information sharing agreements are taking place. Moreover, the efforts on the methodological improvement of market risk measurement for all financial entities providing banking and investment services have been stepped up among regulatory agencies. At the European Union level, two important pieces of relevant legislation on market risk – the Capital Adequacy Directive (CAD) and its complementary Investment Services Directive (ISD) – had come into effect in early 1996. These legislative developments indicate that trading-book activity and, in turn, market risk is becoming equally important as traditional types of banking risk.

The implications of adopting particular methodologies for the precise measurement of market risk on the financial system as a whole warrant thorough investigation. In this study, we point out that regulatory uniformity and harmonization, as already implemented in European Union countries, is not without costs to systemic efficiency. The new path taken by the Basle Committee on Banking Supervision (Basle Committee), and more recently by the European Commission, on the measurement of and accounting for market risk is a step toward accepting the view that a degree of flexibility and variation in the underlying methodology is a vehicle for achieving systemic efficiency and stability. This feature, however, is not present in the EU's Capital Adequacy Directive. Currently, methodological adaptability is becoming the predominant feature of the regulatory treatment of market risk in the United States and the European Union.

3. CAPITAL ADEQUACY OF PORTFOLIOS INVOLVING CLOSED-END EMERGING MARKET COUNTRY FUNDS

3.1. Issues

The focus of this study is on financial institutions' portfolios that include emerging market closed-end funds listed in developed countries' organized exchanges. Such funds are a special form of collective investment under-takings. For the purposes of this study, collective investment undertakings are defined as all joint investments, such as mutual funds, irrespective of their underlying instrument composition, management scheme, or legal form. Along the same conceptual lines, undertakings for collective investments in transferable securities (UCITS), as defined by Directive 85/611/EEC, are viewed as a subset of CIUs and can be subject to the same methodological treatment outlined below.

The capital adequacy treatment for such financial assets has not been dealt until today by supervising entities in a satisfactory manner. The rigid regulatory methodologies in industrialized countries, along with the complexity of these instruments, have created a rather obscure, if not ineffective, framework for a meaningful measurement of CIUs' credit and market risks. Specifically, in the context of the Solvency Ratio of the EEC, which is aligned to the Basle Accord of 1988, all CIUs are assigned a weighting equal to 100% of their book value which is equivalent to a capital charge for credit risk of 8% (Basle Committee, 1993). It is obvious that, for portfolio diversification and economic reasons, such a blanket approach without reference to the composition of the underlying portfolio of primitive assets or the behavior of a CIU itself, is questionable. The problem is magnified when CIUs are part of the trading book of a financial institution subject to capital charges for market risk.

Under the provisions of Directive 93/6/EEC or of the Building Block Methodology of the Basle proposal for the measurement of market risk, a theoretically prudent treatment of CIUs would require access to a continuously updated and detailed composition of the portfolio of the CIU, so that netting of opposite positions can be properly accounted for. The inclusion of new financial instruments in the portfolio of a CIU makes matters even worse. Under such rigid methodological requirements, a straightforward implementa-tion of the Building Block Methodology becomes a grossly inefficient exercise and in most cases an impossible task. The methodological rigidity of the Building Block Methodology can mainly be attributed to the fact that the required information may not be readily available for a variety of reasons, ranging from practical difficulties to legal hurdles associated with the proprietary nature of the CIUs' investment strategy. Even in the theoretical case, however, where all relevant information for the implementation of the BBA methodology is readily available to financial institutions at any time, a direct application of the methodology is difficult to assess whether it contributes to an efficient or effective treatment of market and credit risks of positions in CIUs.

In comparison to existing practice, any attempt based on economic or legal ground to classify CIUs in distinct groups, so that capital charges can be applied in a sensible manner, will be an improvement. At the same time, however, solutions of this nature carry the risk of unfair treatment of the portions of CIUs with lower market or credit risk than the rest of the portfolio. While the purpose of a capital adequacy standard is to impose capital charges in accordance with the degree of market or credit risk, these assessment approaches defeat such purpose by triggering mechanisms of regulatory arbitrage.

The problem with CIUs, whose underlying portfolio elements are financial assets of emerging markets, is acute since any regulatory differentiation between a direct-through a CIU-and an indirect investment strategy would result in market inefficiency and additional regulatory arbitrage. As is known, listed emerging market CIUs of the closed-end type have been the predecessors of many indirect investment schemes and have become the capital market barometers of the performance of these countries. Thus, an efficient methodology for the measurement of the degree of potential loss in these investment vehicles, combined with disclosure requirements for the issuer as well as the investing entity, can provide the basis for harmonization standards in this field, without imposing significant implementation costs or requiring the revelation of sensitive information to outsiders.

3.2. A Model for Measuring Market and Credit Risks

While we do not claim to provide a solution to all methodological and supervisory problems outlined in part 1 above, we propose a specific treatment for the measurement of market and credit risks of CIUs with publicly available net asset values. The empirical application of this proposal is carried out in part 3 below by examining a group of emerging market closed-end funds that are listed in the New York Stock Exchange. The underlying hypothesis is that reasonable measurement of market and credit risks of these assets, when measured in currency units other than the currency of the home country, can serve as a basis for imposing appropriate capital charges for the associated market and credit risks. The proposed market risk measurement is in concordance with the latest "internal models approach" proposal by the Basle Committee and specifically with that of the Value-at-Risk (VaR) methodology, which is anticipated to be a regulatory standard soon, rather than with that of Directive 93/6/EEC. The amount of the relevant empirical literature that has appeared in only a very short period of time is indicative of the momentum on the subject.[2]

We propose that a $100\ (1-a)$ percentage, h-period VaR measure of an investment in a CIU is defined as the percentage c of its market value such that

$$\text{Prob } [\ln(P_t/P_{t-1}) < c] = a$$

where,

P_t is the market price of the CIU, and $\ln(P_t/Pt - 1) = \ln P_t - \ln P_{t-1}$ denotes the percentage change in the market price of the CIU between periods (t) and ($t-1$).
h is the pre-specified holding period, and
c is the tolerated percent loss from changes in a CIU's market value
a is a sufficiently small probability.

The market price P_t is in effect the net asset value of the CIU, while the relevant loss ratio (c) is the proposed capital adequacy ratio. In the case of listed CIU shares, a possible complication arises by the fact that net asset values deviate from the value represented by the market price of the listed CIU. While the presence of closed-end fund discounts from their net asset values should not be of concern for the purposes of capital adequacy, the presence of premiums may be perceived as a complication. In practice, however, this is not a serious drawback since the application of the methodology on a gross basis, i.e. without taking into account the presence of a discount or premium, does not result in significantly different capital charge ratios than an application on a net basis. This becomes obvious when considering the magnitude of the relevant product of a typical VaR level of 10% and a typical premium of 10%. Moreover, the possibility of maintaining short trading positions in other CIUs reduces the overall degree of such measurement errors. In any case, when the benefits from utilizing such a practical methodology are taken into account, the measurement error due to the presence of a discount/premium becomes of secondary importance.

In selecting the levels of the statistical parameters, h and a, as well as the form of the historical VaR simulation, we utilize the minimum quantitative standards designated by the Basle Committee on Banking Supervision (Basle Committee, 1996). These standards are:

(i) a 99th percentile, one-tailed confidence interval;
(ii) a ten-day equivalent holding period; and
(iii) an effective historical observation period of at least one year.

Despite the fact that not all CIU portfolios have the same investment horizons and the distributions of their returns are not identical, utilization of the main

Basle Committee parameters enables to conform with the objectives of common supervisory standards of the "internal models approach" which is in itself a regulatory standard. As explained below, the proposed methodology employs two additional specifications with regard to market risk measurement: the selection of the form of the VaR simulation applied to CIUs and the suppression of one of Basle Committee's quantitative parameters, known as the multiplication factor. Specifically:

The choice of the historical VaR simulation: While the "internal models approach" proposed by the Basle Committee specifies alternative forms of simulations (Variance-Covariance, Monte Carlo), the possible presence of derivative financial instruments or risk management techniques in a CIU would complicate the pre-specification of the relevant probability distribution and, in turn, complicate the whole implementation process. In contrast, the proposed historical simulation provides clear-cut, verifiable and indisputable levels of VaR, which are based on direct market quotations. Judging from the results obtained and presented below, the proposed methodology provides satisfactory results for the measurement of market risk of CIUs. When such measurements are combined with disclosure requirements for the issuing institutions as well as the investing entities, the benefits to all market participants can be substantial.

The issue of the multiplication factor: We argue that the inclusion of the multiplication factor proposed by the Basle Committee is not relevant in the application to listed CIUs whose net asset values are marked-to-market or quoted in a currency other than the currency of denomination of the underlying assets. This is typically the case for all emerging market closed-end funds listed in major organized exchanges (Gatzonas & Papaioannou, 1997). The methodology proposed here aims at extracting the relevant VaR figure from a distribution-free process. The most important aspect, however, is the fact that the selected VaR figure refers to a distribution of returns in a currency other than that of the denomination of the CIU's portfolio assets. By so doing, we have already taken a major step towards the recognition of foreign exchange risk and, as a result, any additional alteration of the VaR figure, such as a multiplication factor, leads to a double counting of the underlying risks. An additional reason for not incorporating the multiplication factor to the VaR figure is diversification. The vast majority of CIUs is managed by professional entities which make a minimum effort in diversifying the relevant portfolio of a CIU. In so doing, while they eliminate significant portions of unsystematic risks (including event and default risks), they leave the CIU exposed to pure market risks, such as foreign exchange risk and/or equity market risk. By design, the proposed methodology handles both of these types of risks without any additional modification and, therefore, it leads to a VaR figure which could be used as the relevant capital charge.

The treatment of specific risks presents typically a problem, especially for non-diversified portfolios. Recent developments in the area of modeling specific risks for the purposes of capital adequacy (Basle, 1997, 1999 (April)) come with a word of caution for supervising entities and institutions. While the theoretical and empirical work on the interaction of market and credit risks in the VaR context has not been sufficiently investigated yet, however, the role of credit, event and default risks is in the case of CIUs suppressed in the sense that the underlying portfolio is sufficiently diversified. To the extent that the relevant portfolio of securities is sufficiently diversified to minimize credit risk exposure, the remaining material exposure is in essence market risk.

3.3. Results and Evaluation

To examine the validity of these methodological arguments, we investigate the daily price behavior of thirteen closed-end emerging market country funds listed in the New York Stock Exchange for the period October 1994 to December 1997. The observed wide variation in the equity performance of the respective markets, as manifested by the daily valuations of these funds in a currency other than the local currency, provides us with the appropriate data set for the application of the proposed methodology, as outlined in Section 2. The results obtained by applying the Basle Committee's (1996) specification of VaR for the measurement of market risk in these emerging market closed-end funds indicate that the measures for capital charges are reasonable, meaningful, and easy to replicate for any listed CIU. The estimated VaR figures range from a minimum of 3.91 percent in the case of the Central European Fund (in March-April 1996) to at least 20.0 percent in the case of the Thai Cap Fund, the Brazilian Equity Fund, the Central European Fund, the Korean Investment Fund, the Malaysian Fund, and the Taiwan Province of China Fund, (at the end of November and beginning of December 1997) (Table 1). For all 13 funds, the overall sample period VaR figure reaches the level of 11.52% which is well above the focal capital adequacy ratio of 8% pursued by most regulatory authorities. The resulting excess average charge of 3.52 (i.e. 11.52–8)% could be justified by making reference to the nature and excess volatility observed in emerging markets. It should also be mentioned that these results prove a sensitivity of the proposed methodology to periods of increased financial turbulence. In a previous study, where we used the sample period of October 1994 to May 1997 – i.e. before the Asian financial crisis, the VaR measurements of market risk of the same 13 funds were uniformly lower than

MICHAEL G. PAPAIOANNOU AND E. K. GATZONAS

Table 1. Value at Risk of Selected Closed-End Funds Listed in the NYSE
[Anticipated Maximum Loss of Holding a Position for 10 Days]
99% Confidence Interval, Actual 10-Day Loss.

	Thai Cap	Brazilian Equity	Central European	Turkish Fund	Chilean Fund	New Germany	India Growth	Korean Invest.	Malaysia Fund	Mexican Fund	First Philippine	Portugal Fund	R.O.C. Taiwan
10/31/95	-17.52%	-25.74%	n.a.	-12.28%	-15.91%	n.a.	-19.42%	n.a.	-13.75%	n.a.	-15.56%	n.a.	n.a.
11/30/95	-17.52%	-25.74%	n.a.	-12.28%	-15.91%	n.a.	-19.42%	n.a.	-13.75%	n.a.	-15.56%	-9.09%	n.a.
12/29/95	-17.52%	-24.12%	n.a.	-12.28%	-15.91%	n.a.	-19.42%	n.a.	-10.67%	n.a.	-15.56%	-9.09%	n.a.
01/31/96	-8.51%	-20.96%	n.a.	-12.28%	-15.91%	n.a.	-19.42%	n.a.	-9.93%	n.a.	-15.56%	-8.08%	n.a.
02/29/96	-8.51%	-15.91%	-3.97%	-12.28%	-15.91%	n.a.	-19.42%	n.a.	-9.93%	-18.33%	-15.56%	-8.08%	-14.13%
03/29/96	-8.51%	-15.57%	-3.91%	-12.28%	-10.96%	-5.00%	-19.42%	-9.00%	-8.51%	-17.65%	-8.20%	-6.60%	-11.49%
04/30/96	-8.51%	-15.57%	-3.91%	-12.28%	-10.96%	-5.00%	-19.42%	-9.00%	-8.51%	-17.65%	-8.20%	-6.60%	-11.49%
05/31/96	-8.51%	-15.57%	-4.86%	-11.11%	-10.96%	-5.00%	-19.42%	-9.00%	-8.51%	-17.19%	-8.20%	-6.60%	-11.49%
06/28/96	-8.51%	-15.57%	-4.86%	-11.11%	-10.96%	-5.00%	-19.42%	-9.00%	-8.24%	-17.19%	-8.20%	-6.60%	-11.49%
07/31/96	-8.57%	-15.83%	-4.86%	-11.32%	-10.96%	-5.00%	-19.42%	-9.00%	-7.98%	-17.19%	-8.20%	-6.60%	-11.49%
08/30/96	-7.55%	-15.83%	-4.86%	-11.32%	-9.36%	-4.95%	-19.42%	-9.09%	-7.83%	-17.19%	-8.20%	-5.83%	-10.98%
09/30/96	-7.55%	-15.83%	-4.86%	-11.32%	-9.36%	-4.95%	-19.42%	-8.75%	-7.83%	-17.19%	-8.20%	-5.83%	-10.98%
10/31/96	-9.35%	-15.83%	-4.86%	-11.32%	-9.36%	-4.95%	-12.71%	-9.09%	-7.83%	-11.76%	-9.02%	-5.83%	-10.98%
11/29/96	-9.35%	-15.83%	-4.86%	-11.32%	-9.18%	-4.95%	-12.71%	-9.72%	-7.23%	-9.62%	-9.02%	-5.83%	-10.98%
12/31/96	-13.68%	-15.83%	-7.69%	-11.32%	-9.18%	-8.70%	-12.71%	-9.72%	-7.89%	-8.93%	-8.09%	-5.15%	-10.98%
01/31/97	-13.68%	-15.57%	-7.69%	-11.32%	-7.14%	-8.70%	-12.71%	-9.72%	-9.49%	-8.93%	-8.09%	-4.63%	-8.86%
02/28/97	-13.68%	-15.57%	-7.69%	-11.32%	-7.14%	-8.70%	-12.71%	-9.72%	-9.49%	-8.93%	-8.09%	-4.63%	-8.86%
03/31/97	-13.68%	-13.33%	-7.69%	-11.32%	-7.82%	-8.70%	-12.71%	-9.72%	-9.49%	-8.62%	-7.69%	-4.04%	-8.43%
04/30/97	-13.68%	-13.33%	-7.69%	-11.32%	-7.82%	-8.70%	-12.71%	-9.72%	-9.86%	-8.62%	-9.85%	-4.63%	-8.43%
05/30/97	-13.68%	-13.33%	-7.69%	-11.32%	-7.82%	-8.70%	-10.42%	-9.72%	-9.86%	-8.62%	-9.85%	-4.63%	-8.70%
06/30/97	-13.68%	-13.33%	-7.69%	-10.91%	-7.82%	-8.70%	-10.42%	-9.72%	-9.86%	-8.62%	-9.85%	-4.63%	-10.00%

Table 1. Continued.

	Thai Cap	Brazilian Equity	Central European	Turkish Fund	Chilean Fund	New Germany	India Growth	Korean Invest.	Malaysia Fund	Mexican Fund	First Philippine	Portugal Fund	R.O.C. Taiwan
07/31/97	-13.68%	-8.80%	-7.69%	-9.09%	-7.73%	-8.70%	-10.10%	-10.00%	-11.48%	-8.20%	-9.92%	-6.67%	-10.00%
08/29/97	-17.24%	-10.22%	-7.69%	-9.09%	-7.73%	-8.70%	-12.09%	-10.00%	-16.25%	-8.20%	-14.36%	-6.67%	-10.00%
09/30/97	-17.24%	-10.22%	-7.69%	-9.09%	-7.73%	-8.70%	-12.09%	-11.02%	-20.00%	-8.20%	-15.34%	-6.67%	-11.11%
10/31/97	-17.24%	-25.20%	-11.67%	-17.57%	-9.95%	-9.40%	-13.98%	-17.78%	-20.00%	-15.56%	-17.44%	-10.30%	-26.52%
11/28/97	-21.00%	-25.20%	-32.11%	-17.95%	-9.95%	-12.61%	-15.88%	-21.11%	-20.00%	-15.56%	-17.44%	-10.30%	-26.52%
12/09/97	-21.00%	-25.20%	-32.11%	-17.95%	-9.95%	-12.61%	-15.88%	-21.11%	-20.00%	-15.56%	-17.44%	-10.30%	-26.52%
Average	-12.93%	-17.00%	-8.64%	-12.01%	-10.35%	-7.56%	-15.66%	-10.94%	-11.27%	-12.76%	-11.36%	-6.69%	-12.63%
STD	4.27%	5.02%	7.65%	2.28%	2.97%	2.46%	3.64%	3.77%	4.24%	4.19%	3.72%	1.88%	5.65%
Average		-11.52%											

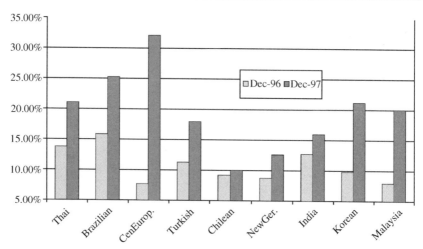

Fig. 1.   Value-at-Risk for Selected Closed-End Funds.

those presented here (Gatzonas & Papaioannou, 1998). Figure 1 shows the
substantial increase in the VaR figures for selected close-end funds between
December 1996 and December 1997. An "order statistics" approach to
determining the VaR levels appearing in Table 1 is provided in the Appendix.

By design, the proposed methodology allows for variation of VaR estimates
on a fund-to-fund basis and it also provides the means for varying the capital
charge in response to recent historical volatility. As shown in Table 1, the VaR
figures vary over time as volatility patterns change while it takes a considerable
amount of time before such levels are actually reduced. For a VaR figure to be
reduced on any particular date, it would take an approximate time interval of
250 trading days (around one year). On the other hand, recent increases in the
stock price volatility of the funds are incorporated into the VaR figures in a
much faster manner. On average, the waiting time for the incorporation of
increased volatility into the calculated VaR is a direct function of the model's
holding period, which in our study is a period of 10 trading days. The flexibility
of the methodology to incorporate recent increases in volatility along with the
ability to adjust the capital charge in accordance with the portfolio's market
risk constitute two key advantages that are not present in the existing capital
adequacy treatment of CIUs.

In comparison with the capital requirements of the Building Block
Methodology, the range of VaR-based capital charges obtained here is also
reasonable. The existing regulatory standard for market risk requires capital

ratios of 12% in a particular equity (8% for net positions and 4% for gross positions), 8% for positions in an equity index and 2.4% in a single position in ten-year government bond. While these charges could be higher when adjusted for other types of market risk (foreign exchange, settlement and counterparty risk), it should also be taken into account that such modifications could be done in the opposite direction through possible offsetting allowances and netting processes, thus reducing the overall capital charge to a focal ratio of around 8%.

4. CONCLUSIONS

The results obtained from the proposed methodology seem to provide better than existing risk-return assessments for the disclosure of the risk profile of portfolios that include regulated CIUs. The historical simulation employed allows for replication of results by any private agency or international organization, and the use of the standardized methodology for rating CIUs. Moreover, even though disclosure of these figures does not reveal the CIUs' investment strategy, it is sufficient to characterize the risk profile of an investment in CIUs.

The proposed standards for the capital adequacy of CIUs combine the characteristics of a market-oriented practice, which enhances the organizational and risk management ability of institutions, with that of a potential solution to the complex problem of risk measurement. The inherent weakness of a large number of EU financial institutions to successfully adopt similar requirements in their management information and risk management systems carries the risk of superficial implementation of such standards. Despite these potential drawbacks, the proposed methodology can provide the basis for a uniform approach towards the measurement of investment risk in CIU shares.

While enhancing a financial institution's risk management systems is equally important to the implementation of the quantitative aspects of the VaR measurement and disclosure methodology, it should be mentioned that alternative proposals, such as the "precommitment approach," as well as other more flexible supervisory risk assessment processes, have taken a vanguard position in latest regulatory developments. Regardless of the final shape of these regulatory proposals, utilization of VaR methodologies for CIUs as independent entities (asset class) or as investment vehicles in portfolios of other institutions is anticipated to gain ground as a prominent risk measurement practice and disclosure requirement.

The issue of the legal form of implementation of this methodology needs to be addressed. From the relevant experience in the European Union, the benefits obtained from the new capital adequacy standards would not have been materialized, had such standards taken the form of a recommendation rather than the legally binding Directive 93/6/EEC. Given the implementation difficulties in a variety of financial institutions in the European Union, mainly banking and investment firms, such a conclusion can easily be justified. These concerns could be avoided as long as the utilized methodology employs the generic but precise specification proposed in this paper.

The legally binding market-risk Directive of the European Union, as well as the recent "internal models approach" to measuring market risk, allows for substantial differentiation in the simulation form and the definition of the underlying statistical parameters. Despite these regulatory breakthroughs, however, none of the existing or recent supervisory developments address directly the issue of CIU market risk in a comprehensive way. This void in the literature of risk measurement and regulatory treatment of CIUs is covered by the present study.

NOTES

1. See, for example, Kupiec (1999), Tattersall (1996), Szego (1995), Kupiec and O'Brien (1995), and Franklin and Mishkin (1995).
2. Beder (1995), Estrella (1995), Hendricks (1996), Hendricks and Hirtle (1997), Hoper (1996), Jorion (1996), Marshall and Venkataraman (1996), Sheldon (1995), Spinner (1996), Stambaugh (1996), Kupiec (1998), Falloon (1999), Smithson (2000), Dowd (2001) and Basak and Shapiro (2001). In addition, the proposals put forward in the 1998 conference of the Federal Reserve Bank of New York seem to set the basis for the future of capital regulation.

REFERENCES

Bank of International Settlements (2001). Basle Committee on Banking Supervision. The New Basle Accord (January). Basle, Switzerland.
Bank of International Settlements (1999). Basle Committee on Banking Supervision. A New Capital Adequacy Framework (June). Basle, Switzerland.
Bank of International Settlements (1999). Basle Committee on Banking Supervision. Credit Risk Modeling: Current Practices and Applications (April). Basle, Switzerland.
Bank of International Settlements (1997). Basle Committee on Banking Supervision. The Treatment of Specific Risk (September). Basle, Switzerland.
Bank of International Settlements (1997). Financial Trends in the Emerging Markets. 67th Annual Report (July). Basle, Switzerland.
Bank of International Settlements (1996). Basle Committee on Banking Supervision. Overview of the Amendment to the Capital Accord to Incorporate Market Risk. Basle, Switzerland.
Bank of International Settlements (1993). Basle Committee on Banking Supervision. The Prudential Treatment of Netting, Market Risks and Interest Rate Risk (April). Basle, Switzerland.

Bank of International Settlements (1988). Basle Committee on Banking Supervision. International Convergence of Capital Measurement and Capital Standards. Basle, Switzerland.

Basak, S., & Shapiro, A. (2001). Value-at-Risk-Based Risk Management: Optimal Policies and Asset Prices. *Review of Financial Studies, 14*(2), 371–405.

Beder, T. S. (1995). VAR: Seductive but Dangerous. *Financial Analysts Journal, 51*(5), September/October, 12–24.

Berkowitz, J., & O'Brien, J. (2001). How Accurate Are Value-at-Risk Models at Commercial Banks? *Federal Reserve Board Discussion Paper* 2001–31 (July). Washington, D.C.

Council of European Communities (1993). Council Directive 93/6/EEC on the Capital Adequacy of Investment Firms and Credit Institutions, March, Brussels.

Dowd, K. (2001). Estimating VaR with Other Statistics. *Journal of Derivatives*, Spring, 23–30.

Estrella, A. (1995). A Prolegomenon to Future Capital Requirements. *Federal Reserve Bank of New York Economic Policy Review, 1*(2), July, 1–12.

Falloon, W. (1999). Growin' up. *Risk*, February, 26–31.

Federal Reserve Bank of New York (1998). Financial Services at the Crossroads: Capital Regulation in the Twenty-First Century, Proceedings of a Conference. *Economic Policy Review, 4*(3), October.

Franklin, R. E., & Mishkin, F. S. (1995). The Decline of Traditional Banking: Implications for Financial Stability and Regulatory Policy. *Federal Reserve Bank of New York Economic Policy Review, 1*(2), July, 27–45.

Gatzonas, E. K., & Papaioannou, M. G. (1997). Premium/Discount Determinants of Emerging Market Closed-End Funds. *Emerging Markets Quarterly*, Spring, 33–39.

Gatzonas, E. K., & Papaioannou, M. G. (1998). Market Risk of Close-End Funds and Other Collective Investment Undertakings in Emerging Markets. In: E. O. Lyn & G. J. Papaioannou (Eds), *Financial Services in the Evolving Marketplace: Approaching the Next Millennium*. Conference Proceedings, The Merrill Lynch Center for the Study of International Financial Services and Markets, Hofstra University, October 1–3, 1998, Hempstead, New York (forthcoming).

Hendricks, D. (1996). Evaluation of Value at Risk Models Using Historical Data. *Federal Reserve Bank of New York Economic Policy Review, 2*(1), April, 39–69.

Hendricks, D., & Hirtle, B. (1997). Bank Capital Requirements for Market Risk: The Internal Models Approach. *Federal Reserve Bank of New York Economic Policy Review, 3*(4), December, 1–12.

Hoper, G. (1996). A New Methodology for Measuring Portfolio Risk. *Federal Reserve Bank of Philadelphia Business Review*, July-August, 19–30.

Jackson, P., Maude, D. J., & Perraudin, W. (1997). Bank Capital and Value at Risk. *Journal of Derivatives, 4*(3), Spring, 73–89.

Jorion, P. (1996). Risk^2: Measuring the Risk in Value at Risk. *Financial Analysts Journal, 52*(6), November/December, 47–56.

Kendall, M., & Stuart, A. (1977). *The Advanced Theory of Statistics, Vol. 1: Distribution Theory*. High Wycombe: Charles Griffin and Company Ltd.

Kupiec, P. H. (1999). Risk Capital and VaR. *Journal of Derivatives*, Winter, 41–52.

Kupiec, P. H. (1998). Stress Testing in a Value-at-Risk Framework. *Journal of Derivatives*, Fall, 7–24.

Kupiec, P. H., & O'Brien, J. M. (1995). Recent Developments in Bank Capital Regulation of Market Risks. *Federal Reserve Board Finance and Economics Discussion Paper*, 1995–51, December, Washington, D.C.

Lopez, J. A. (1997). Regulatory Evaluation of Value-at-Risk Models. *Federal Reserve Bank of New York Staff Reports, 33,* November.
Lopez, J. A. (1999). Methods for Evaluating Value-at-Risk Estimates. *Federal Reserve Bank of San Francisco Economic Review, 2,* 3–17.
Marshall, D., & Venkataraman, S. (1996). Bank Capital for Market Risk: A Study in Incentive-Compatible Regulation. *Chicago Fed Letter, 104,* April, 1–4.
OECD (1996). A Revolution in Securities Markets' Structures. *Financial Market Trends, 65,* November.
Sheldon, G. (1995). A Limit-Risk Capital Adequacy Rule. Swiss *Journal of Economics and Statistics, 131*(4/2), December, 773–805.
Smithson, C. (2000). Beyond VaR. *Risk,* December, 85–87.
Spinner, K. (1996). The VaR Explosion. *Wall Street and Technology, 14*(6), June, 8–11.
Stambaugh, F. (1996). Risk and Value at Risk. *European Management Journal, 14*(6), December, 612–621.
Szego, G. P. (1995). Risk-Based Capital in the European Economic Community. *Journal of Banking and Finance, 19,* 727–729.
Tattersall, J. (1996). A Cost You Can't Ignore. *Banker, 146*(841), March, 30–31.

APPENDIX

In its general specification, VaR is derived from the probability distribution for the future portfolio value, $f(x)$. At a given confidence level, c, the worst possible realization x^* is defined such that the probability of exceeding such a value is c, where

$$c = \int_{x^*}^{\infty} F(x)dx_t \tag{1}$$

or, such that the probability of a value lower than x^* is $1 - c$, where

$$1 - c = \int_{-\infty}^{x^*} F(x)dx_t \tag{2}$$

In other words, the area from $-\infty$ to x^* must sum to $1 - c$, which for empirical applications is typically specified at 1%, or 5%.

In a historical simulation approach to measuring VaR, such a general specification is valid without having to resort to assumptions of normality or serial independence. In an order-statistics context (Kendall & Stuart, 1977), VaR at a probability level p is taken to be equal to the negative of the r-th lowest observation, where r is equal to $100p + 1$. More generally, with n observations, the VaR is equal to the negative of the r-th lowest observation, where $r = np + 1$. The r-th lowest observation (order) determines the position of the relevant VaR level. As presented by Dowd (2001), the order statistics approach to VaR can be applied to any parametric VaR-normal VaR, t-VaR, or even extreme-value VaR. Moreover, provided that sample sizes are not too small, the approach is sufficiently accurate, practical and useful, as calculations can be carried out on a spreadsheet.

For the distribution of net asset value returns, x^*, generated over a historical period of one year after specifying the relevant holding period, h, to be equal to two weeks (10 trading days), the position of the observation such that c percent of the sorted – in ascending order – portion of the distribution is on the right side, can be found by multiplying the significance level $(1 - c)$ by the number of observations in the historical sample. When such a position is specified, the relevant VaR is determined by the corresponding (negative) value x^* of the sorted distribution. The discrete-time specification of (2) utilized in this work is

$$1 - c = \sum_{-m}^{x^*} F(x) \qquad (3)$$

where,

$F(x)$ is the frequency distribution of the 10-day period returns over a one-year historical period (250 working days),

m is the minimum historical value of the array which has been sorted in ascending order, and

x^* is the observation in the array of returns which corresponds to the 99% level of $F(x)$, which is the 3rd observation of the sorted historical distribution, or the $np + 1$ order observation of the array of net asset values. The VaR figures shown in Table 1 correspond to values of x^*, which in turn are specified for one-year historical periods ending at the end of each calendar month in the sample. The underlying array of observations refer to 10-day percentage changes of net asset values of the closed-end funds under investigation.

G-22

|v5| G-12 G-13

6. FRICTIONS AND TAX-ADVANTAGED HEDGE FUND RETURNS

David M. Schizer

ABSTRACT

This article discusses strategies in which taxpayers use derivatives to attain better tax treatment for hedge fund investments. In response to an early planning strategy, Congress enacted the constructive ownership rule of Section 1260. This measure's success has proved surprising, given the similarity of section 1260 to the constructive sale rule of section 1259; the latter rule, which targets a different use of derivatives in tax planning, has proved easy to avoid. Theoretically, either rule can be avoided through relatively modest changes in economic return. While this strategy is common for section 1259, it is much more difficult for section 1260 because securities dealers cannot supply the necessary derivative. Instead, taxpayers have sought tax-advantaged hedge fund returns through strategies involving insurance and offshore corporations.

1. INTRODUCTION

With twin tax provisions, a superficial resemblance can sometimes mask very different personalities.[1] So it is with the constructive sale rule of section 1259

This article is based on a larger work, Fictions as a Constraint on Tax Planning, that was published in volume 101 of the *Columbia Law Review.*

Global Risk Management: Financial, Operational, and Insurance Strategies,
Volume 3, pages 81–95.
ISBN: 0-7623-0982-2

and the constructive ownership rule of section 1260. The provisions use essentially the same statutory language, and each targets a tax-motivated use of derivative securities – either to hedge appreciated assets (section 1259) or to simulate investments in hedge funds and other pass-thru entities (section 1260). Notwithstanding this similarity, however, the measures have prompted very different reactions from taxpayers. Theoretically, either rule can be avoided through relatively modest changes in economic return. While this strategy is common for section 1259,[2] it is much more difficult for section 1260 because securities dealers cannot supply the necessary derivative. Instead, taxpayers have sought tax-advantaged hedge fund returns through strategies involving insurance and offshore corporations. After a description in Section 2 of the transaction targeted by section 1260, Section 3 explains why tactics for avoiding section 1259 are less effective for section 1260. Section 4 considers other strategies involving derivatives that survive under section 1260. Section 5 discusses insurance-based techniques for securing tax-advantaged hedge fund returns. Section 6 is the conclusion.

2. PLANNING TARGETED BY SECTION 1260

In cutting the long term capital gains rate from 28% to 20% in 1997, Congress reduced the attractiveness of investment strategies that involve frequent trading. Most hedge funds use such strategies to earn impressive pretax returns. As partnerships for tax purposes, though, they pass their profits through to investors as short term capital gains, taxable in the current year. In response, investment bankers and their tax advisors developed a way to convert these appealing pretax returns into deferred long term capital gains: a derivative whose return was based on the hedge fund's value. No tax was due until the derivative was settled, and gains were taxed at long term rates if the taxpayer held the derivative for the requisite holding period (eighteen months at the time, and currently one year).[3] When selling such a derivative to a client, the investment bank would hedge its "short" derivative position by investing in the hedge fund. In essence, the investment bank would become a partner in the fund, and would use a derivative to transfer the economic return to clients.[4]

After the transaction attracted media attention, Congress responded by enacting the constructive ownership rule of section 1260. Closely based on section 1259,[5] section 1260 applies to derivatives that simulate the return of a hedge fund or other pass-thru entity[6] by offering the holder substantially all of the risk of loss and opportunity for gain from the underlying asset.[7] If this test is satisfied, certain long term capital gain earned on settlement of the derivative is recharacterized as ordinary income, and an interest charge is imposed to compensate the government for tax deferral.[8]

3. THE CONTRAST WITH SECTION 1259

Notwithstanding the similarity of the two statutory formulae, section 1260 has prompted different planning responses than section 1259. To develop this contrast, this Section begins with the tax benefit from avoiding section 1260 and then considers the non-tax costs, or "frictions," as they are called here, that stand in the way.[9]

3.1. Tax Benefit

Avoiding section 1260 often yields less of a tax benefit than avoiding section 1259, and so taxpayers may not try as hard. Although each transaction offers deferral, and the possibility of tax forgiveness if the taxpayer dies (as long as the basis step-up remains in effect), deferral opportunities are greater in hedging appreciated assets. The reason is that these assets are *already* appreciated when the derivatives transaction begins, so tax would otherwise be due immediately, and deferral erodes this tax burden from the outset. In contrast, a hedge fund derivative is not appreciated from the start. Since it allows taxpayers to pay a preset price for the fund, the derivative becomes valuable only if the underlying fund appreciates. Thus, tax is not deferred from the beginning, but only on gains earned *after* the transaction starts. Even so, avoiding section 1260 offers a benefit, in addition to deferral, that does not arise from avoiding section 1259: halving of the relevant tax rate from almost 40% to 20%.

3.2. Derivatives with a Modified Return

Since section 1260 uses essentially the same statutory standard as section 1259, we might expect a similar strategy: use of derivatives that offer most, but not all, of the fund's return.[10] For a fund interest worth $100, for instance, the taxpayer might bear the full risk of loss below $95 by selling a put with a $95 exercise price, while enjoying opportunity for gain above $115 by purchasing a call with a $115 exercise price. In fact, these "partial return" strategies are uncommon.

3.2.1. Statutory Language
Although frictions ultimately account for the difference, disparities in statutory language should be considered first. Unlike section 1259, section 1260 does

not have legislative history deeming the rule inapplicable when the return on the derivative differs sufficiently from the return on the underlying property. The reason, I suspect, is that the point was well understood because the standard was consciously lifted from section 1259. Even so, the two provisions treat forward contracts differently. Unlike section 1259, section 1260 covers *any* forward contract, even one that omits a portion of the underlying fund's economic return, and so such forwards are not a viable planning strategy.[11] Nevertheless, like section 1259, section 1260 excludes options and equity swaps that do not sufficiently track the underlying asset.[12] If these derivatives are used, strategies like those employed for section 1259 would pass legal muster for section 1260.

3.2.2. Difficulty of Dynamic Hedging

The relative difficulty of avoiding section 1260, then, derives not from the tax law itself, but from frictions – in particular, frictions affecting the dealer counterparty's ability to hedge. Before section 1260 was enacted, the dealer could hedge by holding the fund interest. But now that the derivative must convey *less than all* of the hedge fund's economic return – a requirement for avoiding section 1260 – holding the fund interest is no longer a perfect hedge. For instance, assume the investment bank is asked to sell a call for $115 and buy a put for $95. If the fund appreciates from $100 to $115, this profit goes to the dealer. Yet if the price declines from $100 to $95, the dealer cannot pass this loss on to the client through the put, an outcome that generally is unacceptable under the risk-management policies of major investment banks.[13]

Given this difficulty, why are dealers able to supply derivatives for avoidance of section 1259? After all, a dealer that offers customers a collar on one share cannot perfectly hedge by selling one share short, since the economic returns do not match perfectly.[14] The key difference is that for section 1259, but not section 1260, the relevant derivative is based on a publicly traded asset. As a result, dealers can use hedging strategies that rely on delta, the correlation of the derivative's value with underlying stock prices. For instance, assume a collar leaves a dealer exposed to risk of loss below $90 and opportunity for gain above $110 on 1000 shares of a publicly traded stock currently worth $100. For every dollar change in the underlying stock's value, the collar's value will change by an observable number of cents, which will be less than a dollar. The reason for this divergence is that the collar does not cover the full range of stock returns. There is a gap between $90 and $110. As a result, since the collar is based on 1000 shares, the dealer would not hedge by shorting a full 1000 shares, but an amount *fewer than* 1000 shares. If a $1 change in the asset price induces an $.85 change in the collar's value, the dealer's offsetting short would be 85% as large (i.e. shorting 850 shares to hedge a collar on 1000 shares). Delta will vary as the underlying stock price changes, reflecting different probabilities that the derivative will yield a profit or loss. Thus, the dealer must constantly monitor delta and make corresponding adjustments in the size of the hedge.

For two reasons, then, dynamic hedging is feasible only for publicly traded assets, and not for hedge fund positions. First, computation of delta requires data about the relationship between derivatives and the underlying asset, and such a rich supply of data is available only for a publicly traded asset.[15] Second, constant adjustments in the size of the hedge are feasible only in an extremely liquid market – and certainly not with a hedge fund, which might allow redemptions only once a month.

Although delta hedging is not feasible for a hedge fund derivative, one investment bank was once willing to sell such a derivative without perfectly hedging it – a notorious exception that proves the rule. In 1996, Union Bank of Switzerland (UBS) provided this service to the principals of Long Term Capital Management (LTCM).[16] The economic disparity between the derivative and underlying fund interest proved disastrous for UBS when LTCM failed three years later. This transaction is well known on Wall Street and investment bankers often mention it in explaining why securities dealers are wary of taking risks on these transactions.

4. DERIVATIVES-BASED STRATEGIES THAT SURVIVE UNDER SECTION 1260

Thus, although the language of section 1259 was transplanted into section 1260, methods of avoiding section 1259 are not so easily borrowed, due to the dealers' difficulty in supplying the necessary derivative. Taxpayers have attempted to use modified derivatives to avoid section 1260, with only limited success. This Section describes six of these strategies.

4.1. Call Options

One alternative is for a taxpayer to buy call options. For instance, Bear Stearns sells call options on a "fund of funds" run by Bear Stearns investment managers.[17] The call option sells for one-third the price of a direct investment, has an exercise price of 120% of a direct investment's initial value, and has a term of seven and a quarter years.[18] Presumably, Bear Stearns can offer these options because, as manager of the underlying fund, the firm is better able to hedge satisfactorily.[19] Yet the client's tax analysis is weakened: Since the derivatives dealer and hedge fund manager are related, it might be easier for the government to treat the client's payments to the dealer for an option as, in substance, payments to the fund manager for a partnership interest. There are other disadvantages as well. Instead of choosing which fund she prefers, the taxpayer can invest only in the six funds selected by Bear Stearns. More importantly, call options are costly. The taxpayer must pay a large premium, and will not break even unless the fund appreciates by 53% (so the taxpayer can recover the 33% premium and 120% exercise price).

4.2. Reduced Opportunity for Gain

Another strategy is for dealers to sell a derivative in which they retain opportunity for gain, without taking on risk of loss – on the theory that losses are especially troubling to dealers. Thus, assume a dealer sells the client a $120 call, takes a $100 put in return, and hedges by purchasing a fund interest for $100. The dealer's net exposure would be to profit from appreciation between $100 and $120. Yet although dealers will not object to this exposure, they are reluctant to pay for it, at least at major investment banks. As a result, clients are likely to be charged for the *full* opportunity for gain, without a discount for the $20 of appreciation kept by the dealer. For example, assume a direct investment in the fund would cost $100. For the derivative, the client would pay approximately $103 (i.e. the price of the hedge fund plus a 3% fee). While the tax treatment is better, no pretax profit is earned until the underlying fund appreciates by 20%. This deal makes sense only if a very high pretax return (and thus a high tax bill) are expected on the fund. Eventually, dealers may start paying for this 20% of retained exposure, since this bet clearly has positive value. For instance, less well known investment banks might do so to attract new business, although these dealers would have to consider the effect of a risky hedge fund portfolio on their creditworthiness.

4.3. Catch-Up Structures

Instead of paying for this exposure, dealers have looked for ways to give this return to the client. For example, the client could receive no payment for the fund's first 20% appreciation, while receiving double credit for the next 20%. As the fund appreciates from $120 to $121, the client receives not one, but two dollars. When the fund reaches $140, the client claims $40 of appreciation (i.e. $2 for each dollar of appreciation between $120 and $140). As long as the fund appreciates to $140, the client benefits from *all* appreciation in the underlying fund, sharing none with the dealer.

Yet to avoid section 1260, the return on the derivative and underlying fund must diverge in a meaningful way. In this transaction, a difference arises only if the fund's maturity value is between $100 and $120 (and, to some extent, between $120 and $140). For some funds, the end value is reasonably likely to be in this range. For many funds, though, the likelihood is remote.

4.4. Inclusion of a Third Party

Since the dealer does not value the exposure between $100 and $120 and, for tax reasons, the client should not take it, another approach is to transfer this exposure to an unrelated third party. (The two customers should be unrelated so the government cannot treat the two as one person and deem them, jointly, to be subject to section 1260. Notably, however, section 1260, unlike section 1259, grants no explicit authority to consider the activities of related parties.) The dealer would thus sell the right to this appreciation as a separate "stub" security. Because the dealer will collect payment for the stub, the dealer can reduce the price of the main derivative.

There are challenges in implementing this strategy, though. Since the dealer will not tolerate unhedged exposure for any amount of time, the dealer cannot keep the stubs as inventory, to be sold whenever a suitable customer is found. Rather, two unrelated customers must appear simultaneously, and must want to invest in the same fund. In addition, if one customer wishes to terminate the derivative prior to maturity (e.g. to claim tax losses), the other must be compelled to do so because the dealer cannot hedge one without the other. In effect, the stub must have an uncertain term, terminating whenever the main derivative terminates. This requirement would reduce the price an investor would pay.

4.5. Offshore Vehicles

Instead of changing the derivative's economic return, the taxpayer can hold the derivative through an offshore corporation. As a result, the taxpayer will no longer own a derivative, at least not directly. Instead, she will own common stock in a corporation, an investment not explicitly covered by section 1260. Nor will section 1260 apply to the corporation itself, as long as the entity is not subject to U.S. tax. Even so, this structure has two potential vulnerabilities. First, passive investments in offshore corporations can trigger other anti-abuse rules, including the passive foreign investment company (PFIC)[20] and controlled foreign corporation (CFC)[21] rules. While a comprehensive examination of these regimes is beyond this article's scope, the bottom line is that careful planners can often thread these needles.[22] The real vulnerability, instead, is the government's regulatory authority under section 1260 (which might be used retroactively) to cover "transactions . . . that have substantially the same effect" as those explicitly covered in the statute.

4.6. Modification of the Underlying Property: Managed Accounts, Indices, and Compound Derivatives

Still another possibility is to change the subject matter of the derivative. For instance, what if the derivative is based not on a hedge fund, but on the performance of a specified portfolio of securities held by an investment bank (a so called "managed account")? Section 1260 applies only to derivatives based on "financial assets," defined as "any equity interest in any pass-thru entity."[24] The term is arguably not broad enough to include a free-standing portfolio (even if managed by a hedge fund manager or, for that matter, by the taxpayer herself).[25] Because the portfolio is not held in an entity such as a partnership or trust, some argue that section 1260 should not apply. In a similar strategy, the derivative could be based on an "index" that reflects the trading strategy of a particular hedge fund, rather than the hedge fund itself. Whatever the merits of this technical argument,[26] the Treasury could override it through retroactive regulations.[27]

Other strategies also game the definition of "financial asset." What if the derivative is based on a hedge fund (which admittedly is a financial asset) and something that is not a financial asset, such as a commodity index? Some argue that this transaction avoids the regime, although the government could reach it through regulations, for instance, by bifurcating the derivative into a constructive ownership transaction and a separate position.[28] Under a plausible reading of the statute, though, this transaction is already covered, at least if a swap or forward contract is used. These derivatives are caught if the taxpayer "receive[s] credit" for changes in a financial asset's value – presumably, even if other factors, such as a commodity index, also influence the forward's or swap's value.[29] For instance, assume the hedge fund appreciates by $100 and the commodity index appreciates by $75, yielding a $175 profit on the derivative. The taxpayer has "received credit" for the $100 hedge fund profit.[30]

5. INSURANCE-BASED STRATEGIES

Section 1260 thus has impeded the use of derivatives to attain better tax treatment for hedge fund returns. To an extent, taxpayers can still pursue this goal with deals involving insurance. This section discusses two of these transactions.

5.1. Variable Life Insurance and Annuity Contracts

One strategy – a "variable" life insurance policy or annuity whose return is based on a hedge fund[31] – is a novel twist on an old practice. Favorable treatment of life insurance and annuities is longstanding. Even so, the tax treatment of these products can be less favorable than the treatment of derivatives before section 1260 was enacted. Like these early derivatives, annuities and life insurance offer deferral. Taxpayers do not owe tax while the hedge fund appreciates (as hedge fund partners do), and are taxed only upon receiving cash. But unlike these early derivatives, which offered long term capital gain, annuities yield ordinary income and, except in two scenarios, life insurance shares this disadvantage. The first exception is that payments are tax free when the insured dies (so tax character is irrelevant).[32] Although helpful to those who are investing for their heirs, this boon is useless to taxpayers who want to spend their gains. Second, policy loans and certain withdrawals are sometimes available tax free, but only if the life insurance policy is not a "modified endowment contract" (MEC), and even then complex restrictions may apply. Esoteric details aside, the main way to avoid MEC status is by staggering the payment of policy premiums over seven years, instead of investing a single premium up front.[33] Yet this slow pace carries a cost. Funds that have not yet been invested cannot begin enjoying tax deferred or tax free investment growth.

In addition, these deals present frictions of their own. First, the taxpayer must place a mortality bet so that the contract will qualify as life insurance for tax purposes. Second, significant fees and out-of-pocket costs erode the investment return. For policies issued by a U.S. insurance company, state excise taxes and a federal "deferred acquisition" (DAC) tax are approximately 4% of premiums. This cost is lower for policies issued by offshore insurers, which are subject only to a federal excise tax of 1%.[34] Fees must be paid to the money managers, as well as the insurance broker, insurance company, and bank custodian. Third, the taxpayer must accept less control over invested funds. U.S. insurance companies traditionally offer a slate of approved money managers, which might not include the taxpayer's preferred manager; offshore funds are more accommodating, since the regulatory environment is more flexible. Yet even then, the U.S. tax analysis is stronger if taxpayers limit their role in investment decisions.[35] Finally, although offshore insurance companies offer lower excise taxes and more flexibility, their credit may be less well established, and the regulatory environment can inspire less confidence.

A further risk is that section 1260 arguably could extend even to insurance and annuities. The Treasury has regulatory authority to cover transactions having "substantially the same effect" as the enumerated ones.[36] This language arguably is broad enough to reach annuities and insurance contracts that offer tax deferred hedge fund returns, although there is a credible argument to the contrary.[37] Notwithstanding these drawbacks, insurance is becoming an increasingly common method of securing tax advantaged hedge fund returns.

5.2. Offshore Hedge Fund Reinsurers

Instead of buying an insurance policy, taxpayers can invest in an offshore insurance or reinsurance company whose assets are managed by a hedge fund manager – in effect, a hedge fund that also sells insurance. The fund is structured as a corporation rather than as a partnership. Thus, investors are not liable every year for tax on the fund's trading profits. Rather, investors pay no tax until they sell their fund interest, and are taxed at long term capital gain rates if they have held the fund for at least a year. The fund itself will not pay U.S. (or other) income tax if it is incorporated in a tax haven such as Bermuda. Such offshore "incorporated pocketbooks" are an old strategy, targeted by several regimes. Most relevant are the PFIC rules, which generally apply to firms, such as hedge funds, that are engaged in investing and other "passive" businesses.[38] If this regime applies, there is no tax advantage over a domestic partnership. Investor returns would be recharacterized as ordinary income, and an interest charge would be imposed, as under section 1260. The trick here is that the PFIC regime does not apply to insurance companies, a statutory exception not yet elaborated by regulations.[39]

What factors help a fund qualify as an insurance company for purposes of the PFIC regime? Obviously, the fund must sell insurance, and thus must bear some mortality or casualty risk.[40] In some cases, these risks can substantially erode returns. Yet because these risks are actuarially predictable, many taxpayers will accept marginal increases as the price of a lower tax. In addition, the fund's ability to reinvest profits must be limited. The purpose of the fund's investments supposedly is to fund insurance liabilities. If these reserves dwarf the liabilities, it is not credible to claim that the fund is an insurance company.[41] Furthermore, to satisfy credit rating agencies and insurance regulators, firms cannot invest all their reserves in hedge funds; 40% is commonly thought to be the maximum. Finally, the firm must set up a real infrastructure, for instance, by hiring employees to manage insurance liabilities.

6. CONCLUSION

In sum, similar statutory language does not necessarily make for similar tax planning. The reason is that other key variables – business realities or "frictions" – are at work. Thus, a strategy that is common in one context can prove rare in another, despite similarities in the governing statutes.

NOTES

1. This article is part of a larger work that compares sections 1259 and 1260. See David M. Schizer, *Frictions as a Constraint on Tax Planning*, 101 Colum. L. Rev. 1312 (2001). A similar excerpt appeared in the *Journal of Taxation of Financial Products*. Statutory references are to the Internal Revenue Code of 1986, as amended.

2. For a discussion, see id. at 1339–68. Section 1259 targets strategies in which taxpayers who have appreciated property use derivatives to simulate a sale without triggering a current capital gains tax.

3. See Section 1234A. For a discussion, see New York State Bar Association Tax Section, Comments on H.R. 3170, *Tax Analysts, Tax Notes Today*, July 16, 1998, LEXIS, 98 TNT 136-38.

4. Because investment banks mark securities to market under section 475, they suffer no adverse consequences from holding the hedge fund. For a discussion, see David M. Schizer, *Sticks and Snakes: Derivatives and Curtailing Aggressive Tax Planning*, 73 S. Cal. L. Rev. 1339, 1343 n.10 (2000), at 1367–72.

5. See Barbara M. Flom, Constructive Ownership Transactions: The Sound of One Shoe Dropping. *J. Tax'n Fin. Products*, Summer 2000, at 19, 28 n.5 ("[T]he drafters viewed 'constructive ownership' as the mirror image of 'constructive sale.'").

6. Other pass-thru entities include regulated investment companies, real estate investment trusts, S corporations, passive foreign investment corporations, and foreign personal holding companies. I.R.C. § 1260(c)(2).

7. The definition of a constructive ownership transaction is based on, and closely tracks, section 1259's definition of a constructive sale. Compare section 1259(c)(1) with section 1260(d)(1).

8. Id. § 1260(b) (imposing interest charge on recharacterized gain). Two other tax motivated uses of hedge fund derivatives were not explicitly addressed. First, tax-exempt hedge fund investors can potentially earn taxable UBTI. Id. § 512(a)(1). In addition, foreign hedge fund investors can potentially earn two types of income that would be subject to U.S. tax, either "fixed or determinable annual or periodical gains, profits, and income" (FDAP), or "effectively connected income" (ECI). Id. § 871(a)(1)(A) (defining FDAP); id. §§ 864(c), 897(a)(1)(B) (defining ECI). By investing instead in derivatives, these investors can avoid these consequences in some cases. Section 1260 does not recharacterize gain as either UBTI or ECI. See Flom, supra note 5, at 19, 25–26 (arguing that section 1260 is unlikely to reach UBTI-avoiding strategies of tax-exempt organizations, but could conceivably reach FDAP- and ECI-avoiding strategies for foreign taxpayers, for instance, through regulations or case law).

9. The term "frictions" is borrowed from Myron S. Scholes & Mark A. Wolfson, *Taxes and Business Strategy: A Planning Approach* 7 (1992).

10. For a discussion of strategies for avoiding section 1259, see Schizer, supra note 1, at Part II.

11. See I.R.C. § 1260(d)(4) (defining forward contract as "any contract to acquire in the future (or provide or receive credit for the future value of) any financial asset"). In contrast, section 1259 does not cover forward contracts in which the amount of property delivered varies significantly with the value of the underlying property. See id. § 1259(d)(1) (defining forward contract as "a contract to deliver a substantially fixed amount of property (including cash) for a substantially fixed price"). Section 1260 covers such variable delivery forward contracts, but regulatory authority is provided to exclude them. Id. § 1260(g)(2). The Treasury has not yet used this authority.

12. With a pair of options, the regime is avoided as long as their exercise prices are not "substantially equal." Id. § 1260(d)(1)(C) (providing that regime is triggered by holding a call and selling a put, but only if "such options have substantially equal strike prices and substantially contemporaneous maturity dates"). Similarly, section 1260 clearly applies only to swaps offering the entire return (i.e. "substantially all" risk of loss and opportunity for gain) of the hedge fund – but not to swaps offering only some of this return. See id. § 1260(d)(3)(A), (B) (providing that a person has a "long position under a notional principal contract," and thus is covered by statute, if the person has "the right to be paid (or receive credit for) all or substantially all of the investment yield (including appreciation) on such financial asset for a specified period," and "is obligated to reimburse (or provide credit for) all or substantially all of any decline in the value of such financial asset"). The standard under section 1259 is identical in all relevant respects. See id. § 1259(d)(2)(A), (B) (defining "offsetting notional principal contract" as any agreement which "includes . . . a requirement to pay (or provide credit for) all or substantially all of the investment yield (including appreciation) on such property for a specified period," and a "right to be reimbursed for (or receive credit for) all or substantially all ofany decline in the value of such property").

13. For a discussion of these policies, see Schizer, supra note 1, at 1373–1374.

14. Assume the dealer sells a $95 put and buys a $115 call, giving the dealer risk of loss below $95 and opportunity for gain above $115. A short sale of a single share does not offer complete protection. The dealer will lose $15 on the short sale as the stock rises from $100 to $115, but will not make this money back on the collar because opportunity for gain on the call begins only at $115.

15. If the dealer knew the details of the fund's trading strategy, the dealer might be able to use this information to hedge. Yet funds are secretive about their trading strategies, a trade secret that justifies high management fees.

16. Nicholas Dunbar, *Inventing Money*, 170–172 (2000).

17. Geraldine Fabrikant, For the Rich, a Hedge Fund with an Eye on Taxes, *N.Y. Times*, July 1, 2001, at BU 7 (describing warrants that Bear Stearns is offering on its fund of funds).

18. Id.

19. I do not know how Bear Stearns hedges this position, but four possibilities come to mind. First, after selling a call to an investor, the derivatives dealer might, in turn, buy an identical call option from the underlying fund. Obviously, it is easier for the dealer to secure this accommodation from a fund run by Bear Stearns, as opposed to an

unaffiliated fund. The net effect would be that direct investors in the fund receive a call premium in exchange for sharing gains above 20% with optionholders.

Alternatively, the derivatives dealer might use its knowledge of the funds' trading practices to hedge dynamically. The dealer would have to track the trading practices of each fund, establish offsetting positions, and then adjust these offsetting positions as prices (and thus deltas) change and as the funds' portfolios change. The trick is that the dealer must have adequate information about the funds' trading practices – something that is not usually possible. Yet this strategy might be feasible here because the fund manager is a Bear Stearns affiliate.

Third, the fund might have a "stop loss" strategy in which the fund liquidates its portfolio and invests in safe assets, such as Treasuries, after losing a specified amount of money. Obviously, this is not the norm for hedge funds, but the derivatives dealer could choose only funds that adopt such strategies (and the dealer obviously could trust the fund manager to implement this strategy, since the manager would be an affiliate).

Finally, if the derivatives dealer simply holds the underlying fund interests, the call premium protects the dealer from losses of up to one-third of the fund interests' value. For instance, if the master fund's value declines from $1 million to $700,000, Bear Stearns will lose $300,000 on the fund, but will keep the $330,000 call premium, for a net gain of $30,000. This cushion obviously would not be adequate for a more dramatic decline in value, as UBS discovered. Yet Bear Stearns has the advantage of diversification here, since the option is based on the value of six funds. In choosing which funds to include, moreover, Bear Stearns could have chosen funds that are less volatile and do not correlate with each other. For added protection, Bear Stearns could add a "knock out" feature in which the call option would expire upon declining below a certain threshold (e.g. 70%) unless the investor were to pay an additional premium.

20. I.R.C. §§ 1291, 1293–1298.

21. Id. §§ 951–962, 964.

22. For a discussion, see Schizer supra note 1, at n. 256.

23. Id. § 1260(d)(1)(D). Taxpayers can strengthen their argument that retroactive regulations should not apply by differentiating the economic return on their common stock from the economic return on the derivative. For instance, the offshore corporation could hold other assets, such as mortgages. Yet addition of these other assets would increase transaction costs. Moreover, the regulations might still apply, as long as the government undertakes to bifurcate or look through the common stock.

24. I.R.C. § 1260(c)(1)(A). The term also means: "to the extent provided in regulations – (i) any debt instrument, and (ii) any stock in a corporation which is not a pass-thru entity." Id. § 1260(c)(1)(B).

25. Jeffrey J. Lonsdale, *What LIES Beneath* the Investor's Quest for a Scalable Capital Gain Holding Period?, *J. Tax'n Fin. Products*, Spring 2001, at 5, 8 (analyzing transaction in which taxpayer invests with hedge fund and the investment is not for a partnership interest, but for "an index investment tied to a mathematically defined, market neutral hedging strategy").

26. Even without section 1260, the government might argue that the client is the real tax owner of the managed account. While the merits of this argument turn on the particular facts, the government's case is strengthened considerably if the client is giving directions about how the account should be traded.

27. Under section 1260(g), "[t]he Secretary shall prescribe such regulations as may be necessary or appropriate to carry out the purposes of this section." I.R.C. § 1260(g).

Section 1260(c)(1)(B) authorizes the Secretary to expand the definition of "financial asset" to include debt and common stock. Id. § 1260(c)(1)(B). Further authority can be found in section 1260(d)(1):
"[A] taxpayer – enter[s] into a constructive ownership transaction with respect to any financial asset if the taxpayer . . .
(D) to the extent provided in regulations prescribed by the Secretary, enters into one or more other transactions (or acquires one or more positions) that have substantially the same effect as a transaction described in any of the preceding subparagraphs."
Id. § 1260(d)(1), (d)(1)(D). Some do not view this last phrase as authority to reach a managed account. The argument is that this language, which is part of section 1260(d)'s definition of a "constructive ownership transaction," does not broaden the definition of a "financial asset," which is defined in a different section (section 1260(c)). Once the taxpayer has a derivative based on a "financial asset," it is argued, this language reaches various derivatives *of this type*, including those with slightly different forms (e.g. contingent notes) or economic returns. Yet I'm inclined to read this "catch all" language more broadly. Congress's purpose, in my view, is to reach transactions that have a similar effect, and Congress did not limit itself to a particular *type* of similarity.
  28. See Flom, supra note 5, at 27.
  29. I.R.C. § 1260(d)(3) (treating notional principal contract as constructive ownership transaction if the taxpayer "(A) has the right to be paid (*or receive credit for*) all or substantially all of the investment yield . . . and (B) is obligated to reimburse (*or provide credit for*) all or substantially all of any decline in the value of such financial asset" (emphasis added)); id. § 1260(d)(4) (defining "forward contract" as "any contract to acquire in the future (*or provide or receive credit for the future value of*) any financial asset" (emphasis added)).
  30. For knotty questions raised by this reading, see Schizer supra note 1, at n. 265.
  31. In a "variable" contract, the size of death benefits (for life insurance) or annual payments (for annuities) depends upon the performance of specified assets, chosen by the taxpayer from a range of options.
  32. I.R.C. § 101 (excluding death benefit from income tax). If structured so that the policy is excluded from the taxpayer's estate, life insurance can offer the added benefit of avoiding estate tax.
  33. See I.R.C. § 7702A(b) (providing "7-pay" test to define MEC).
  34. I.R.C. § 4371.
  35. Limiting the taxpayer's role in managing the investment and supervising the fund manager is helpful under general principles of tax ownership. The point is for the insurance company, not the taxpayer, to be regarded as the real owner of invested assets. See generally David S. Miller, Taxpayers' Ability to Avoid Tax Ownership: Current Law and Future Prospects, 51 Tax Law. 279, 303–04 (1998); see also Rev. Rul. 81–225, 1981–2 C. B. 13 (one of the so-called "investor control" rulings, which offers a series of fact patterns for purposes of determining whether mutual fund shares underlying an annuity contract are owned by contract holder or life insurance company).
  36. I.R.C. § 1260(d)(1)(D).
  37. The counterargument is that the effect is not "substantially the same" because the economics of the transaction are different (given the mortality risk) and because the tax result is different (given the ordinary character). Indeed, one of section 1260s consequences – recharacterization of long term capital gain as ordinary income – applies awkwardly to contracts that yield either ordinary income or no income, although

section 1260s interest charge presumably could be applied. While these objections have force, their persuasiveness depends on the scope of the regulations (e.g. whether they exempt policies with more than a requisite concentration of mortality risk) and, ultimately, on the degree of discretion the Treasury is thought to have in writing regulations. If section 1260 is not adequate authority, moreover, the Treasury might attack these contracts on other grounds, such as the degree of "investor control." For a discussion, see supra note 35.

38. See I.R.C. §§ 1291, 1293–1298. Other regimes include the controlled foreign corporation regime, see id. §§ 951–962, 964, and the foreign personal holding company regime, see id. §§ 551–558. But these rules generally apply only if U.S. taxpayers own more than a minimum percentage of the entity.

39. Specifically, the PFIC regime does not treat as passive "any income . . . derived in the active conduct of an insurance business" if the corporation "is predominantly engaged in an insurance business" and would be subject to tax under the Code's special regime for insurance in subchapter L. Id. § 1297(b)(2).

40. Under regulations implementing subchapter L, the key factor is, in effect, whether the "primary and predominant" business of the corporation is selling insurance and annuities. Treas. Reg. § 1.801–3(a)(1) (as amended in 1972).

41. See Treas. Reg. § 1.801–4(a) (as amended in 1972) (defining "life insurance reserves"); see also S. Rep. No. 100–445 (1988), [2001] 13 Stand. Fed. Tax Rep. (CCH) ¶ 31,620, at 57,413–14 ("Thus, income derived by entities engaged in the business of providing insurance will be passive income to the extent the entities maintain financial reserves in excess of the reasonable needs of their insurance business").

F23

G-13

F31

7. FINANCIAL VERSUS OPERATIONAL HEDGING

Bhagwan Chowdhry

ABSTRACT

Multinational firms will engage in operational hedging only when both exchange rate uncertainty and demand uncertainty are present. Operational hedging is less important for managing short-term exposures, since demand uncertainty is lower in the short term. Operational hedging is also less important for commodity-based firms, which face price but not quantity uncertainty. For firms with plants in both a domestic and foreign location, the foreign currency cash flow generally will not be independent of the exchange rate. Consequently the optimal financial hedging policy cannot be implemented with forward contracts alone but can be implemented using foreign currency call and put options, and forward contracts.

1. INTRODUCTION

When should a multinational corporation adopt financial hedging policies to manage risk? Under what conditions should it resort to operational hedging? When should it use both simultaneously and how should these policies be implemented? These questions are addressed in this paper.

Of course, in perfect capital markets, we obtain the standard Miller-Modigliani capital structure result that corporations need not hedge exchange risk at all since investors can do it on their own. There is a large literature on

Global Risk Management: Financial, Operational, and Insurance Strategies,
Volume 3, pages 97–103.
© 2002 Published by Elsevier Science Ltd.
ISBN: 0-7623-0982-2

how market imperfections, such as taxes, agency problems, asymmetric information, dead-weight costs associated with financial distress, provide incentives for corporations to hedge risk. A number of finance scholars and practitioners have discussed how firms could use *financial* instruments to hedge financial price risk (see references in Chowdhry & Howe, 1999).

In addition to using financial contracts, a firm could manage its risk exposure through *operational* hedging. An example of an operational hedging policy would be to locate production in a country where significant sales revenues in the local (i.e. foreign) currency are expected. The effect of unexpected changes in exchange rates and foreign demand conditions on domestic currency value of sales revenues is hedged by similar changes in the domestic currency value of local production costs. Operational hedging motives thus may provide a reason for direct foreign investment by firms and may further explain the existence of multinational firms with production facilities at several foreign locations.

The costs of implementing a financial hedge are likely to be an order of magnitude smaller than those of implementing an operational hedge. After all, in order to implement an operational hedge, a firm may be required to open a production plant in another country whereas to implement a financial hedge may simply require a phone call to the firm's bank. What could, then, be the advantages of operational hedging policies?

If the quantity of foreign currency revenues the firm is expected to generate is certain, it is easy to hedge the exchange risk exposure associated with it by using a forward contract for that certain quantity. This eliminates the associated transaction exposure completely with a relatively simple financial hedge.

However, fluctuating foreign currency cash flow represents an additional source of uncertainty for many multinationals. For certain products, demand conditions can swing dramatically from year to year, inducing large changes in foreign currency revenues. If the quantity of foreign currency revenues is uncertain (and not perfectly correlated with the exchange rate), no financial contract (that must be agreed upon ex ante) that is contingent only on ex post observable and non-manipulable variables such as the exchange rate, can completely eliminate the exchange risk. One of the advantages of an operational hedge is that it allows the firm to align domestic currency production costs and revenues more closely. It is as if the firm had a forward contract whose quantity is contingent upon sales in the foreign country. Clearly, this dominates a fixed quantity forward contract. An operational hedge, by aligning local costs with local revenues amounts to self-insurance by the firm against demand uncertainty; market insurance for demand uncertainty is not feasible because of the severe moral hazard problem since sales can be manipulated by the firm.

2. A SIMPLE MODEL

Consider a firm based in the U.S. that generates revenues denominated in foreign currency, denoted $R(FX)$, at some date in the future. The dollar value of this future foreign currency revenue, denoted $R(\$)$, then will depend on the spot price of the foreign currency in terms of dollars, denoted $e(\$/FX)$. Algebraically,

$$R(\$) = e(\$/FX)R(FX).$$

2.1. Certain Foreign Currency Revenues

If $R(FX)$ is known with certainty today, it is easy to see that a forward contract to sell $R(FX)$ units of foreign currency at the forward foreign currency price, denoted $f(\$/FX)$, hedges the uncertainty in dollar value of foreign currency receivables completely because the cash flow then can be written as

$$R(\$) = f(\$/FX)R(FX)$$

where both $f(\$/FX)$ and $R(FX)$ are known in advance.

2.2. Uncertain Foreign Currency Revenues

What happens, however, when $R(FX)$ is uncertain? $R(FX)$ could be thought of as foreign currency revenues which are a product of the price of the good in foreign currency, denoted $p(FX)$, and the quantity sold, denoted q. Algebraically,

$$R(FX) = p(FX)q.$$

Uncertainty in foreign currency revenues thus could arise if demand for the product, q, is uncertain. The dollar value of the foreign currency cash flow

$$R(\$) = e(\$FX)p(FX)q$$

then has two sources of uncertainty, the exchange rate, e, and the demand, q.

2.3. Market Insurance vs. Self-Insurance

It is feasible to write a contingent contract on any variable that is publicly observable and which cannot be manipulated by the any contracting party. The exchange rate, e, is such a variable so it is feasible to write a financial contract contingent on e. A forward foreign currency contract is indeed an example of such a financial contract. Using a financial contract for hedging essentially amounts to buying market insurance for the risk one is facing.

The quantity of goods sold, q, or the sales revenue, $p(FX)q$, however, can be manipulated by the firm and therefore, the firm would not be able to write a contract contingent on q. Since this rules out market insurance, the firm may have to rely on self-insurance to hedge the risk associated with uncertain demand conditions. Operational hedging by firm essentially amounts to self-insurance by the firm.

2.4. Operational Hedging as Self-Insurance

Hedging is accomplished by identifying a variable that is highly correlated with the risk one is trying to insure against. In the problem we are analyzing, we need to find a variable that is highly correlated with the quantity of the good sold by the firm. Notice that variable costs in dollars, denoted $C(\$)$, also depend on the quantity produced and sold by the following relation:

$$C(\$) = e(\$/FX)c(FX)q$$

where $c(FX)$ denotes per unit cost denominated in units of foreign currency. We will now see that locating variable costs where revenues are generated thus amounts to self-insurance by operational hedging.

The dollar value of profits or cash flows, denoted $CF(\$)$, thus can be written as:

$$CF(\$) = e(\$/FX)\{p(FX) - c(FX)\}q.$$

It is easy to see that the larger the variable costs, the more effective is the operational hedge. But given that the per unit variable cost, $c(FX)$, will be smaller than the unit price of the good, $p(FX)$, there is some residual variability in $CF(\$)$ caused by the uncertainty in $e(\$/FX)$ that must be hedged by financial contracts. Alternatively, if the firm has operations both domestically and at foreign location, it can shift some of its domestic production abroad to increase the total variable costs that are incurred at the foreign location. Optimal operational hedging thus implies a bias towards locating production at foreign location in general.

In the simple case that we are analyzing in which the firm has operations only at the foreign location, it is easy to show that the financial hedge that minimizes the variance of the dollar value of cash flow, $CF(\$)$, is a forward contract to sell

$$E[\{p(FX) - c(FX)\}q]$$

units of the foreign currency. The expected hedged profits can then be shown to be equal to

$$f(\$/FX)E[\{p(FX) - c(FX)\}q].$$

2.5. Production Flexibility when Firm has Operations at Multiple Locations

So far, we have argued that operational hedging makes sense when there is quantity uncertainty in addition to exchange rate certainty. Though, operational hedging may be more expensive than financial hedging because it may entail large fixed costs, when the firm has operations at multiple currency locations, demand uncertainty implies that sometimes the firm will have excess capacity at some locations. This excess capacity creates a real option to switch production to the location that has the smallest costs of production. It is easy to see that this flexibility will create value for the firm by increasing its expected profits.

The effects of the production flexibility on optimal financial hedging contracts, however, are a bit more subtle. If the domestic and foreign cash flows, denoted $CF(\$)$ and $CF(FX)$, are independent of the exchange rate $e(\$/FX)$, the financial contract that minimizes the variance of the dollar value of total cash flows is a forward contract for $E[CF(FX)]$ contracts. With production flexibility and excess capacity (caused by demand uncertainty), however, the cash flows $CF(\$)$ and $CF(FX)$ must depend on the exchange rate $e(\$/FX)$ because the exchange rate changes the relative dollar value of the costs of production. The optimal financial contract in this case cannot simply be a forward contract but requires the use of call and put options in addition (see Chowdhry & Howe, 1999).

2.6. Extending the Simple Model

The simple model we have analyzed can be extended to consider other latent variables that are correlated with demand to explore other financial hedging instruments. It seems unlikely though that it will be feasible to eliminate all uncertainty caused by demand or quantity uncertainty. The results of our simple model thus seem quite robust to this generalization.

The model could also be generalized to consider costs of shipping products from one location to another. While this would change the exact nature of the operational hedging contracts and the trigger points at which the firm would switch production decisions from one location to another to respond to changes in costs brought about by exchange rate changes, the central qualitative results of the model are likely to remain unchanged.

A useful and promising extension of the model will be to consider mechanisms that alleviate moral hazard and thus allow for better financial hedging contracts which might decrease the dependence on operational hedging for managing risk.

3. CONCLUSION

The key insight in the paper is that a multinational firm will engage in operational hedging only when both exchange rate uncertainty and demand uncertainty are present. The intuition is clear. If there is no exchange rate uncertainty, the only residual uncertainty is demand uncertainty which can be hedged only if we can create an instrument that is correlated with demand; it cannot be hedged by operational production decisions. On the other hand when there is exchange rate uncertainty but no demand uncertainty, the exchange rate can be hedged entirely by using financial contracts, i.e. forward contracts, which obviates the need for relatively expensive operational hedging.

We now make a few empirical observations. Firms whose main products are commodities, e.g. oil, copper, grains, are exposed only to price uncertainty not quantity uncertainty. Furthermore, the relevant prices, such as the spot prices of the commodities as well as the exchange rates, cannot be manipulated by any single firm. It follows from our analysis that we would expect such firms to hedge their exposure using mainly financial instruments; operational hedging by such firms would be rare. Some survey evidence in Bodnar, Hayt, Marston and Smithson (1995) indicates that the percentage of firms that use financial derivatives for hedging is the highest for firms that are classified as commodity based than for firms in any other classification.

Our insight is also consistent with the empirical observation that firms often seem to use financial instruments to hedge short-term exposure but not long-term exposure. It seems plausible that demand uncertainty will be smaller for shorter horizons than for longer horizons as firms will be able to forecast their sales more accurately in the short term. Our analysis thus predicts that firms are likely to use financial instruments to a greater extent to hedge short term exposure and rely on operational hedging more heavily to hedge long term exposure.

We leave it to future research to generalize our results and to empirical test its predictions.

ACKNOWLEDGMENTS

This paper is based on my paper with Jonathan Howe (see references). The paper was written for the conference held as the Second International Business Research Forum sponsored by the Institute of Global Management Studies and the Advanta Center for Financial Services at Temple University in April 2001.

REFERENCES

Bodnar, G. M., Hayt, G. S., Marston, R. C., & Smithson, C. W. (1995). Wharton Survey of Derivatives Usage by U.S. Non-Financial Firms. *Financial Management, 24,* 104–114.

Chowdhry, B., & Howe, J. T. B. (1999). Corporate Risk Management for Multinational Corporations: Financial and Operational Hedging Policies. *European Finance Review, 2,* 229–246.

PART III:
INTERNATIONAL RISK

F31 F23

8.   EXCHANGE RATE EXPOSURE:
A SIMPLE MODEL

Gordon M. Bodnar and Richard C. Marston

ABSTRACT

This study develops a model of foreign exchange exposure dependent on only three variables, the percentage of the firm's revenues and expenses denominated in foreign currency and its profit rate. The model demonstrates that foreign exchange exposure elasticities should be largest for pure exporting and importing firms, especially those with low profit margins. Exposure elasticities should be smaller for multinational firms that match their foreign currency revenues and costs. Such operational hedges may help to explain why previous studies have found low or negligible levels of exposure when they studied the sensitivity of share prices to foreign exchange rates.

1. INTRODUCTION

This paper develops a simple model to measure a firm's exposure elasticity to exchange rate changes without the need to use stock return data. The model is that of a monopoly firm whose revenues and expenses are exposed to changes in exchange rates. It demonstrates that measured exposure elasticities are fundamentally functions of net foreign currency revenues, and profit margins. Large exposure elasticities arise in firms with large imbalances in foreign currency revenues and costs and low profit margins. In contrast, firms that develop operational hedges, in which they offset foreign currency revenues and

Global Risk Management: Financial, Operational, and Insurance Strategies,
Volume 3, pages 107–115.
Copyright © 2002 by Elsevier Science Ltd.
All rights of reproduction in any form reserved.
ISBN: 0-7623-0982-2

costs, can shield themselves from the large-scale effects of exchange rate changes. In these cases, exposure elasticity remains a decreasing function of the profit margin, except in the case when the proportion of revenues and costs exactly match, in which case the profit margin plays no role in the exposure elasticity.

Empirical studies of the foreign exchange rate exposure of U.S. firms (for example, Jorion, 1990; Bodnar & Gentry, 1993; Amihud, 1994; Choi & Prasard, 1995; Griffin & Stulz, 2001; Allayannis, 1997), typically find low or negligible levels of exposure for most firms, even when the firms examined have significant foreign operations. This has been considered somewhat of a puzzle. None of these studies are based explicitly on a model of firm behavior, so it is difficult to interpret their findings of low exposure in terms of economic behavior[1]. When calibrated for various operational conditions, this model provides a possible explanation why many of these studies have had difficulty documenting significant exposure elasticities from equity returns.

2. MODEL BASICS

To develop a measure of foreign exchange exposure, we need to start with an operational definition of a firm's value. As is common in finance, we assume that the value of a firm can be expressed in terms of a stream of present and future cash flows as

$$V = \sum_{t=1}^{\infty} \frac{CF_t}{(1+\rho)^t} \tag{1}$$

where CF_t represents the expected cash flows of the firm at time t, which are equal to after-tax profits less net investment, and where ρ is the discount rate. In order to keep the model tractable we assume that the net investment of the firm is equal to zero and that cash flows are expected to be constant from year to year. In that case, the present value can be written

$$V = \frac{CF}{\rho} = \frac{(1-\tau)}{\rho}\pi \tag{2}$$

where τ is the corporate tax rate and π is profit before taxes. The basic measure of foreign exchange exposure is dV/dS, where S is the exchange rate expressed as home currency/foreign currency. This measures the nominal value (in home currency) that is exposed to the exchange rate. With taxes and the discount rate constant, foreign exchange exposure can be expressed as:

$$dV/dS = [(1-\tau)/\rho]d\pi/dS \tag{3}$$

Exchange exposure, measured as a dollar amount, is proportional to the derivative of current profits with respect to the exchange rate. It is this latter derivative, $d\pi/dS$ that will be measured explicitly below in a more detailed setting.

3. EXCHANGE RATE EXPOSURE

3.1. Nominal Value Exposure

To investigate foreign exchange exposure across a variety of firms, we must adopt a model of the firm that is versatile enough to take into account different forms of exposure. Exchange rates may affect a firm through a variety of channels:

  (i) a firm may produce at home for export sales;
 (ii) a firm may produce with or sell imported components;
(iii) a firm may produce the same product or a different product at plants abroad.

The model of the firm must be broad enough to capture all of these channels. The firm described below is a multinational firm, producing and selling at home and abroad, using both foreign and domestic components. Let's define the following variables:

X, X^* = sales of the domestic good at home and abroad, respectively.
Z, Z^* = sales of the foreign-produced good at home and abroad, respectively.
     This good is produced by the domestic firm in a foreign plant.
S = exchange rate (i.e. the dollar price of the Euro).
C, C^* = cost functions, denominated in dollars and Euros, respectively, representing the cost of producing the domestic goods $(X+X^*)$.
K, K^* = cost functions, denominated in dollars and Euros, respectively, representing the cost of producing the foreign goods $(Z+Z^*)$.

Combining these variables, we can state the profits of the firm as net revenues earned by selling both domestic products and foreign products:

$$\pi = XD(X) + SX^*D^*(X^*) - C(X+X^*) - SC^*(X+X^*)$$
$$+ ZF(Z) + SZ^*F^*(Z^*) - K(Z+Z^*) - SK^*(Z+Z^*) \qquad (4)$$

Because the firm is producing two products for two different markets, there are four first-order conditions for this firm to be a profit maximizer. Taking the derivative of profits with respect to the choice of each quantity gives us the following four relations:

$$(d\pi/dX) = D(X) + XD_0(X) - C_0(X+X^*) - SC_0^*(X+X^*) = 0 \qquad (5a)$$

$$(d\pi/dX^*) = SD^*(X^*) + SX^*D_0^*(X^*) - C_0(X+X^*) - SC_0^*(X+X^*) = 0 \quad (5b)$$

$$(d\pi/dZ) = F(Z) + ZF_0(Z) - K_0(Z+Z^*) - SK_0^*(Z+Z^*) = 0 \qquad (5c)$$

$$(d\pi/dZ^*) = SF^*(Z^*) + SZ^*F_0^*(Z^*) - K_0(Z+Z^*) - SK_0^*(Z+Z^*) = 0 \quad (5d)$$

In these expressions, the derivative of each function with respect to output is denoted by a subscript 0.

The exchange rate exposure of the firm is proportional to the derivative of the profit equation with respect to the exchange rate as denoted in Eq. (3):

$$d\pi/dS = [d\pi/dX](dX/dS) + [d\pi/dX^*](dX^*/dS) + [d\pi/dZ](dZ/dS)$$

$$+ [d\pi/dZ^*])dZ^*/dS) + \{[X^*D^*(X^*) - C^*(X+X^*)]$$

$$+ [Z^*F^*(Z^*) - K^*(Z+Z^*)] \qquad (6)$$

According to this expression, there are two ways that profits adjust to changes in the exchange rate. First, output can change in response to the change in the exchange rate (these are the $dX/dS(dX^*/dS)$ and $dZ/dS(dZ^*/dS)$ terms on the top line of Eq. (6)). Second, profits adjust in proportion to the initial level of net revenue denominated in foreign currency (this is the effect on the second line of Eq. (6)).

This expression can be simplified by recognizing that the first order condition given in Eq. (5) require the response of profits to changes in the various outputs to be equal to zero at the current equilibrium. Thus if the firm was initially at a profit maximizing point, only the direct effect of the exchange rate on profits remains.[2] The means the expression for exposure simplifies to:

$$d\pi/dS = \{[X^*D^*(X^*) - C^*(X+X^*)] + [Z^*F^*(Z^*) - K^*(Z+Z^*)] \qquad (7)$$

The exchange rate exposure of the firm is equal to the initial level of *net* revenue denominated in foreign currency. This measure of exposure is proportional to the nominal value exposure, dV/dS, as it measures the amount of current period cash flow exposed to the exchange rate. Under simple assumptions about future cash flow expectations, this exposure measure will relate to the nominal value exposure by the factor $(1 - \tau)/\rho$.

3.2. Exposure in Elasticity Form

While $dV/dS = ((1 - \tau)/\rho) \, d\pi/dS$ is the actual measure of cash flow exposure, the empirical literature on exposure typically measures the exposure elasticity (i.e. the percentage change in firm value (return) per percentage change in the exchange rate) rather than the nominal value exposure. The exposure elasticity, which we define as delta, δ, is given by:

$$\delta = d\ln\pi/d\ln S = S\{[X^*D^*(X^*) - C^*(X+X^*)] + [Z^*F^*(Z^*) - K^*(Z+Z^*)]\}/\pi$$

(8)

As long as the tax rate and cost of capital are assumed constant, this measure will be identical to the elasticity of the firm value with respect to the exchange rate. This expression can be simplified if we define several new variables:

R = total revenue = $XD(X) + SX^*D^*(X^*) + ZF(Z) + SZ^*F^*(Z^*)$.

M = total cost = $C(X+X^*) + SC^*(X+X^*) + K(Z+Z^*) + SK^*(Z+Z^*)$.

h_1 = foreign currency-denominated revenue as a percent of total revenue
   = $S[X^*D^*(X^*) + Z^*F^*(Z^*)]/R$

h_2 = foreign currency-denominated costs as a percent of total costs
   = $S[C^*(X+X^*) + K^*(Z+Z^*)]/M$

r = the profit rate (i.e. profits as a percent of total revenues) = π/R

We can then rewrite the expression for delta in terms of h_1, h_2, and r:

$$\delta = h_1(R/\pi) - h_2(M/\pi) = (h_1/r) - h_2((1/r) - 1)$$

(9a)

$$\text{or } \delta = h_1 + (h_1 - h_2)((1/r) - 1)$$

(9b)

In this model, delta is a function of only three variables, h_1, h_2, and r. The partial derivative of delta is positive with respect to h_1, and negative with respect to h_2. These results are quite intuitive as greater foreign currency revenues lead to a greater increase in firm value in response to a depreciation of the home currency ($dS > 0$) and greater foreign currency costs lead to a greater decrease in firm value in response to a depreciation of the home currency. The partial derivative of delta with respect to r is a negative function of the net foreign currency revenue position of the firm ($h_1 - h_2$). The basic effect is that an increase in profit margin makes the exposure elasticity smaller in size (i.e. closer to zero). This is because an increase in profit margin increases firm value, V, without changing the nominal value exposure, dV/dS, which is purely a function of the net foreign currency position (see Eq. (7)). As a result, the exposure elasticity, which is related to the nominal-value exposure over firm value ($(dV/dS)/V)$), is smaller for more profitable firms because the increase in profit margin corresponds to a higher firm value.

4. EXPOSURES ACROSS TYPES OF FIRMS

Despite its simplicity, the expression for delta is general enough to encompass a variety of different firms. Consider the following examples of different types of firms:

1. Pure Exporter

This firm is assumed to produce all of its output at home and to sell a fraction, h_1, abroad for foreign currency revenue. Moreover, all of the components needed for production are produced at home (so $h_2 = 0$). As a result, its exchange rate exposure elasticity is given by

$$\delta = h_1/r$$

For example, let's assume this firm sells 40% of its product abroad as exports for foreign currency revenues ($h_1 = 40\%$) and its profit rate is 10% ($r = 0.1$). Under these assumptions the firm's delta would be:

$$\delta = h_1/r = 0.40/0.1 = 4.0$$

A delta of 4.0 means that the firm's profits vary four times as much in percentage terms as the exchange rate. So a 10% depreciation (appreciation) of the domestic currency leads to a 40% rise (fall) in profits for this firm. Thus, a pure exporting firm is a leveraged play on exchange rate depreciation (because it has no offsetting foreign currency costs) and has a corresponding large exposure elasticity to such an exchange rate change. This is the type of firm that is explicitly modeled in Bodnar, Dumas and Marston (2002).

2. Pure Importer

This firm is assumed to sell nothing abroad so $h_1 = 0$, but it imports components from abroad for local production and sales, so $h_2 > 0$. As a result, this firm's delta is given by

$$\delta = - h_2((1/r) - 1)$$

For example, let's assume the firm imports inputs with foreign currency costs that constitute 40% of its total costs ($h_2 = 0.4$) and its profit rate, r, is again 10%. In this case, the firm's delta would be:

$$\delta = - h_2((1/r) - 1) = - 0.4((1/0.1) - 1) = - 3.6$$

Like the pure exporter, this firm has large foreign exchange exposure, but its exposure is opposite in sign to that of the exporter. It is a leveraged play on a domestic currency appreciation rather than on a domestic currency depreciation. For similar levels of foreign activity (40%) and profit margin, notice that the exposure elasticity of the importer is slightly smaller in magnitude than for the exporter. This is because the import firm is not as the leveraged a play on the exchange rate as the exporter, because the costs (the exposure for the pure importer) are smaller than the revenues (the exposure for the pure exporter) in a profitable firm.

3. Multinational Firm

A multinational firm generally both produces and sells abroad so it will have both foreign currency revenues and foreign currency costs. Thus we will have positive values for both h_1 and h_2. For example, let's assume that this firm produces goods abroad to sell to the foreign markets. If foreign production is local then it is likely the case that $h_1 = h_2$. In this case, from Eq. (9b) this firm's delta is given by:

$$\delta = h_1$$

More specifically, let's assume the firm produces and sells half its output abroad. With local production, half of its revenues and half of its costs will be in foreign currency, so $h_1 = 0.5$ and $h_2 = 0.5$. In this case the firm's delta would be

$$\delta = h_1 = 0.5$$

By producing abroad all of the products it sells in foreign markets, the foreign currency costs have created an "operational hedge" for its foreign revenues. In this case, only its profits from foreign operations remain exposed. The exposure is the percentage of profits in foreign currency (this turns out to be the same percentage as the revenues and costs in foreign currency). Notice that with $\delta = 0.5$ this multinational firm has a much smaller exposure elasticity than either of the previous two examples despite being more international (50% of sales and costs as opposed to 40% in the previous examples). This demonstrates that operational hedging can dramatically reduce the size of the exchange rate exposure elasticity relative to a pure importer or pure exporter.

Let's consider another example of a multinational firm. In this case, the multinational firm has 45% of its revenues in foreign currency ($h_1 = 0.45$) and 50% of its costs in foreign currency ($h_2 = 0.5$). Once again we will assume the profit margin to be 10% ($r = 0.1$). In this case the firm's delta would be:

$$\delta = h_1 + (h_1 - h_2)((1/r) - 1) = 0.45 + (0.45 - 0.5)((1/0.1) - 1) = 0$$

This multinational firm has zero exposure. We would describe it as having a perfect natural hedge. With its profit margin of 10%, because it has 10% more of its costs in foreign currency than its revenues, it is naturally hedged. As a result, despite significant foreign currency activity, this firm would not be materially affected by changes the exchange rate.

5. IMPLICATIONS FOR EMPIRICAL STUDIES

It is not difficult to see that for certain operational arrangements, a multinational firm can actually have a negative exposure, in contrast to the common assumption that multinationals gain when the dollar depreciates. This model makes clear that typical multinational firms with reasonably balanced foreign currency revenues and costs will not be likely to have large exposure elasticities, despite potentially heavy foreign activity. Multinationality has commonly been a screening mechanism for identifying samples in previous empirical studies in exposure. This model provides a possible explanation as to why these studies fail to find significant exposures. In contrast, it suggests that pure exporters or importers, especially those in low profit activities should be expected to have the largest exposure elasticities. This would suggest an completely new approach to choosing firms for empirical exposure studies.

6. CONCLUSION

This paper develops a simple model of foreign exchange exposure to explain why previous studies have found such low exposure in most U.S. and foreign firms. The model is that of a firm that both produces and sells at home and abroad. The derived expression for exchange rate exposure is simple enough so that exposure can be approximated easily without share price data. It requires only three informational inputs about the firm: the percentage of revenues denominated in foreign currency, the percentage of costs denominated in foreign currency, and the profit rate. While proxies for the first and last data are readily available in U.S. firms' public disclosures, information on the percentage of costs denominated in foreign currency is typically not disclosed and is available only to insiders of the firm. As a result, this model is most directly applicable to managers or other insiders wishing to gain a quick measure of their firm's sensitivity to the exchange rate. For broader research purposes, the use of this model would require the collection of information on foreign currency costs through interrogation or survey of corporate managers.

The conclusions from this model are that for many firms, especially multinational firms with significant revenues and costs in foreign currency, foreign exchange exposure may be low because the firms match their proportion of foreign currency revenues and costs. Such operational hedging is an effective way to reduce exposure to modest levels. The firms that must contend with large foreign exchange exposure are those with unbalanced revenue or cost streams. For those firms, sizable financial hedges may be necessary to moderate their exposure.

NOTES

1. Bodnar, Dumas and Marston (2002) provide an explicit theoretical model and they find relatively high levels of exposure. But their model is estimated for a group of Japanese firms that have been chosen because they are likely to have high levels of exposure, since their purpose is to investigate the link between pass-through and exposure behavior in firms that have high levels of exposure. Other theoretical studies of exposure include Adler and Dumas (1984), Hekman (1985), Shapiro (1975), Flood and Lessard (1986), von Ungern-Sternberg and von Weizsacker (1990), Levi (1994) and Marston (2001).

2. This result is discussed in detail in Marston (2001). As discussed in Marston, this result continues to hold under some but not all forms of oligopoly. For a more general discussion of the envelope theorem on which this analysis is based, see Varian (1992, pp. 490–492).

REFERENCES

Adler, M., & Dumas, B. (1984). Exposure to Currency Risk: Definition and Measurement. *Financial Management*, Summer, 41–50.

Allayannis, G. (1997). The Time-Variation of the Exchange-Rate Exposure: An Industry Analysis, Darden School Working Paper, University of Virginia DSWP No. 97-29, December.

Amihud, Y. (1994). Exchange Rates and the Valuation of Equity Shares. In: Y. Amihud & R. Levich (Eds), *Exchange Rates and Corporate Performance*, 49–59. New York: Irwin.

Bodnar, G. M., Dumas, B., & Marston, R. C. (2002). Pass-through and Exposure. *Journal of Finance*, February, 199–232.

Bodnar, G. M., & Gentry, W. M. (1993). Exchange Rate Exposure and Industry Characteristics: Evidence from Canada, Japan, and the USA. *Journal of International Money and Finance*, February, 29–45.

Choi, J. J., & Prasad, A. (1995). Exchange Risk Sensitivity and Its Determinants: A Firm and Industry Analysis of U.S. Multinationals. *Financial Management*, *24*, 3.

Flood, E., & Lessard, D. R. (1986). On the Measurement of Operating Exposure to Exchange Rates: A Conceptual Approach. *Financial Management*, Spring, 25–37.

Griffin, J. M., & Stulz, R. (2001). International Competition and Exchange Rate Shocks: Cross-Country Industry Analysis of Stock Returns. *Review of Financial Studies*, *14*, 215–241.

Hekman, C. (1985). A Financial Model of Foreign Exchange Exposure. *Journal of International Business Studies*, Summer, 83–99.

Jorion, P. (1990). The Exchange-Rate Exposure of U.S. Multinationals. *Journal of Business*, July, 331–345.

Levi, M. D. (1994). Exchange Rates and the Valuation of Firms. In: A. Yakov & M. L. Richard (Eds), *Exchange Rates and Corporate Performance* (pp. 37–48). New York: Irwin.

Marston, R. C. (2001). The Effects of Industry Structure on Economic Exposure. *Journal of International Money and Finance*, April, 149–164.

Shapiro, A. C. (1975). Exchange Rate Changes, Inflation, and the Value of the Multinational Corporation. *Journal of Finance*, September, 485–502.

von Ungern-Sternberg, T., & von Weizsacker, C. C. (1990). Strategic Foreign Exchange Management. *Journal of Industrial Economics*, June, 381–395.

Varian, H. R. (1992). *Microeconomic Analysis*. New York: Norton.

9. THE IMPACT OF THE ASIAN FINANCIAL CRISIS ON U.S. MULTINATIONALS

F23 F31
O16
G13 G15

George Allayannis and James P. Weston

ABSTRACT

This paper examines the impact of the Asian crisis on U.S. firms. We find that while neither the average U.S. firm nor the average U.S. multinational was affected by the crisis, U.S. multinationals with presence in East Asia were negatively and significantly affected. On average, these firms experienced a sizable (−1.43%) abnormal return per month during the crisis period. We also find that currency derivatives use and potential operational hedging strategies did not significantly protect firms from the East Asian crisis. This is perhaps due to the magnitude of the shock and the resultant lack of liquidity in the derivatives markets during and after the crisis.

1. Introduction

The Asian financial crisis was an event that crippled many economies in East Asia. Many feared that the crisis would trigger a global demise. U.S. multinationals, with large presence in these countries would be hard-hit. Not only did the buying power of the local population go down, but also the precipitous devaluation of the local currencies vs. the dollar should have long-lasting effects on the bottom line of U.S. firms that rely on such markets to sell

Global Risk Management: Financial, Operational, and Insurance Strategies,
Volume 3, pages 117–130.
ISBN: 0-7623-0982-2

their products. On the other hand, many of these firms engage in financial or operational hedging strategies, which may help them weather such a crisis.

In this paper, we examine whether the Asian crisis affected the stock returns of U.S. multinationals and compare the effects of the crisis for firms that have a presence (subsidiaries) in East Asia to those that do not. We also examine whether the use of financial or operational hedging strategies protected these firms from the crisis.[1] We find that, while U.S. multinationals with no presence in East Asia were not significantly affected by the crisis, U.S. multinationals with presence in the region incurred large drops in their market values. Specifically, our estimates suggest that the Asian crisis reduced returns for these firms by 1.4% per month (in excess of what the CAPM would predict). We also find that the use of currency derivatives or the presence in multiple countries (i.e. operational hedges) did not significantly help mitigate the impact of the crisis on these firms.

2. PRIOR LITERATURE

Several theories suggest that operational hedging is valuable for a firm as it allows the firm to increase its flexibility and shift production elsewhere in response to adverse exchange-rate movements (see e.g. Mello, Parsons & Triantis, 1995). More recently, Chowdhry and Howe (1998) suggest that operational hedging is important in the presence of both exchange rate and demand uncertainty. In their framework, operational hedging is less important for managing short-term exposures, since demand uncertainty is relatively small in the short term.

In addition to theories that are specific to operational flexibility and hedging, several earlier theories have pointed out the beneficial effect of geographic diversification (multinationality) on firm value. For example, the internalization theory predicts that foreign markets are important for firms that have intangible assets, such as superb production skills, consumer goodwill, or technological know-how. By internalizing these foreign markets for their intangible assets, firms can increase their value.[2] In contrast, some authors have suggested that multinationality arises from managers who are "empire-builders" and is hence a value-destroying strategy.

Errunza and Senbet (1981, 1984), Morck and Yeung (1991) and Bodnar, Tang and Weintrop (1997) find that multinationality is associated with higher value, although Morck and Yeung (1991) only find this positive effect for firms with significant intangible assets as proxied by R&D expenditures, thereby confirming the internalization theory. In contrast to the above studies, Christophe (1997) and Denis, Denis and Yost (2002) find that multinationality decreases value. Morck and Yeung (1991) is one of the few papers in the finance literature that have used the number of subsidiaries and the number of countries that a firm operates in as a measure of multinationality for a sample of firms during 1978.[3] Most commonly, papers use a dummy which equals to one if a firm has subsidiaries abroad or foreign sales (sales from operation abroad), or use the percent of foreign sales as a proxy for the degree of multinationality.

Furthermore, several papers have examined whether the location of the subsidiaries (not merely their number or the presence of a foreign subsidiary) is important for the value of a multinational corporation. The multinational network hypothesis affirms that location is important as it might influence a firm's ability to enter segmented markets that exist in certain parts of the world (regions), exploit tax-arbitrage opportunities that may exist or construct operational hedges that effectively counteract exchange-rate movements across the network of subsidiaries (see, e.g. Kogut & Kulatilaka, 1994; Buckley & Casson, 1998). Doukas and Travlos (1988) and Allen and Pantzalis (1996) provide indirect evidence consistent with the multinational network hypothesis, by showing that firms that expand through acquisitions are creating value, only if the acquisitions are located in countries where the multinationals did not previously operate. More recently, Pantzalis (1998) directly examines the multinational network hypothesis for a sample of firms during 1990 and finds that firms with presence in countries in less developed regions are generally more valuable than similar firms that only operate in advanced regions. His study therefore confirms the importance of location (country) factors on firm value.

Firms can also use financial derivatives to mitigate currency risk and improve value. Several recent theories of financial hedging suggest that hedging can be a value-increasing strategy for firms, as it may reduce underinvestment [see, e.g. Froot, Scharfstein & Stein, 1993; Smith, Smithson & Wilford, 1990; Stulz, 1990), costs of financial distress (Smith & Stulz, 1985), or the information asymmetry between managers and investors (DeMarzo & Duffie, 1995). Several papers have examined the validity of the above theories and have generally found evidence confirming of the theories [see, e.g. Visvanathan, 1998; Geczy, Minton & Schrand, 1997; Mian, 1996; Nance, Smith & Smithson, 1993).

More recently, several authors have examined the effect of financial derivatives on risk. For example, Guay (1999) finds that firms' exchange rate and interest rate risk goes down after the initiation of financial hedging programs, while Allayannis and Ofek (2001) find similar results for a large cross-section of U.S. firms and across several currencies, and He and Ng (1998) find similar results for a sample of Japanese firms. Finally, and most related to this paper, Allayannis and Weston (2001) examine the effect of foreign currency derivatives on firm value and find that the use of derivatives increases value.

In this paper we test the value of operational and financial hedging for a sample of U.S. multinationals during the Asian crisis. The Asian crisis is a natural experiment in the sense that it was largely unpredictable and the magnitude of the shock was very large. Our data on foreign currency derivatives use and on the location of subsidiaries allow us to test specific hypotheses on the impact of the crisis to U.S. firms and differ with respect to their operational and financial hedging activities. In contrast to previous papers, we are able to distinguish between a multinational firm that operates in East Asia vs. one that does not, and one that operates in East Asia and uses currency derivatives vs. a similar firm that also operates in East Asia but does not use derivatives.

3. SAMPLE DESCRIPTION

Our main sample consists of all U.S. non-financial firms that are in the Compustat database that have assets above $100M during 1996–1998 and which report the presence of at least one foreign subsidiary. The total number of firms that meets our selection criteria is 225. In a few of our tests, we employ a larger sample, which consists of all firms with assets above $100M (regardless of whether they have foreign sales or not). This broader sample contains a total of 521 firms.

For our sample firms we hand-collect level-1 subsidiary data from the National Registry. Level-1 subsidiaries are those that are majority-owned by the corporation. We limited our subsidiary data information to level-1 subsidiaries, as these subsidiaries constitute the majority of the firms' main exposure to the alternative regions; this also made the data collection process more tractable. We then construct a dummy that equals 1 if a firm has a subsidiary in East Asia (Thailand, Malaysia, Indonesia, Vietnam, Cambodia, Laos and the Philippines) and 0 otherwise, as well as a continuous variable defined as the ratio of a firm's East Asian subsidiaries to total subsidiaries, reflecting the importance of the region for a firm. Unfortunately, it is not possible to obtain foreign sales at the country level for U.S. multinationals, nor is it possible to obtain foreign sales at the country level for U.S. multinationals related to those countries, or any countries for that matter. Our maintained hypothesis is that those subsidiaries proxy for the net exposure to this region in the sense that an appreciating dollar may hurt the overall operations of the U.S.

multinational. To the extent that there are significant importing operations for U.S. firms from this region, then, it is conceivable that a dollar appreciation is a net benefit for them. Ultimately, this is an empirical question that we turn to in this paper.

For the firms in our sample, we also collect data from their annual reports on the potential use of foreign currency derivatives. In particular, we construct a foreign currency derivatives dummy which equals 1 if the firm reports the use of any foreign currency forwards, futures, options, or swaps. Unfortunately, firms are not required to disclose the currencies that derivatives are denominated in, so we do not know whether these derivatives are directly applied to exposures in South East Asia or not. In this sense, we do not know whether the use of derivatives may help mitigate any exposures or not. Again, this is an empirical question that we will address in the paper.

Table 1 presents summary statistics on the main variables that we use in our paper. On average, firms in our sample have $11,724M in sales (median of $4,843) and approximately $3,315M in foreign sales (median of $946). On average, a firm's foreign sales amounts to 31% of total sales. Note that there are several firms in our sample which have zero foreign sales although they have at least one foreign subsidiary, suggesting that some of the subsidiaries may be marketing or importing facilities. On average, firms in our sample operate in 11.5 different countries around the world and about 54% of them have at least one subsidiary in East Asia. These statistics suggest that our sample's exposure to East Asia may potentially be quite significant; the average exchange-rate exposure is 0.17 suggesting that a 1% appreciation of the dollar reduces returns

Table 1. Summary Statistics.

Descriptive Variables	Obs	Mean	Std.	5%	Median	95%
Total Sales	225	11,724	19,668	974	4,843	46,287
Total Foreign Sales	225	3,315	6,679	0.00	946	14,610
Foreign Sale/Total Sales	225	0.31	0.25	0.00	0.30	0.75
Number of Countries	225	11.54	12.46	1.00	8.00	36.00
FX Derivatives Use Dummy	225	0.77	0.42	0.00	1.00	1.00
East Asian Dummy	225	0.54	0.50	0.00	1.00	1.00
East Asian Subsidiaries	225	0.09	0.12	0.00	0.05	0.33
Return on Assets	225	4.70	6.69	−4.89	4.87	14.50
Average Abnormal Returns	225	−0.01	0.04	−0.07	−0.01	0.04
Exchange-Rate Exposure	225	0.17	1.33	−1.72	0.16	2.26
Market-to-Book Ratio	225	1.71	1.56	0.49	1.13	4.86

by 0.17% on average. Perhaps mitigating this exposure is the fact that on average, 77% of the firms in our sample employ foreign currency derivatives. Finally, our sample firms' return on asset (market-to-book ratio) is on average 4.7% (1.71).

4. THE EAST ASIAN CRISIS AND U.S. MULTINATIONALS

In this section we examine the impact of the East Asian Crisis on U.S multinationals. One way to test for this is by examining the abnormal returns for our sample firms during the period of the crisis. Figure 1 shows a graph of the rate of return on the JP Morgan East-Asian exchange-rate index. Although it is difficult to pinpoint the exact beginning and ending date of the crisis, as it can also be seen from the graph, it seems that the period between June 1997 and May 1998 covers the majority, if not all of the crisis.[4] By the end of 1997, most East Asian currencies were down 30% against the U.S. dollar.

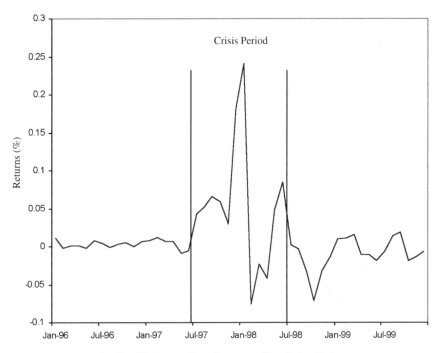

Fig. 1.   Exchange Rate Returns – East Asian Index
January 1996–December 1999.

4.1. Abnormal Returns During the East Asian Crisis

We estimate abnormal returns during the crisis using the following model for each firm;

$$R_{i,t} = a_0 + \gamma_i I_{event} + \beta R_{m,t} + \varepsilon_{i,t}^2$$

where $R_{i,t}$ is the return for firm i in month t and $R_{m,t}$ is the market return in month t. The event indicator variable is equal to 1 between June 1997 and May 1998 and zero otherwise. Hence, our measure of γ_i is our estimate of the abnormal return for firm i. For each firm i, we use return data during January 1996 – December 1998 and obtain the time series returns from CRSP.

Our hypothesis is that firms with presence in East Asia were hurt by the crisis. This implies negative and significant abnormal return (γ_i) for these firms during the crisis. Table 2 shows univariate results for alternative samples. Row 1 shows results for a sample of U.S. firms with assets above \$100 million during 1996–1998. The sample contains a total of 251 firms; 122 firms that have subsidiaries in South East Asia; 103 firms without any subsidiaries in South East Asia but subsidiaries in some other region of the world; and 296 firms that have no foreign subsidiaries at all. The average abnormal return for the entire sample of U.S. firms is positive but small in magnitude (0.00055 per month) and statistically insignificant. This suggests that on average, U.S. firms were not affected by the crisis. Examining further the abnormal returns of the subsample of firms with foreign subsidiaries (regardless of their location) reveals that U.S. multinationals were on average hurt by the East Asian crisis.

Table 2. Abnormal Returns During the East Asian Crisis.

Sample of Firms	Obs.	Mean	Std.	Median	T-stat.
1. All firms	521	0.00055	0.0396	0.00259	0.317
2. Firms with foreign subsidiaries	225	−0.00924	0.0352	−0.00924	−3.942
3. Firms with foreign subsidiaries but no subsidiaries in East Asia	103	−0.00320	0.0341	−0.00290	−0.952
4. Firms with foreign subsidiaries in East Asia	122	−0.01435	0.0354	−0.01170	−4.475
5. Firms with foreign subsidiaries in East Asia that do not use FX derivatives	13	−0.01354	0.0436	0.00177	−1.120
6. Firms with foreign subsidiaries in East Asia that use FX derivatives	109	−0.01444	0.0345	−0.01182	−4.365

Note: Standard deviations and *T*-statistics for our measure of abnormal returns are based on the standard deviation of γ_i.

The abnormal returns are negative and statistically significant (–0.00924 per month) (row 2). The more interesting result arises when we split U.S. multinational firms into those that have no subsidiaries in East Asia and those that do (rows 3 and 4). While multinational firms with no subsidiaries in East Asia were generally not affected by the Asian crisis (abnormal returns are negative but statistically insignificant), those firms that have subsidiaries in East Asia were significantly hurt by the crisis. On average, we find that the abnormal returns for this group of firms is negative, large in magnitude (–0.01435 per month), and statistically significant.

The last two rows show results for the sample of firms with East Asia subsidiaries that do not use currency derivatives (row 5) and for those that do (row 6). The former sample is quite small; only 13 firms with subsidiaries in East Asia are not using currency derivatives. In contrast, about 109 firms with subsidiaries in East Asia employ currency derivatives. Despite the use of currency derivatives, U.S. multinationals with subsidiaries in East Asia were significantly affected by the crisis. Specifically, the average abnormal return for firms in this sample is negative and statistically significant (–0.0144). Firms which do not use derivatives also have negative abnormal returns on average, but the impact is not statistically significant, potentially due to the low power of the test given the small number of observations.

4.2. Exchange-Rate Exposure

Before we examine the impact of the Asian crisis on U.S. multinationals in a multivariate framework, we examine the exchange-rate exposure of these firms prior to the crisis. This ex-ante exposure should reveal whether firms with presence in East Asia were in fact exposed to FX risks or not. By examining the exposure prior to the crisis we want to mitigate the endogeneity that may arise if we measure exposure and performance during the same period. To estimate exposure we use a two-factor model, shown below, commonly used in the prior exposure literature (see, e.g. Jorion, 1990).

$$R_{i,t} = a_0 + \beta_{FX}FX_t + \beta_m R_{m,t} + \varepsilon_{i,t}^2$$

where $R_{i,t}$ is the return for firm i in month t, $R_{m,t}$ is the market return in month t and FX_t is the return on the JP Morgan East Asian foreign exchange index. The estimate of β_{FX} is our measure of the firms' foreign currency exposure.

Table 3 shows univariate results of exchange-rate exposure for alternative samples of firms. Consistent with our expectations, we find that, while firms with no foreign subsidiaries in East Asia were not significantly exposed to East Asian exchange-rate movements, firms with East Asians presence were

Table 3. Foreign Currency Exposure (Pre-Crisis Period).

		Firms that use FX derivatives	Firms that do not use FX derivatives
Firms with foreign subsidiaries but no subsidiaries in East Asia	*N*	65	38
	Mean	0.022	0.057
	Standard Deviation	1.385	1.147
	(*T*-Statistics)	(0.128)	(0.310)
Firms with foreign subsidiaries in East Asia	*N*	109	13
	Mean	0.311	0.131
	Standard Deviation	1.378	1.046
	(*T*-Statistics)	(2.354)	(0.451)

Note: Reported averages are the equally-weighted cross-sectional means of β_{FX} over the sample.

significantly exposed. The average exposure of these firms is 0.311 suggesting that a 1% appreciation in the dollar vs. a basket of East Asian currencies would reduce returns by 0.311%. These exposures are significantly higher than the average exposures documented in prior literature (see, e.g. Allayannis and Ihrig (2001) where the average exposure for U.S. industries is about 0.13).

4.3. Determinants of Abnormal Returns and Profitability Changes During the Asian Crisis

In Section 4.1 we documented in univariate tests that U.S. multinationals with subsidiaries in East Asia had negative abnormal returns during the crisis. In this section we will examine the validity of this finding using a multivariate framework. It is possible that the negative abnormal return documented in these univariate tests is due to some other factor and not necessarily their presence in East Asia. Table 4 presents the results of our multivariate test. Column 1 shows results using the East Asian dummy variable, while column 2 shows results using our continuous variable, the ratio of East Asian subsidiaries to total subsidiaries.

Consistent with our hypothesis and our univariate findings, we find that U.S. multinationals with a subsidiary in East Asia experienced negative abnormal returns (the coefficient on the East Asian dummy variable is –0.923 and is statistically significant), suggesting that the Asian crisis had a severe and adverse effect on them. Consistent with our earlier finding in this paper (but opposite to previous findings on derivatives use) we find that the use of

Table 4. Determinants of Abnormal Returns During the Asian Crisis.

Dependent Variable: Abnormal Returns		
Exposure	−0.309	−0.292
	(0.067)	(0.084)
Foreign Sales/Total Sales	−2.201	−2.265
	(0.098)	(0.091)
East Asian Dummy (= 1 if the firm has subsidiaries in East Asia)	−0.923	
	(0.042)	
Ratio of East Asian Subsidiaries to Total Subsidiaries		−4.182
		(0.078)
FX Derivatives Dummy (= 1 if the firm uses derivatives)	0.257	0.092
	(0.688)	(0.887)
Constant	0.114	0.123
	(0.855)	(0.843)
N	225	225
R^2	0.071	0.075

Note: Standard errors are reported below coefficient estimates.

derivatives had a positive but not significant effect on abnormal returns. This may be explained by the magnitude of the shock, or by the inability of the derivatives market to remain liquid when the crisis hit.[5] The coefficients on the control variables are consistent with our expectations; firms that had a higher ex-ante exposure to exchange-rate risk experienced negative returns and firms with a high percentage of foreign sales as a percentage of total sales were also adversely affected by the crisis. Using a continuous variable (the ratio of East Asian subsidiaries to total subsidiaries) does not alter our inferences; we find that the higher the ratio of East Asian subsidiaries to total, the lower (the more negative) the abnormal returns for the firm. This result suggests that firms with a large presence in East Asia were more severely affected by the crisis than firms with a small presence.

Our last test examines the impact of the Asian crisis on U.S. multinationals' profitability. Specifically, we examine whether the presence in East Asia was linked to changes in profitability between 1996 and 1998. Table 5 presents the results of this test. Consistent with our hypothesis we find that presence in East Asia had a negative and significant impact on changes in profitability as measured by changes in ROA between 1996 and 1998. Although the coefficient on the use of foreign currency derivatives is positive, suggesting that the use of derivatives benefited firms' profitability, the effect is not significant. Similarly,

Table 5. The Effect of the Asian Crisis on Firm Profitability.

Dependent Variable: Changes in ROA	
East Asian Dummy	−3.125
	(0.050)
FX Derivatives Dummy	0.357
	(0.742)
Ln (Number of Countries)	0.529
	(0.424)
Size (Log of Total Sales)	−0.084
	(0.972)
Market-to-Book Ratio	2.011
	(0.004)
Debt to Equity	−0.011
	(0.000)
Growth (Capital Exp/Sales)	−18.381
	(0.057)
Advertising/Assets	−49.465
	(0.486)
Constant	−0.690
	(0.512)
N	225
R^2	0.071

Note: P-values are reported below coefficient estimates.

the coefficient on our proxy for operational hedges (number of countries) that a firm operates in) is positive but not significant. This suggests that, similar to financial hedges, operational hedges were not effective in protecting U.S. multinationals.[6] Most of the control variables we use are significant and have signs consistent with our expectations. For example, firms with high investment opportunities as proxied by the market-to-book ratio experienced an increase in profitability; firms with high leverage experienced a decline in profitability; in contrast to the coefficients on the market-to-book ratio, both the coefficients on capital expenditures and advertising (as a percentage of sales and assets respectively) were negatively related to changes in profitability, suggesting that high growth firms (riskier firms) suffered during the crisis.

5. CONCLUSIONS

In this paper we examine the impact of the Asian crisis on U.S. multinationals. We find that while the East Asian crisis had an insignificant impact on the average U.S. firm and the average U.S. multinational, it had a severe adverse effect for U.S. multinationals that had a presence in East Asia. The effect was larger, the larger the firm's presence in East Asia and amounted to 1.44% per month. Finally, although the use of currency derivatives and potential operational hedging were positively related to abnormal returns and profitability changes during the crisis, their effect was not statistically significant. We suggest that the magnitude of the shock (and the resultant lack of liquidity) may have mitigated their effectiveness.

NOTES

1. Francis, Hasan and Pantzalis (2000) examine the impact of the Asian crisis on the exchange-rate risk of U.S. multinationals and find that the mean exposure of U.S. multinationals was significantly higher during the crisis than during the pre-crisis period.

2. See, e.g. Coase (1937), Dunning (1973), etc.

3. Recently, Allen and Pantzalis (1996), and Francis et al. (2000) have employed several subsidiary and country-based measures of multinationality.

4. On July 2, 1997, the Bank of Thailand announced a managed float of the Baht and called on the IMF for "technical assistance". Upon announcement, the Baht devalued by about 20%; this event is considered by many as the onset of the Asian crisis. (see http://stern.nyu.edu/nroubini/ for a detailed timeline of the Asian crisis).

5. See Allayannis, Brown and Klapper (2002) for more details on the impact of the crisis on East Asian firms and the derivative markets illiquidity during the crisis.

6. Allayannis, Ihrig and Weston (2001) examine financial and operational exchange-rate hedging strategies for U.S. multinationals in a broader context. They find that operational hedging strategies improve value only when used in conjunction with financial hedging strategies.

ACKNOWLEDGMENTS

We would like to thank Jane Ihrig, Chris Pantzalis, and Betty Simkins for their many helpful suggestions. The first author also wishes to thank the Darden School Foundation and the Batten Institute for summer support.

REFERENCES

Allayannis, G., Brown, G., & Klapper, L. (2002). Capital Structure and Financial Risk: Evidence from Foreign Debt Use in East Asia. Working Paper, Darden Graduate School of Business, University of Virginia.

Allayannis, G., & Ofek, E. (2001). Exchange-Rate Exposure, Hedging, and the Use of Foreign Currency Derivatives. *Journal of International Money and Finance, 20,* 273–296.

Allyannis, G., & Ihrig, J. (2001). Exposure and Markups. *Review of Financial Studies, 14*(3), 805–835.

Allayannis, G., Ihrig, J., & Weston, J. (2001). Exchange-Rate Hedging: Financial vs. Operational Strategies. *American Economic Review Papers and Proceedings, 91*(2), 391–395.

Allayannis, G., & Weston J. (2001). The Use of Foreign Currency Derivatives and Firm Market Value. *Review of Financial Studies, 14*(1), 243–276.

Allen, L., & Pantzalis, C. (1996). Valuation of Operating Flexibility of Multinational Corporations. *Journal of International Business Studies, 27*(4), 633–653.

Bodnar, G., Tang, C, & Weinrop, J. (1997). Both Sides of Corporate Diversification; The Value Impact of Geographical and Industrial Development. NBER Working Paper #6224, October.

Buckley, P., & Casson, M. (1998). Models of the Multinationals Enterprise. *Journal of International Business Studies, 29*(1), 21–44.

Chowdhry, B., & Howe, J. (1999). Corporate Risk Management for Multinational Corporations: Financial and Operational Hedging Policies. *European Finance Review, 2*, 229–246.

Christophe, S. (1997). Hysteresis and the Value of the U.S. Multinational Corporation. *Journal of Business, 70*, 435–462.

Coase, R. (1937). The Nature of Firm. *Econometrica, 4*, November, 386–405.

DeMarzo, P., & Duffie, D. (1995). Corporate Incentives for Hedging and Hedge Accounting. *Review of Financial Studies, 8*.

Denis, D., Denis, D., & Yost, K. (2000). Global Diversification, Industrial Diversification and Firm Value. *Journal of Finance* (forthcoming).

Doukas, J., & Travlos, N. (1988). The Effect of Corporate Multinationalism on Shareholders' wealth: Evidence from International Acquisitions. *Journal of Finance, 43*(5), 1161–1175.

Dunning, J. (1973). The Determinants of International Product. *Oxford Economic Papers, 25*, 289–336.

Errunza, V., & Senbet, L. (1981). The Effects of International Operations on the Market Value of the Firm: Theory and Evidence. *Journal of Finance, 36*(2), 401–417.

Errunza, V., & Senbet, L. (1984). International Corporate Diversification, Market Valuation, and Size Adjusted Evidence. *Journal of Finance, 39*(3), 727–743.

Francis, B., Hasan, I., & Pantzallis, C. (2000). Operational Hedges and Coping With Foreign Exchange Exposure: The Case of U.S. MNCs during the Asian Financial Crisis of 1997.

Froot, K., Scharfstein, D., & Stein, J. (1993). Risk Management: Coordinating Corporate Investment and Financing Policies. *Journal of Finance*, December.

Geczy, C., Minton, B., & Schrand, C. (1997). Why Firms Use Currency Derivatives? *Journal of Finance, 52*, September.

Guay, W. (1999). The Impact of Derivatives on Firm Risk: An Empirical Examination of New Derivative users. *Journal of Accounting and Economics, 26*.

He, J., & Ng, L. (1998). The Foreign Exchange Exposure of Japanese Multinational Corporations. *Journal of Finance, 53*, 733–753.

Jorion, P. (1990). The Exchange Rate Exposures of U.S. Multinationals. *Journal of Business, 63*(3), 331–345.

Kogut, B., & Kulatilaka, N. (1995). Operating Flexibility, Global Manufacturing, and the Option Value of a Multinational network. *Management of Science, 40*(1), 123–139.

Mello, A., Parsons, J., & Triantis, A. (1995). An Integrated Model of Multinational Flexibility and Financial Hedging. *Journal of International Economics, 39*, 27–51.

Mian, S. (1996). Evidence on Corporate Hedging Policy. *Journal of Financial and Quantitative Analysis, 31*, September.

Morck, R., & Yeung, B. (1991). Why Investors Value Multinationality? *Journal of Business, 64*.

Nance, D., Smith, C., & Smithson, C. (1993). On the Determinants of Corporate Hedging. *Journal of Finance*, March.
Pantzalis, C. (1998). Does Location Matter? An Empirical Analysis of MNC Market Valuation. Working Paper, University of South Florida.
Smith, C., & Stulz, R. (1985). The Determinants of Firms' Hedging Policies. *Journal of Financial and Quantitative Analysis, 20*, December.
Smith, C., Smithson, C., & Wilford, D. S. (1990). *Managing Financial Risk*. New York: Harper and Row.
Stulz, R. (1990). Managerial Discretion and Optimal Financing Policies. *Journal of Financial Economics, 26*, 3–27.
Visvanathan, G. (1998). Who Uses Interest Rate Swaps? A Cross-sectional Analysis. *Journal of Accounting, Auditing and Finance, 13*(3), 173–200.

10. MANAGING POLITICAL RISK IN
THE AGE OF TERRORISM

Llewellyn D. Howell

ABSTRACT

*Although political risk assessments have incorporated political violence
and acts of terrorism into consideration of where the dangers lay for many
decades, the acts of September 11, 2001 have shifted the focus of what is
more impactful in international business and investment. Handling many
of the risks to foreign investors remains a task for company managers but
the nature of this new form of war has forced an interaction with
government and international institutions that will be a new challenge for
investors. What will remain is the necessity for managers of foreign
enterprises to assess political risk along with economic and financial risk
and then to determine which management tools are appropriate in dealing
with specified risks. This essay discusses the relationship between risks
and responses and delineates management methods that can be deployed
in response.*

1. FORECASTING POLITICAL RISK FOR A PURPOSE

Long before September 11, 2001, foreign investors in every country understood
the risks to be faced in doing business in unfamiliar environments. In planning
a foreign investment in today's globalized and yet still diverse international
system, the international manager has to become immediately aware of the
general socio-political climate in which the investing firm must operate. That

Global Risk Management: Financial, Operational, and Insurance Strategies,
Volume 3, pages 131–153.
Copyright © 2002 by Elsevier Science Ltd.
All rights of reproduction in any form reserved.
ISBN: 0-7623-0982-2

is, instead of being simply grounded in the financials and economics of business, today's foreign investors have to be sociologists, anthropologists, and political scientists if they expect to compete and survive in multifaceted environments.

There is both offense and defense in international investment. Offense consists of having good management, controlling the financial situation of the company, and strong marketing of the product or service. Defense is protecting the company against competitive challenges of other companies, responsiveness to geological and physical surroundings, and, most importantly today, an ability to maneuver in complex and very conflictual social, religious, cultural, and political environments.

Political risk assessment and management deal with this latter need. Neither identifying political risk nor dealing with it are skills ordinarily at hand for managers when first venturing into the world of cross-border investments. But these are skills that can be taught and learned, once it is understood that socio-political dangers are real and that most business managers are not initially equipped to deal with these social, cultural, and political phenomena. Fortunately, the necessary capabilities can be acquired, either through training or by hiring consultants.

Managers must first identify specific firm vulnerabilities, determine sources of risk that underlay them, and then match those vulnerabilities with attributes of the socio-political climate. Once these are identified, they must take the critical managerial step of applying the appropriate management tools to avoid, block, alter, or compensate for the sources of risk and possible losses to the investor. My purpose here is to walk through these stages, tying the existing and readily available means of assessment with proposed tools as a guide to managers who are facing increasing instances of political risk in rapidly emerging markets.

2. PROFESSIONAL POLITICAL RISK ASSESSMENT

Many companies provide political risk assessments as their product in this evolving global economy. These are profit making companies and some evaluation of their success can be found in the longevity or "market test" of each. Formal country and political risk assessments date to the 1960s, well prior to the period of the Iran debacle in which no governments or firms were really paying attention to assessments. What is now Business Environment Risk Intelligence (BERI) was originally "Business Risk Intelligence Information" and in the mid-1960s began its analysis of a limited number of countries, with a 10-variable 'political risk index'. The International Country Risk Guide

(ICRG) began in an early format shortly thereafter. With several adjustments in structure, including the most recent in 1997, ICRG continues to provide a Country Risk assessment (political, financial, and economic risk) with its political risk index being the best known. Other well known attribute models are those of the Economist Intelligence Unit (EIU), The Economist (see, e.g. "Countries in Trouble," 1986; Howell, 1992), S. J. Rundt & Associates, Moody's Investors Services, and Standard & Poor's Ratings Group (for a description of all of these, see Howell, 2001).

Both BERI and ICRG are attribute models that provide country-level analyses for all foreign investors in the host country, with what has come to be known as a "macro" analysis. By attribute models, I mean those risk forecasting models that rely on characteristics of the government or the society to determine some level of danger to foreign investors. Attribute models are in contrast to models such as that of The PRS Group (Political Risk Services, dating from 1979) that project central government decisions that might be adverse to foreign investors. Most models used in ratings systems today rely on attributes rather than projected decisions but I will make reference to both attribute and government decision models in this study.

Ratings systems generally are a summed total of a number of variables that are theorized to collectively reflect the level of risk to foreign investors. Although there is reasonably wide variance in the composition of the lists, there are some common components. These lists include: (1) attributes of the government and of political behavior (including political violence) in the host country; (2) attributes of the culture and social system; and (3) attributes of the international circumstances of the country. These attributes are considered to be the sources or possible causes of losses to investors.

A widely used example of such source categorizations is the ICRG. This model includes the following variables and weights:

ICRG Political Risk Components

Government Attributes
- Government Stability 12 pts
- Investment Profile 12 pts
- Democratic Accountability 6 pts
- Law and Order 6 pts
- Military in politics 6 pts
- Religion in Politics 6 pts
- Bureaucracy Quality 4 pts

Societal Attributes
  • Internal Conflict 12 pts
  • Corruption 6 pts
  • Ethnic Tensions 6 pts
  • Socioeconomic Conditions 12 pts

International Environment
  • External Conflict 12 pts

Each variable has a weight that reflects its relative importance in the configuration of attributes that contribute to risk. For the published ratings, these are fixed for all investors. The maximum total number of political risk points is 100. The Actual Risk Points (ARP) achieved are interpreted on the following scale (see Howell, 2001, p. 188).

Very High Risk	00.0 to 49.9%
High Risk	50.0 to 59.9%
Moderate Risk	60.0 to 69.9%
Low Risk	70.0 to 79.9%
Very Low Risk	80.0 to 100%

But this is just general advice. It gives a general idea of the magnitude of risk and possible problems in the investment environment. But what about management advice? There is really none of that here.

Similar methods exist for the attribute models mentioned above. The main categories are the same and many of the variables are similar, with some relatively minor variations.

The PRS decision model also contains twelve variables. Several of these can be considered to be attributes, especially "Political Turmoil," which would fall into the 'attributes of the social system' category. The others are all deemed to be the results of direct or indirect government decisions. The model never uses all the variables in a single risk application but instead variables are used selectively in three areas of investment: (1) Financial transfers; (2) Direct investment; and (3) Exports. For each, a letter grade is provided that parallels the usual evaluation system with 'A' at the top and 'D' at the bottom. The full set of variables provided is:

PRS Political Risk Components

Societal Attributes
  • Political Turmoil

Government Policies Related to:
- Limitations on Equity
- Operations Restrictions and Interference
- Taxation Discrimination
- Repatriation Restrictions
- Exchange Inhibitions or Controls
- Tariff Discrimination
- Non-tariff Barrier Discrimination
- Payment Delays
- Fiscal and Monetary Expansion
- Labor Cost Fluctuation
- Foreign Debt Magnitude

I will refer to management tools below that relate to government decisions as distinct from government or societal attributes. However, these decisions may also be looked at as acts generating losses that are a function of attributes such as those listed for ICRG. Theoretically, or methodologically, the PRS variables – with the exception of political turmoil – can be looked at as intervening variables. That is, Limitations on Equity may have been set as a result of nationalism and ethnic or religious tension in the country. For another example, the ICRG attribute 'poor bureaucracy quality' may be the cause of the PRS government decision 'payment delays.' Although bureaucracy quality is probably not the only cause of payment delays, it may be that, to some extent, a management response may be applied to both.

Political risk assessment is intended to assist foreign investors in managing their businesses located in foreign countries.[1] A country's political risk rating, such as a score of '74' from BERI or ICRG or a letter rating like 'B +' from PRS or 'BBB' from Standard and Poor's, is a statement about the country's overall political risk. Overall risk is an indicator of many possible types of losses to the investing firm and will emanate from many sources. The types of losses can range from straightforward expropriation to subtle operations interference in a local assembly plant to civil strife damage from tribal warfare. Eight types of losses generated from political sources are: (1) Inconvertibility; (2) Expropriation; (3) War damage; (4) Civil strife damage, including the direct effects of terrorism; (5) Contract repudiation; (6) Negative government actions; (7) Process deterioration; and (8) Event intervention (See Howell, 2001). The first five of these are coverable by political risk insurance from institutions such as OPIC, MIGA, or AIG (the latter an example from among many private insurers). These loss types are characterized as vulnerabilities. The sources can be as wide-ranging as ethnic or linguistic fractionalization to extensive involvement of the military in political decision making.

The point of identifying political risk probabilities with accurate assessments is to be able to avoid the costs of a probable loss or to manage the circumstances to reduce or even eliminate any damage. How does a country rating of '74' or 'B +' tell us about the source of the risk or about which management tool to apply? The answer is that it doesn't. The country rating can say "Don't go there!" (if it's a 'D') or it can say "Don't worry!" (if it's an 'A +'). For managing macro level concerns, the standardized country-level analyses can potentially be useful for the right circumstances. But relatively little actual risk today is at the macro level. This level of assessment was useful in the 1960s and 1970s when socialist or Communist governments were coming into power in the wake of the colonial era. Countrywide expropriations or control of currency were common and governments in the emerging states treated all foreign investors alike. We have passed that era.

In the 21st Century, selective and creeping expropriation is much more likely. Particular types of businesses are targeted by governments who pick out cash cows with little import-component dependency to exploit. International war has diminished greatly only to be replaced with an expansion of ethnic wars and terrorist activity that are often contained in particular parts of the country. International politics and nationalistic attitudes sometimes enter the picture and even the nationalities, religions, and races of the investors become the basis of selective actions by governments or guerrilla groups.

So what if it's an in-between rating, like most are? What does a 'B' rating tell us about the chances of civil strife damage? About potential contract interference? About any of the specific dangers that foreign investors face? Obviously, very little. That is, the manager who is trying to figure out what to do in the way of dealing with risk, instead of just running from it, doesn't gain much from this unfocused assessment. If political risk is high, a foreign investor may choose to avoid the risk entirely by not investing or investing in a different national location. But this will also result in lost opportunity, and doesn't involve much in the way of management.

3. INDUSTRY, FIRM, OR PROJECT RISK AS DISTINCT FROM COUNTRY LEVEL RISK

In addition to quantitative ratings, most political risk firms also provide qualitative assessments in the form of text. The text may provide more detail on specific problems in the country and narrow the sources of risk. But this type of writing has to be general to address the many potential types of firms that may be investing. As noted above, PRS ratings are narrowed to three investment areas: financial transfers, foreign direct investment (manufacturing, mining, any investment with equity in the host country), and exports. Even this, however, is not enough.

If a financial firm has no facilities in the host country, it probably would incur little in the way of damaging consequences from the PRS variable Political Turmoil. If, however, the firm has a branch or two in the capital city with physical property, then there might be more danger of damage and loss from riots, racial conflicts, or civil war. If it has 20 branches spread around the country, the danger would be much greater. The variable could be included or excluded from the rating calculation, depending on whether or not there were physical assets at risk. At minimum, the variable should be weighted according to the impact on the particular investor. It's clear that there is no 'one size fits all' for political risk assessments.

Charles Kennedy has noted managerial perceptions of risk from particular variables across a wide range of industries (Kennedy, 1987). On a zero to three scale, managers in the pharmaceutical industry and petroleum industry felt that political instability would have a great effect on them, rating it at 2.9. On the other hand, those in automobile exports scored instability only at 1.5. Other perceptions range widely in between. Both as a matter of perception and reality, risk varies according to industry, firm, and project.

The consequence of this realization is that country ratings should be viewed not as the end product but rather as the medium by which individual variable ratings are provided to the end user. That is, the most valuable component of a quantitative risk rating package is the data, not the country rating. The user can then develop a rating to fit its own needs. How does this process work?

What is necessary is that each individual investor look first at its own vulnerabilities for any foreign investment situation. These may be drawn from the eight categories suggested or drawn more narrowly. Then once these are identified, work backward to identify the sources of the particular risk (see Fig. 1).

The investor needs to begin by identifying its particular vulnerabilities in the foreign environment. What types of losses might occur for this industry, firm, or project? Then what are the sources of those losses. This next stage has to be a causal analysis. Given the context and practice of foreign investment, this doesn't have to have a formal mathematical analysis, but rather should be a sit-down session with knowledgeable managers and consultants, including both those familiar with the firm and its operations and those who know the host country well. This can always be a situation where company managers undertake the entire analysis with the help of published text country

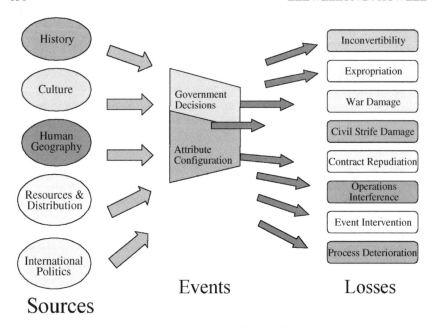

Fig. 1.   Origins of Socio-Political Losses.

assessments but there is always much missing in any written study. These are also written for a general audience.

Here's an example of how this would work. If we are talking about a mining company, it is likely that: (1) a contract with the government is entailed; (2) a large number of local employees will be hired; (3) ore will be shipped from a host country port facility; (4) the facility will be located in a remote and rural area of the country; and (5) there is considerable equity in buildings, general infrastructure, and equipment. There are always more elements to the situation than this but these will serve to illustrate the problem and the process.

If there is a government contract, the vulnerability is to contract repudiation. The investor needs to know, first, what situational characteristics or attribute types have historically led to abrogation or disputes over terms of contracts. It then needs to know if any of those characteristics are present in the host country government. And it is important to understand that repudiation or interference can occur at many levels, specifically national, provincial, city, village, or even tribal.

If there are a large number of employees, the company's human resource office will have to deal with intercultural sensibilities among the employees, cross-cultural sensitivity between the employer and the employees, government determined hiring policies, affirmative action requirements, and gender parity problems related to the particular society. The firm's employee base will invite a variety of types of both negative government actions and negative events such as politically motivated strikes.

If a port facility is required, the firm will be vulnerable to any action affecting that port or the exporting ability of the host country. Sanctions and blockades in diplomatic controversies could be one problem but so would acts of war or sabotage conducted by another country, including the home country. War damage is not common but has remained a central category of political risk insurance coverage for a reason. The terrorist acts that destroyed the World Trade Center towers would normally fall under this heading and the need for this form of political risk insurance has grown dramatically since September 11, 2001.

If the firm is operating in a remote area of the country, it could be vulnerable to civil strife damage. There is a vulnerability on two counts. The first is that conflicts between ethnic groups or between guerrilla groups and the government usually arise and are fostered in remote areas. The second is that host government forces are usually arrayed in urban areas and around the seat of government. It takes them longer to get to confrontations in the more remote areas, if they ever get there. In the meantime, otherwise preventable damage could be done.

Terrorist actions that are taken directly against a foreign firm may fall into a category not readily identified as either war damage or civil strife damage (Howell, 2002). With Islamic terrorists like those that attacked the World Trade Center and the Pentagon, there was no national entity behind them that could provide an identity that would enable the acts to be described as "war," despite the widely used term to characterize the response as a "War on Terrorism." And yet, terrorist acts on behalf of an international cause cannot be clearly defined as civil strife in the insurance sense. Perhaps a separate category of terrorist damage is now merited.

Any firm with equity is vulnerable to expropriation. In today's world, that includes many forms of "creeping" expropriation, as well as nationalizations and seizures. And, of course, expropriation can occur at all the same levels as contract repudiation, from national to tribal.

There are more vulnerabilities than these for this firm but these provide examples to work with and illustrate the process of initial identification of possible problems for a firm no matter where it is located. Some of these vulnerabilities can be responded to directly or have to be. Others can be dealt with at their sources. The next step is to determine if the conditions that lead to exploitation of these vulnerabilities are present in the host country, and in the region of that country where the project is located.

4. UNDERSTANDING THE SOURCES OF VULNERABILITIES

Let's follow up on two examples of the vulnerabilities and hypothesize a bit about how losses in these categories might arise. The two examples are civil strife damage and expropriation. Expropriation is the most notorious of losses, dating especially to the anti-colonial period of the 1960s and 1970s. Civil strife damage was the most common political risk insurance claim paid by OPIC in the 1990s.

For Civil Strife Damage, the example of Freeport McMoRan in Indonesia is instructive. In 1996, Freeport was struck by rioting at its copper mine in Irian Jaya, the eastern-most island of Indonesia. Buildings were damaged, with windows broken and other damage occurred as well: mining and personal use vehicles were hit, and production was halted for three days (*Financial Times*, 1996). Underlying the complaints of the rioters were several familiar situational attributes found in political risk models. These included: (1) Ethnic Tension (ICRG, Economist, BERI); (2) Political Fractionalization (BERI); (3) Religion in Politics (ICRG, Economist); and Poor Socioeconomic Conditions (ICRG).

The region around the Irian Jaya mine is populated by tribal peoples who are a distinct racial group from the Indonesian leadership in Java and from Indonesians generally in the rest of the country. Moreover, these people are also subdivided among themselves into tribes with different cultures and agendas. The latter account for one element of political fractionalization. Another arises from within Indonesia itself, where the political culture of Jakarta, thousands of miles away, fails to reach into many of the hundreds of populated islands that compose the country. Many employees and villagers in the area surrounding the mine look to Freeport McMoRan as the local government. That in turn, increases the concern and intervention of the national government in Jakarta that wants both to continue to receive the income from the mine and maintain its political control. Add to the picture the fact that most Indonesians are Muslim (about 95%) while the Irian Jaya population is mostly Christian and other local religions. In socioeconomic terms, the area has been neglected by the Indonesian government and is among the poorest in a very poor country.

The mélange of racial, religious, cultural, political, and economic disparities make a volatile mix, already resulting in several major losses to Freeport McMoRan. More importantly for our purposes, it's a useful illustration of societal attributes and vulnerability to "civil strife damage." These sources of strife were evident to any trained eye well before the initiation of work at the mine. The question is 'were the responses of managers prepared in advance for these likely events?'

What about expropriation? Without going into as much detail as in the example above, acts of expropriation can also be seen in attributes and projected decisions of national or local governments. (1) Authoritarian (Economist, ICRG, BERI) institutions are more likely to have the opportunity and leverage to expropriate. (2) When the military is heavily involved in politics (ICRG, Economist), legal principles are more likely to be ignored. (3) Unstable political leadership (ICRG) often finds it necessary to take drastic actions to justify its existence, especially new governments coming to power with a widely variant political philosophy from the previous government. (4) When radical – and especially leftist – forces take over a government (BERI) both ideology and a sense of nationalist ownership create an environment in which seizures and expropriation become more likely. And (5) a weak legal system (ICRG) often leaves little or no recourse in the courts for a foreign investor to obtain a return of equity seized by a government at any level.

As was suggested above in noting the two model types – attributes and decisions – management response to risk can occur at either or both of the levels described. In the first example, there are responses to both the underlying causes (e.g. ethnic tension) and the social outcome (e.g. civil strife damage). For the second, management principles may be applied in dealing with a weak legal system (for example, externally guaranteed contracts) and with expropriation itself (expropriation insurance). Some tools are multiple-use tools; others are specific to the task.

5. IDENTIFYING MANAGEMENT TOOLS

For companies that pay attention to political risk, there are five possible general responses that a firm can take. To make some distinction between these broader responses and more specific actions that can be taken by investment managers, I will refer to the broad responses as 'Level I' tools and to the more specific as 'Level II.' While all five of the Level I responses are decisions that company or investment managers make – and all therefore can be referred to as 'management' – each entails a different strategic approach to handling the effort to prevent losses arising from socio-political risk. The general process of political risk assessment and then ensuing risk management is described in Fig. 2.

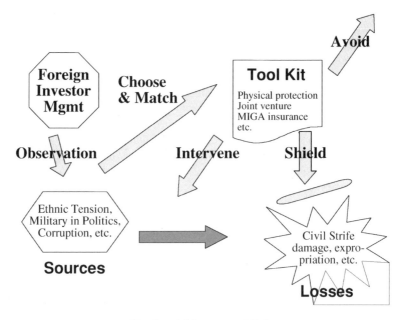

Fig. 2. A Management Path.

5.1. Level I Management Tools

The first is *avoidance*. If a firm finds that it has no ability to deal with a particular risk or a set of risks in a country, it can make a decision either to not invest abroad at all or to shift its investment interests to another country or location with less risk. Both of these options are common, with the former more common than the latter, at least until the era of globalization.

The second is *deterrence*. In this process, the investing firm can act to prevent particular problems from arising. It is now recognized that political risk insurance can sometimes play a role as a deterrent. This can be referred to as "impact" political risk insurance, as distinct from "compensation" political risk insurance. These are discussed further below. If a firm is known to have political risk insurance from the Overseas Private Investment Corporation (OPIC), for example, a government might be less likely to expropriate assets of that firm because it knows that OPIC-insured properties become the possession of the U.S. government if it pays the insurance claim.[2] Insurance from the Multilateral Investment Guarantee Agency (MIGA) of the World Bank has the same effect, also including possible consequences affecting lending from the World Bank and its affiliates. This approach can have its own dangers. Historically, many firms have deterred government interference by creating an alliance with the government in power. Since the government has a stake in business development, it is less likely to dispute its own source of profits. But if the government has a dramatic loss of support or is ousted in a coup or rebellion, that same firm can suddenly find itself on the side of the new government's enemy.

The third is *process management*. It is in this category that most options occur. Here management recognizes a source of danger and intervenes to prevent it from reaching its culminating effects. For example, if a mining firm is aware of local ethnic rivalries that could result in violence in the workplace, the firm's managers can exercise discretion in placement of supervisors, in numbers of particular ethnic group employees hired, and in an appropriate balance in training, advancement, and awards.

The fourth is *compensation protection*, otherwise known as political risk insurance. For the most part, political risk management means making decisions that keep the firm or business from harm. Political risk insurance has its primary use in dealing with the aftermath of damage, reducing it rather than preventing it. Since political risk insurance usually involves a deductible and often payments are a result of negotiation rather than set amounts, this does not amount to full recovery of losses. The deductible may be 10% and thus still amounts to a considerable loss to the firm. In addition, peripheral damage often occurs that is not or cannot be covered by insurance. For example, Keene Industries in Liberia suffered a number of losses in the early 1990s in Liberia when attacked on several occasions by elements of an ongoing rebellion in that country (see Howell, 1998). Keene was partially compensated for losses of vehicles, food stores, equipment, and some product but received no compensation on lost production, evacuation costs for expatriate personnel, or wages to employees who had to be paid despite a lack of actual work. Note that compensation political risk insurance should be distinguished from impact political risk insurance as being from two different categories of response.

Separate from political risk insurance, investors can buy terrorism insurance. Such insurance already existed before September 11, 2002 but interest obviously rose after that event, as did the obvious need. In May of 2002, American Airlines, United Airlines, and other U.S. carriers proposed creating a company that would provide terrorism insurance at half the cost of existing coverage. Commercial insurers had limited war-risk coverage for airlines and increased premiums after the September 11 attacks, which forced carriers to seek alternatives and more financing for insurance (Hughes, 2002). Frequent warnings from the U.S. government about future terrorist activity in the U.S. and elsewhere has led investors and businesses to give considerably more attention to this type of insurance than had ever been the case previously.

Fifth is *a risk offset*. In this instance a loss is balanced in a larger picture by reducing overall risk by making "a substantial part of [the firm's] profits in another part of the value-added chain or in related operations" (Wells, 1998, p. 33).

5.2. Level II Management Tools

In today's context of high information, knowing the risk and its nature should be able to put investors in a position of being able to counter the risk with management actions that alleviate the level of risk. Referred to as process management above, there are many options for managers who seek to head off or resolve socio-political threats to their firms. Here is a set of possibilities that can be regarded as a "tool kit" for managers and investment decision-makers. The vulnerabilities (loss categories) to which the management tool might apply are underlined:

Get Expertise for Identifying Risk
The foreign investor needs two kinds of expertise. The first is expertise on the firm in order to determine vulnerabilities. This kind of expertise usually has to come from within the firm, although outside consultants familiar with the industry can help. The second is expertise on the host country. This almost always has to come from outside the firm. One of the biggest mistakes an investing firm can make is to send the company's VP to the capital city of the host country, to stay in a five-star hotel and meet with host country nationals who speak the language of the investor. True country experts are necessary to give a full and unbiased picture of the business environment. They can get beyond the English language news sources and have a "feel" for the country that investors ordinarily don't have. Country expertise is needed no matter what the form of political risk or potential loss.

Purchase Impact Political Risk Insurance
By "impact" political risk insurance I mean insurance that has an impact on the government of the country prior to any political acts that might compromise the investor. This is especially important for situations of potential expropriation, limits on currency conversion, government interference with operations, or contract repudiation. Impact insurance is that which plays a role in preventing negative government actions. For example, if an investor has OPIC insurance,

the government will know that if the investor loses equity to them, the U.S. government will become the owner of the equity after payment of a claim and that the U.S. will come after compensation from the host government. After the Indonesian government expropriated Mid-American Energy's two power plants in 1998 and OPIC paid the claim in 1999, the U.S. actively discouraged other loans and assistance to the Indonesian government until the Indonesian government agreed to pay the $290 million lost by MidAmerican (and therefore by the U.S. government). OPIC and MIGA have guarantee agreements with host country governments. Importantly, they have the power to back them up.

Negotiate Better Profit Margins
Where the host country is a seller's market for foreign investors (and most are), conditions in the country that discourage such investment can be dealt with by asking the government to waive or alter limitations that would ordinarily be placed on the investor. For example, if ethnic divisions in the country are high, and if there is a limit on the percentage of profit that can be repatriated, then the investor might negotiate to take home a larger percentage as insurance against the possibility that the ethnic tension might result in conflict with damage to facilities. The investment, of course, has to have some advantage for the host government. This tool would be useful in any situations where there are the makings of domestic conflict that is beyond the direct control of the government and, ultimately, civil strife damage, event intervention (like kidnapping), or other acts generated by the society.

Obtain or Provide Physical Protection
Some of the larger investors have chosen to protect their facilities by hiring armed guards, purchase and use of armored cars, placing protective perimeters and other barriers, forming their own small armies, or 'hiring' components of the national army of the host country. This protection ranges from that against kidnapping to the guarding of oil pipelines against civil strife and event intervention damage. There is also considerable danger here, too, in that some protective forces get out of hand and some have been charged with human rights abuses, creating more risk than they inhibit.

Enter International Alliances
Louis T. Wells (1998) has detailed a number of approaches to political risk management at what might be called the 'micro' level. From a broad company perspective, one way to manage risk in one country is to spread it across countries. That is, one firm can open investments in several countries, some

with lesser levels of risk, to help bear the burden if one has difficulty. More effective is to develop a consortium with other firms in the same industry to spread resources over a larger number of projects. This may be across countries or simply in different regions of the same country. Although this may increase the possibility of some loss, it can eliminate the probability of a large loss. International alliances are especially effective where the host government is likely to be involved in the potential loss, areas like expropriation, inconvertibility, and contract repudiation.

Share Investment with Other Firms
Joint venturing with other foreign firms in the same industry can spread any possible losses. Of course, profits are spread too. The tool is useful for those cases where the only recourse seems to be loss reduction, such as in civil strife damage or war damage, rather than for those instances where some intervention with the government might work.

Build Local Political Alliances
In order to head off problems in the local community that arise in response to the presence of the investor operation, it is necessary – at minimum – to be fully aware of the nature of the local political structure and know who the players are. Without taking sides in an explicit sense, cooperative relations with local governments and institutions (such as welfare agencies) is more than a matter of good public relations. By making itself known as a positive force in community development, the investor can head off local government operations interference and contract abrogation. The focus here is on relations between the investor and government processes.

Build Community Indebtedness
Just as the investor can deal from the start with government institutions to head off misunderstandings and eliminate distance between them, the investor can likewise direct efforts at building a relationship with the social community itself. Allies can be created in the population to deter effects of xenophobia and mistrust, thereby heading off acts of [event] intervention that occur between the community and outsiders. Singapore companies operating in the Indonesian islands of the Riau group, for example, have taken such steps as providing scholarships to local high school students, in an area where funding for high school tuition and books (and even clothing) can make a difference in educational accomplishments and local development.

Apply Knowledgeable Human Resource Management

Every community in which an investor operates has its divisions. The investor cannot be seen to be taking sides, and yet many do so unknowingly. In many Southeast Asian countries there are local Chinese communities that provide a pool of educated and skilled personnel, often experienced in business, management, and technology at a level beyond that of other ethnic groups. On a purely skill basis, it always tempting to hire proportionally larger numbers from this group. But the investor has to be concerned about relations among employees of different racial, religious, linguistic, and cultural backgrounds, especially including those between supervisors and other workers. Local resentments can pour into the workplace and disturb and disrupt production. This form of event intervention can not only limit production but can explode into larger acts of civil strife, all stemming from disputes over opportunity distribution. Attention has to be given to all forms of fragmentation in the local community: race, religion, language, gender, social standing, tribal affiliation, caste, even physical size. HR personnel need to be extremely knowledgeable about the local culture to be able to prevent problems that can easily arise in environments where the investor is a newcomer. And this particular intervention of good management has to occur at the earliest possible stage of the investment. Mistakes made early on often set the tone and cannot be overcome later.

Make Money in Related Operations

Where there is a value-added chain for an investor, that chain can be segmented in terms of political risk. The investor can then focus on making profits in the less risky segments of the chain. Wells uses the example of Enron in India, which could have chosen to make its profits in the supply of fuel to its Maharashtra power generation plant rather than from operation of the power plant itself. "If the core project is squeezed, peripheral activities may assure adequate returns." (p. 33) This can be a useful technique for management of risks of expropriation and operations interference (see Wells, 1998).

Joint Venture with a Local Partner

Sometimes a JV with a local partner can reduce the impact of some risk, especially where the foreign investors may be the target of nationalism or xenophobia, and thereby of civil strife damage or event intervention. Great care must be taken, however, in the choice of the partner. A partner from the wrong side in local disputes may make the investor a target when it might not otherwise be.

Avoid Blame Associated with Privatization
Privatization often entails price increases for the product of the industry taken out of government assets or ownership. If an investor buys in at an early stage, blame is likely to be directed at the foreigner. Investors can anticipate this and require that any price increases take place before it takes over. This tool is useful in circumstances of potential civil strife damage or local government negative actions that might be in response to societal conditions or concerns (see Wells, 1998).

Prepare for Regulation
Particularly at a point of new or recent privatization, few or no regulations will have been established. Anticipating the possibility that the firm might be out of step with future regulations, exemptions can be sought or the government can be asked to establish private sector regulations before funds are committed. Managing this problem will help fend off contract disputes, negative government actions (national and local), and event intervention in the society where the investor must operate (see Wells, 1998).

Involve Strong International Interests
Like with impact political risk insurance, if influential partners are involved in a project there is less likelihood of some forms of negative government actions. This is particularly so if projects are funded by institutions such as the Asian Development Bank or the IMF. International organizations may also have an effect but these seem to be declining in importance in recent years (Wells, p. 35). Negative actions such as expropriation, declarations of inconvertibility, limitations on remittances, or contract repudiation can be inhibited via the power of the international partner, especially when it is a lending institution from which the host government would hope to get further funding. When risk is high, it might be worthwhile seeking out a particular lender to get this kind of protection (see Wells, 1998).

Seek Sensible Methods of Dispute Settlement
In a globalized system, it is no longer a sign of lack of trust to seek international arbitration or to build mechanisms for such adjudication into initial contracts. This tool is most effective for larger investments but sometimes can be utilized for smaller ones if negotiations are handled carefully. It can be applied where there is a concern about possible operations interference, contract repudiation, or expropriation (see Wells, 1998).

Design Financial Structure to Minimize Risk

"The record for honoring debt from parents and other affiliates seems almost as strong as that of debt from independent financial institutions. As a result, a financial structure that depends heavily on debt may provide more security than one with a lower debt/equity ratio" (Wells, pp. 34–35). This tool will be useful if there is a vulnerability to expropriation, negative government actions, or contract frustration (see Wells, 1998).

Choose Defensible Process for Negotiating Entry

Transparency is increasingly expected in the world of the WTO and globalization. Unfortunately, the level of secrecy remains high in the competitive world of multinational and international business. Companies still too often think in terms of getting a special deal or "engage in bargaining processes that are not competitive" (Wells, p. 36). In the darkness of some of these negotiations, illegalities, favoritism, and unreasonable terms often characterize the outcome. Investors can avoid negative government actions later by keeping the deal open and clean from the beginning. In effect, the investment manager should plan from the beginning how he will be able to navigate both the judicial system of the host country and the court of public opinion (see Wells, 1998).

Look for Innovative Forms of Agreement

In sensitive areas of investment, such as those dealing with natural resources, monopolies, and basic services, it is sometimes useful to separate ownership from control and earnings. The investment can be structured such that nominal ownership is in the hands of host country nationals while major decisions and sufficient earnings are kept in the hands of the foreign investor. This tight structuring obviously has to be done at the front end of the investment. In the long run it can protect against civil strife directed at the firm and from both national and local operations interference. Building change into an agreement anticipates the need for contracts to evolve and heads off a perceived need by the government to alter or repudiate contracts. 'Build, operate, and transfer' (BOT) arrangements are one form of anticipating the problem of staleness of contracts (see Wells, 1998).

The Slippery Slope of Bribery

No realistic discussion of political risk management is complete without some discussion of the role of bribery and other forms of corruption and favoritism. It has to be recognized that payoffs to prevent problems (strikes, sabotage, delays, unwanted regulations, etc.) are sought widely, in both emerging and developed markets. And, of course, the use of these techniques can provide some short-term solutions. But more than any other tool that is at the hand of the foreign investor, corruptive acts lay the groundwork for far more problems than they resolve (see Howell, "Asian Corruption . . .", 2002). Not the least of these is product deterioration. Hiring the relatives of an influential local official can, for example, mean that the most skilled managers or workers are not employed. Corruption can often lead to production shortcuts to make up the cost of money lost in process. Favoritism is always recognized in local communities and is seen as side taking, leading to the possibility of cleavages that can be more of a problem than anything that was resolved. Most importantly, even in most places where corruption is common, it is also illegal. This is particularly a threat for American companies where it is also illegal in the U.S. as well as in the local context. This is a tool that is available but is clearly a double-edged sword and is best left in the toolkit.

6. MANAGING RISK: SPECIFIC KNOWLEDGE AND SPECIFIC SKILL

This list is only partial. It represents an effort to link management tools with vulnerabilities and to make the manager aware of the fact that there are tools available for dealing with political risk. But vulnerabilities still need to be linked with country or regional attributes and government decision proclivities in order to determine whether the recommended tools should be applied. The investor will have vulnerabilities no matter where he/she chooses to invest. The key question is 'can the vulnerabilities be exploited in the chosen investment country (or sub-region)?' Here is the management task then: (1) match the investment and the firm with vulnerabilities (for example) . . .

Expropriation
Contract Repudiation
Civil Strife Damage
Event Intervention
et al.

. . . then (2) match vulnerabilities with sources of risk . . .

For example, for Event intervention (Kidnapping of managers and workers), the sources might be:

Ethnic tension
Military power abuses
Religion in politics
Xenophobia

. . . then match the exploitable vulnerabilities and their causal sources to tools:

For **ethnic tension,**
Build local political alliances
Build community indebtedness
Include physical protection
Develop alliances
Purchase compensation political risk insurance.

Since impact political risk insurance is not going to stop ethnic warfare, compensatory insurance has an important role here. It is also important to know which form of political risk insurance to contract for. In this case 'civil strife' or 'political violence' damage insurance would be needed, as distinct from inconvertibility, expropriation, war damage, or contract repudiation insurance.

Several tasks are therefore laid out for the managers of a foreign investment in dealing with political risk. First, they have to know the investment climate well, but they must also know their own firm and operations well in order to determine vulnerabilities. This may seem obvious and in many cases is. But it is still often the case that investors get caught off guard by unfolding events in emerging markets and end up with significant losses. We only need to check the claims lists at the companies providing political risk insurance.

Managers have to be able to investigate the local sources of loss outcomes. That is, someone in the firm or someone hired by the firm has to be able to dissect Indonesia but also Irian Jaya if that is where the firm is going to be located. That dissection involves both societal and governmental processes, including at the local level.

Finally, a political risk manager has to know what the management tools are that are available from the very beginning of an investment project. There is an array of tools, at two levels, that a manager can apply to specific problems generated by the society and political system in which they must operate. The manager must know specifically what those tools are and what they can do, but most importantly, the manager has to know that there is a resource pool of management techniques to employ in dealing with political risk. Use of those tools is necessary at the earliest stages of a foreign investment and must be a part of the plan from the start. Political risk insurance is a good reminder. Insurance can only be purchased before the business or project is started. It can't be purchased after the project is underway and it is suddenly discovered that it is located in the middle of a religious conflict. At the same point the manager is making a decision about political risk insurance, he must also make at least preliminary decisions about which management tools he will apply. In emerging markets, he will certainly need to employ some. And as with any other aspect of good business practice, planning ahead is the key for dealing successfully with political risk. The tools are there. Managers have to know enough to employ them.

NOTES

1. And by 'foreign investor' here I mean any investor not operating in its home cultural and/or political system. Since most political risk assessment systems provide ratings of developed as well as developing countries, a foreign investor here could be a Singaporean company investing in the U.S. or vice versa.

2. OPIC is an agency of the U.S. government that offers political risk insurance to qualified American companies investing abroad. For a brief description of OPIC and a case where the U.S. government pursued a government after it had expropriated two power plants, see Llewellyn D. Howell, The Overseas Private Investment Corporation (OPIC): An Application of Risk Management – MidAmerican Energy in Indonesia. In: L. D. Howell (Ed.), *The Handbook . . .* , 2001.

ACKNOWLEDGMENTS

This chapter is an expansion and updating of a previous study, Llewellyn D. Howell, Dealing with Political Risk: A Manager's Toolkit. In: L. D. Howell (Ed.), *Political Risk Assessment: Concept, Method, and Management.* East Syracuse, NY: The PRS Group, Inc., 2001, pp. 167–188.

REFERENCES

Bernstein, P. (1998). *Against The Gods: The Remarkable Story of Risk.* NY: John Wiley & Sons, Inc.

Countries in Trouble: who's on the skids? *Economist, 301,* 69–72. December 20, 1986.

Hodgetts, R. M., & Luthans, F. (1991). In: R. M. Hodgetts & F. Luthans (Eds), *International Management* (pp. 118–119). NY: McGraw-Hill, Inc.

Howell, L. D. (2002). Asian Corruption Undermines Development. *Honolulu Star Bulletin, 7,* 109, D-5.

Howell, L. D. (2001). Dealing with Political Risk: A Manager's Toolkit. In: L. D.Howell (Ed.), *Political Risk Assessment: Concept, Method, and Management* (pp. 167–188). East Syracuse, NY: The PRS Group.

Howell, L. D. (Ed.) (2001). *The Handbook of Country and Political Risk Analysis* (3rd ed.). East Syracuse, NY: The PRS Group.

Howell, L. D. (2002). Is the New Global Terrorism a Clash of Civilizations?: Evaluating Terrorism's Multiple Sources. In: C. W. Kegley Jr. (Ed.), *The New Global Terrorism.* Prentice Hall.

Howell, L. D. (1998). Keene Industries in Liberia: A Political Risk Case Study and Teaching Note. *International Studies Notes, 23*(2), 18–28.

Howell, L. D. (1997). Operationalizing Political Risk in International Business: The Concept of a Politically-based Loss. In: J. Rogers (Ed.), *Global Risk Assessments Book 4.* Riverside, CA: GRA Inc.

Howell, L. D. (1992). Political Risk and Political Loss for Foreign Investment. *International Executive, 34*(6), 485–498.

Howell, L. D. (Ed.) (2001). *Political Risk Assessment: Concept, Method, and Management.* East Syracuse, NY: The PRS Group.

Hughes, J. (2002). New Insurer to Cover Terrorism Proposed. *Honolulu Advertiser* (May 22), D-2.

Irian Jaya Mine Resumes Work. *Financial Times*, March 15, 1996.

Kennedy, C. R., Jr. (1987). *Political Risk Management.* NY: Quorum Books.

Monti-Belkaoui, J., & Riahi-Bekaoui, A. (1998). *The Nature, Estimation, and Management of Political Risk.* Westport, CN: Quorum Books.

Moran, T. H. (Ed.) (1998). *Managing International Political Risk.* Malden, MA: Blackwell Publishers.

Moran, T. H. (1998). *Foreign Direct Investment and Development.* Washington D.C.: Institute for International Economics.

OPIC (2001). Insurance Claims Experience to Date, September 30.

Political Risk Services. In: L. D. Howell (Ed.), *The Handbook of Country and Political Risk Analysis* (3rd ed.). East Syracuse, NY: The PRS Group.

Wells, L. T., Jr. (1998). God and Fair Competition: Does the Foreign Direct Investor Face Still Other Risks in Emerging Markets? In: T. H. Moran (Ed.), *Managing International Political Risk* (pp. 15–43). Malden, MA: Blackwell Publishers.

PART IV:
INSURING RISK

11. SECURITY MEASURES AND DETERMINATION OF CAPITAL REQUIREMENTS

6-22

Jean-Pierre Berliet

INTRODUCTION

Policyholders have a keen interest in the quality of the guarantee offered by insurance companies. They need to have assurances that their claims will be paid fully and promptly. They view capital as one major determinant of the quality of the contracts offered by insurance companies. They believe that more capital is better; with more capital, the likelihood that their insurance company will not perform on its obligations decreases.

At the most intuitive level, policyholders, regulators and insurance executives see that the level of security (or quality of guarantee) offered by a company is directly related to the probability of the company defaulting (i.e. having insufficient financial assets) in relation to its obligations to policyholders.

This paper explains that:

- the probability of default is an incomplete measure of the security offered to policyholders
- another measure of security, the "Economic Cost of Ruin" provides superior information about the security offered by a company

Global Risk Management: Financial, Operational, and Insurance Strategies,
Volume 3, pages 157–162.
Copyright © 2002 by Elsevier Science Ltd.
All rights of reproduction in any form reserved.
ISBN: 0-7623-0982-2

- ECOR measures of security have important advantages over probability of default measures to help a company:
  - ○ determine its aggregate capital requirements
  - ○ attribute capital to individual business segments correctly.

The example that follows demonstrates these points. It also suggests that probability of default measures can lead to erroneous conclusions about capital requirements and result in inappropriate attribution of capital across business segments.

2. MEASURING POLICYHOLDER SECURITY

The following tables compare the security offered by two insurance companies (A and B) which have the same basic financial resources, measured by total assets, expected losses, and probability of default – and yet offer a different level of security to their policyholders.

Company A	Assets	Probability	Liabilities	Payment	Policyholder Deficit
Scenario 1	10,000	97%	8,784	8,784	0
Scenario 2	10,000	2%	10,000	10,000	0
Scenario 3	10,000	1%	28,000	10,000	18,000
Expected	10,000	100%	9,000	8,820	180

Company B	Assets	Probability	Liabilities	Payment	Policyholder Deficit
Scenario 1	10,000	97%	8,505	8,505	0
Scenario 2	10,000	2%	10,000	10,000	0
Scenario 3	10,000	1%	55,000	10,000	45,000
Expected	10,000	100%	9,000	8,550	450

Company A and Company B have the same probability of default of 1% under Scenario 3, but offer policyholders very different levels of security. Company

A exposes its policyholders to maximum losses of 18,000 (the difference between their claims of 28,000, represented by the company's liabilities, and the 10,000 of assets available to pay these claims), while Company B exposes its policyholders to losses of 45,000. Under Scenario 3, policyholders of Company A will suffer an economic loss of 64.3% (18,000/28,000) of their claims, while policyholders of Company B will suffer an economic loss of 81.8% (45,000/55,000). The quality of the guarantee offered by Company A is clearly higher than the quality of the guarantee of Company B, even though both companies have the same probability of default.

This observation leads us to the view that an insurance company needs to assess the security offered to policyholders in relation to the expectation of economic loss that can be suffered by policyholders, the expected economic cost of ruin.

Expected ECOR for Company A above is 180 (i.e. 18,000 cost of ruin with a 1% probability), while expected ECOR for Company B is 450. In relation to expected liabilities, Company A's expected ECOR ratio is 2.0% while that of company B is 5.0%. Both absolute and relative ECOR measures correctly show that company B offers less security to its policyholder than Company A at the level of assets, i.e. also capital needed to meet a 1% probability of default constraint.

3. ASSESSING CAPITAL REQUIREMENTS AND ATTRIBUTING CAPITAL TO BUSINESS SEGMENTS

The use of probability of default risk measures and probability of default risk constraints also leads to erroneous determination of capital requirements and faulty attribution of capital across segments (in the language of mathematicians, the probability of default is not a "coherent" risk measure). This can be seen from the following example in which we look at the capital requirement of Company C which combines the businesses of Company A and Company B discussed in the previous section.

The distribution of losses of Company C is obtained by convolution of the distributions of the results of Company A and Company B. The following table shows this distribution, with scenarios arranged in order of increasing loss, the related deficits for policyholders, and the absolute and relative ECOR measure of security, under the assumption that Company C has assets needed to meet the 1% probability of default constraints that were imposed on Company A and Company B.

			Company C			
Scenarios	*Probability*	*(Loss) Liability*	*Required Assets*	*Payments*	*ECOR*	*ECOR Ratio*
A1 × B1	94.09%	17,289	38,000	17,289	0	
A2 × B1	1.94	18,505	38,000	18,505	0	
A1 × B2	1.94	18,784	38,000	18,784	0	
A2 × B2	0.04	20,000	38,000	20,000	0	
A3 × B1	0.97	36,505	38,000	36,505	0	
A3 × B2	0.02	38,000	38,000	38,000	0	
A1 × B3	0.97	63,784	38,000	38,000	25,784	
A2 × B3	0.02	65,000	38,000	38,000	27,000	
A3 × B3	0.01	83,000	38,000	38,000	45,000	
Total/Expected	100.00%	18,000	38,000	17,740	260	1.4%

Note that at the 1% probability of default constraint, Company C needs assets of 38,000, that is 18,000 more assets than Company A and Company B would need on a separate basis. The 1% probability of default measure implies a counterintuitive diversification penalty when Company A and Company B are combined to form Company C. This result is obtained because the loss distributions of Company A and Company B are not correlated uniformly across the range of outcomes of their activities. With regard to this characteristic of their business, the probability of default risk measure is "incoherent." Expect this to be the case across many insurance businesses, especially those whose volatility cannot be simply described by their mean variance characteristics or involve heavy tails.

Using ECOR measures of risk as constraints for the determination of capital requirements and the attribution of capital across business segments produces results that are substantially different and consistent with conventional wisdom. They show that diversification reduces capital requirements at a given security level.

The following table compares the capital requirements of Companies A, B and C under:

- a 1% probability of default, which yields a 1.4% expected ECOR ratio
- a 1.4% expected ECOR ratio constraint

	At 1% Probability of Ruin			At 1.4% Expected ECOR Ratio	
	Minimum Assets	Expected ECOR	Expected ECOR Ratio	Minimum Assets	Expected ECOR
Company A	10,000	180	2.0%	15,039	130
Company B	10,000	450	5.0	42,039	130
Company C	38,000	260	1.4	38,000	260
Sum of A and B	20,000			57,078	
Diversification Benefit/(Penalty)	(18,000)			19,078	

The 1.4% expected ECOR ratio is used to calculate the minimum assets that Company A and Company B require to offer policyholders the level of security implied by the 38,000 of assets needed by Company C to meet the 1% probability of default constraint. With a 1.4% expected ECOR ratio constraint, Company A needs 15,039 of assets, while Company B, which has been shown to be riskier needs 42,039 of assets. The sum of the capital requirements of Company A and Company B operating on a stand-alone basis is 57,078, which is greater than the 38,000 needed by the companies combined operations (Company C), revealing that the combination provides a diversification benefit of 19,078, a theoretically and intuitively correct result.

4. CONCLUSION

The choice of the measure used to assess the security of an insurance company, determine its aggregate capital requirement and drive attribution of capital to business segments has a significant impact on the outcome of the analyses performed. This memo suggests that the intuitively and widely accepted probability of default measure can produce seriously erroneous results. It also suggest that the serious difficulties created by the use of the probability of ruin can be avoided by the use of the expected ECOR ratio as a measure of security and as a risk constraint for the determination of capital requirements and for capital attribution across business segments.

REFERENCES

Artzner, P., Delbaen, F., Eber, J. M., & Heath, D. (1999). Coherent Risk Measures. *Mathematical Finances*, *9*, 203–228.

Embrechts, P., McNeil, A., & Strauman, D. (1999). *Correlations and Dependency in Risk Management*. 30th ASTIN Colloquium, Tokyo, Japan.

Wirch, J., & Hardy, M. (2000). *Ordering of Risk Measures for Capital Adequacy*, Proceedings of the AFIR Colloquium, Tromsö, Norway.

12. INTEGRATING REINSURANCE STRATEGY WITH ASSET STRATEGY TO ACHIEVE CAPITAL EFFICIENCIES

Joan Lamm-Tennant

G∂∂

D81

INTRODUCTION

In 1999, the property-casualty insurance industry faced significant challenges. The industry's average return on equity was 6.6%, down from 9.2% in 1998 and 11.9% in 1997. The return of 6.6% is only marginally higher than current United States Treasury rates. Clearly property-casualty insurers and their owners were not adequately compensated for taking risk.

There are many forces at play that can offer an explanation for the 1999 results. Pricing pressure continues to erode underwriting results, as evidenced by the 1999 industry combined ratio of 107.9, which declined from 105.6 in 1998 and 101.6 in 1997. Excess capital continues to drag down return on equities (ROEs), with the industry net written premium-to-surplus ratios being less than 1.0. In this environment, insurance decision makers must consider alternative strategies to improve their returns.

Although there are many strategies for improving returns, this article will explore one such strategy that involves integrating the reinsurance decision with the asset allocation choice. This strategy is based on standard financial principles utilized by many industries to achieve optimal capital choices. The strategy is used in conjunction with sound actuarial and operational practices to

Global Risk Management: Financial, Operational, and Insurance Strategies,
Volume 3, pages 163–169.
© 2002 Published by Elsevier Science Ltd.
ISBN: 0-7623-0982-2

improve an insurer's ROE in accordance with the company's risk tolerance. An important element of this strategy is recognition and illustration of how reinsurance costs can be offset through capital market opportunities.

2. SETTING THE STAGE: A SIMPLE EXAMPLE

An example demonstrates the opportunity afforded by integrating the reinsurance choice with the asset allocation decision.

We created a hypothetical property-casualty insurance company whose only decisions are:

• how much catastrophe reinsurance to purchase; and
• how to allocate the assets between equity and fixed income securities.

For simplification purposes we limited the firm's reinsurance choices to the following:

• none;
• 2 million retention; or
• 10 million retention.

The asset allocation choices included:

• low return/low risk securities – mostly fixed income; and
• high return/high risk securities – mostly equity.

The company begins with approximately U.S.$80 million in policyholder surplus and expects to write premiums of U.S.$80 million during the coming year. There are assets of approximately $150 million at the beginning of the year.

The underlying investment and underwriting assumptions include:

Net Retention	Mean Combined Ratio	Standard Deviation
Gross	100.5%	8.3%
High Retention	101.6%	5.5%
Low Retention	102.1%	4.6%
Ceded Cover	**Ceded Loss Ratio**	**Standard Deviation**
High Retention	37.9%	287.5%
Low Retention	53.0%	203.3%
Asset Class	**Mean Return**	**Standard Deviation**
Low return/low risk	6.0%	6.0%
High return/high risk	10.0%	15.0%

Low risk asset returns are 50% correlated with high risk asset returns.

3. IDENTIFYING THE OPTIMAL REINSURANCE STRATEGY AND THE OPTIMAL ASSET STRATEGY INTERDEPENDENTLY (NOT INDEPENDENTLY)

Given this information, the goal is to solve the posed questions and derive optimal returns for the company's owners. With this interdependent approach, investment managers allocate assets using specified guidelines and risk tolerances. A historical response to the challenge would be to resolve the asset allocation decision independently from the reinsurance strategy. One resorts to this approach because it offers ease and simplicity. Independently, risk managers might base their reinsurance purchases on corporate underwriting guidelines. While the historical approach produces optimal outcomes within the distinct worlds of asset management and corporate underwriting, the result is not necessarily optimal for the firm as a whole. Company owners, who view these operations as an entire universe, derive more value from an interdependent approach. By defining corporate risk guidelines in an integrated fashion, through simultaneously varying the investment and the reinsurance choices, one can more readily identify and exploit synergies between the two markets. These synergies result in higher expected ROEs at the same or lower levels of risk. This process begins by bringing together decision makers from underwriting, actuarial and finance departments. Through facilitation we achieve consensus on perception and measurement of risk and return. We then evaluate the risk and return tradeoff between various strategies by integrating the reinsurance choice with the asset allocation exercise. The most efficient combination of reinsurance and assets are identified as those providing the greatest expected return per unit of risk.

4. HOW DO WE PERCEIVE AND MEASURE RISK?

While the purpose here is not to evaluate the efficacy of different risk measures, the choice of measure can lead to different conclusions and should not be minimized. Risk is perceived, and therefore measured, differently within an organization. Because risk is subjective and its meaning varies from one individual to another, its measurement is very difficult. Some define risk as the uncertainty of either overestimating or underestimating return, typically measured by the standard deviation of the ROE. Others focus on a "downside" measure – the probability of under-performing. In this case, risk managers are concerned with limiting the chance of returns falling below a specific benchmark (e.g. "We want no more than a 2% chance of a 10% fall in surplus!"). From an enterprise perspective, this fear of loss/risk can be measured using either the probability of surplus decline or a measure called average excess value loss (AEL).

The AEL indicates the average amount of loss experienced once the firm exceeds its tolerance limit. For example, if the firm tolerates a 10% decline in surplus, the AEL is the average dollar amount of the loss in excess of the 10% surplus decline. We can express the AEL in dollar terms or in terms of additional surplus decline. The advantage of the AEL is that it blends not only the probability of a 10% surplus loss (frequency), but also the amount by which the loss exceeds the 10% decline (severity).

5. EVALUATION OF THE RISK/RETURN TRADEOFFS AFFORDED BY INTEGRATING REINSURANCE STRATEGY WITH ASSET STRATEGY

Continuing our example, we generated underwriting results and cash flows under each of the reinsurance options as previously defined. The output of the models are then evaluated with different asset allocation strategies to compare both the return and the risk inherent to each strategy.

In Fig. 1, we graphed the risk and return results for the situation in which reinsurance is not purchased and the asset allocation is varied (starting with

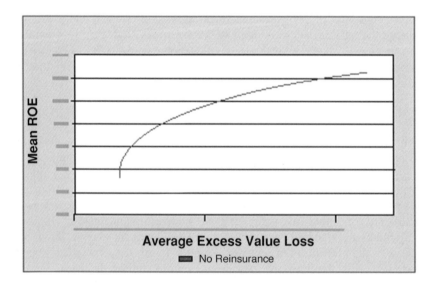

Fig. 1.   ROE vs. Excess Value Loss.

100% of assets invested in low risk securities, then shifting into equities in 5% increments). The lowest risk position indicates an asset portfolio solely comprised of low risk securities. As the insurer opts to take more risk on investments and shifts into higher risk/return securities, its aggregate ROE increases along with the enterprise risk. In this limited framework, the corporation will generally increase its appetite for equities as long as it:

- does not exceed corporate risk tolerance;
- is paid for taking risk (as the curve flattens horizontally, the corporation is adding risk to the profile without a corresponding increase in return); and
- does not raise regulatory or rating agency concerns.

Carrying this analysis further, we reran the exercise showing the results for a corporate retention of $10 million and $2 million.

The results of the model under these scenarios are displayed in Fig. 2.

In this graph, reinsurance purchases add new points above (higher return/ same risk) and to the left (lower risk/same return) of points on the "No Reinsurance" curve. This makes intuitive sense from the nature of the reinsurance transaction: in an efficiently priced market the ceding insurer trades volatility in exchange for a risk charge. If asset allocation is held constant, ROE

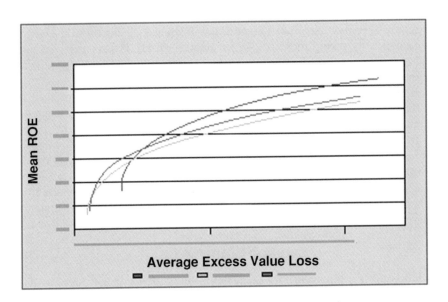

Fig. 2.   ROE vs. Excess Value Loss.

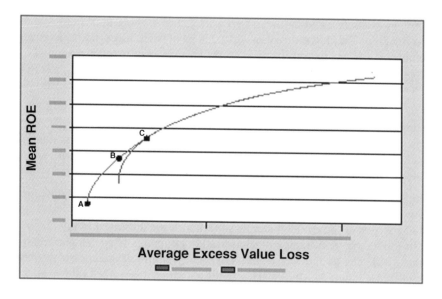

Fig. 3. Efficient Frontier.

and volatility will both decline. However, if the insurer recognizes that the purchase of reinsurance releases some "risk tolerance," it can offset the cost of reinsurance by taking more risk in its asset portfolio. For returns on equity below 8.5%, the introduction of reinsurance, coordinated with sound asset management, increases the insurer's ROE and reduces risk.

By merging the choices from the entire spectrum, we are able to produce an "efficient frontier" that identifies optimal asset allocation and reinsurance strategy for a given risk tolerance. This frontier is displayed in Fig. 3.

In this graph, points A through B were made available to the company through purchases of reinsurance. These points provide similar or lesser returns for the company at lower risk tolerances that were unachievable under the "No Reinsurance" strategy. Points B through C illustrate identifiable opportunities where integrated reinsurance purchasing and asset management strategies increase the insurer's ROE, without increasing the enterprise risk.

6. SUMMARY

We presented a framework for analyzing a trade of risk across an individual balance sheet. By examining investment strategy and reinsurance strategy in an integrated fashion, three things become clear:

(1) The existence and use of reinsurance creates additional optimal capital opportunities that otherwise would not exist.
(2) For some levels of enterprise risk, the risk released through purchasing reinsurance may be reinvested in the capital markets for an improved enterprise return.
(3) The only way to identify these synergies is to examine reinsurance and asset decisions in an integrated framework.

An ancillary benefit of this approach is increased collaboration among the different departments within the insurance organization. This will produce an increased sense of teamwork and improved communication within the organization.

REFERENCE

Insurance Information Institute (1999). Year End Financial Results < http://www.iii.org >

(handwritten: collected countain?)

13. THE "FLIGHT TO QUALITY," GLOBAL CAPACITY AND U.S. REINSURANCE PRICES

Joon-Hai Chung and Mary A. Weiss

ABSTRACT

The puzzle of underwriting cycles and insurance crises in property-liability insurance has led to numerous economic hypotheses and analyses, yet no single theory seems capable of explaining all of its aspects. Reinsurance is hypothesized to be a potential factor in observed cycles in the primary market; despite this, few underwriting cycle studies focusing on reinsurance exist. The purpose of this research is to apply two principal underwriting cycle theories: the capacity constraint and risky debt hypotheses, to non-proportional property and casualty reinsurance in the U.S. Non-proportional reinsurance is highlighted, since it is designed to cover the tail of the loss distribution and is considered to be relatively riskier than proportional reinsurance as a result. Two professional U.S. reinsurer samples are studied, one for property and one for casualty; U.S. reinsurers in each sample were chosen on the basis of their non-proportional property (casualty) writings. The sample period is 1991 to 1995. The results support both the capacity constraint hypothesis and the risky debt hypothesis, and this is the first research to do so. A major innovation in this study is the use of capacity variables that are broken down by major region of the world.

Global Risk Management: Financial, Operational, and Insurance Strategies,
Volume 3, pages 171–205.
Copyright © 2002 by Elsevier Science Ltd.
All rights of reproduction in any form reserved.
ISBN: 0-7623-0982-2

1. INTRODUCTION

Historically, underwriting profit in the U.S. property/liability insurance industry appears to follow a six year (on average) cycle in which soft markets with falling premiums and profits are followed by hard markets with rising premiums and profits. In some, but not all instances, the bottoming out of a soft market triggers a crisis, which is characterized by affordability, availability, and adequacy of insurance coverage problems. The two most recent "crises" in liability insurance occurred in the medical malpractice line in the mid-1970s and in the general liability line in the mid-1980s. The suddenness of the turn in the market and the dramatic increase in premiums associated with these crises have attracted significant economic study (Cummins, Harrington & Klein, 1991).

Two major theories have been advanced to explain the occurrence of underwriting cycles and sporadic crises, the capacity constraint hypothesis and the risky debt hypothesis (Winter, 1994; Gron, 1994; Cummins & Danzon, 1997). The Winter-Gron model is one of a time series while the Cummins and Danzon one is cross-sectional. Both theories suggest that profitability and pricing may be related to the supply of insurer capital. Under the capacity constraint hypothesis, prices and profitability are hypothesized to be inversely related to the supply of capital such that insurance prices are bid up when capital is scarce and fall when capital is plentiful (Winter, 1994; Gron, 1994). On the other hand, the risky debt hypothesis predicts the opposite; higher surplus is associated with higher financial quality for which policyholders pay higher premiums (Cummins & Danzon, 1997). The potential role of reinsurance as a substitute for primary insurers' capital is regarded as possibly important in these theories, although no existing empirical studies incorporate this variable.

More recent market developments highlight the role of reinsurance in industry operations. Hurricanes Andrew and Iniki and the Northridge earthquake increased demand for catastrophe cover (e.g. per occurrence excess of loss reinsurance), leading to a capacity shortage in property catastrophe reinsurance. Similarly, the crisis at Lloyd's of London in the early 1990s created a temporary capacity shortage and resulted in the formation of new reinsurers in Bermuda. A so called "flight to quality" under which (re)insurer size is equated with financial strength and quality is said to be occurring. Thus, the reinsurance industry is well suited to test underwriting cycle theories relating to capacity (level of capital) and financial quality.

The effect of recent market developments is particularly important for non-proportional reinsurance because this coverage is designed to cover the tail of the loss distribution and is triggered only when losses are unexpectedly high. Non-proportional reinsurance premiums assumed by U.S. reinsurers exceeded $12.5 billion dollars in 1995; but this figure understates the importance of non-proportional reinsurance to U.S. insurers. In 1995, 41.6% of U.S. reinsurance premiums were ceded to alien reinsurers all over the world (Reinsurance Association of America, 1997). Further, ceded premiums from North America were $40 billion or 39% of total world ceded premiums in 1997 (Swiss Re, 1998). Thus, the international marketplace potentially significantly impacts pricing and profitability in the U.S.

Study of reinsurance, especially non-proportional reinsurance, is important for several additional reasons. Increased globalization of business makes U.S. businesses more sensitive to catastrophes in other parts of the world, tending to increase the need for property catastrophe protection. Study of reinsurance can provide more insight into how alternative risk financing arrangements from capital markets may complement or substitute for reinsurance.

The purpose of this research is to test two mainstream theories of underwriting cycles, the capacity constraint hypothesis (Winter, 1994; Gron, 1994) and the risky debt hypothesis (Cummins & Danzon, 1997). In this process, factors affecting price in U.S. non-proportional property and casualty reinsurance will be identified. The models control for capacity in the reinsurance markets outside of the U.S. (i.e. the London market, Bermuda, and other reinsurance markets). The sample period is 1991 to 1995. This period encompasses the occurrence of three major catastrophes (i.e. Hurricanes Andrew and Iniki and the Northridge earthquake) which affected property catastrophe coverage in the U.S. This period also includes the crisis period at Lloyd's of London and subsequent introduction of corporate capital there and the formation of new reinsurers in Bermuda. The sample consists of a panel of U.S. reinsurers writing non-proportional property or casualty reinsurance over the sample period. Two models are estimated, one for property and another for casualty non-proportional reinsurance.

The remainder of this paper is organized as follows. In the next section, an overview of the U.S. and alien reinsurance markets is provided. Then underwriting cycle theories and empirical tests are discussed. Emphasis is on the capacity constraint hypothesis and the risky debt hypothesis. The next section contains the model, sample selection procedures and variable specifications. Following this, data sources are described. Finally, the results are reviewed, and the last section concludes.

2. REINSURANCE MARKET DEVELOPMENTS

2.1. U.S. Reinsurance Market

The U.S. reinsurance market has grown rapidly in the last two decades. *Non-proportional* reinsurance premiums, as a percentage of total net premiums written for the U.S. insurance industry, jumped from 1.77% in 1975 to 4.82% in 1995, reflecting an average 4.9% annual increase.[1] In contrast, the general liability line and the medical malpractice line accounted for 6.22 and 1.81% of total premiums in 1995; growth in line shares from 1975 to 1995 for general liability and medical malpractice was 0.7% and 0.1%, respectively (*Best's Aggregates and Averages*, 1996).

The majority of U.S. non-proportional reinsurance premiums not ceded internationally are underwritten by U.S. professional reinsurers. For example, in 1995, 83 professional reinsurers wrote 81.5% of these non-proportional net premiums written, while 436 primary insurers wrote the rest (*Best's Aggregates and Averages*, 1996). For this reason, the discussion below focuses on professional reinsurers.

Underwriting results in the U.S. non-proportional reinsurance market are presented in Table 1. This table shows the trends in accident year loss ratios.[2] The loss ratios for property non-proportional reinsurance are very volatile in contrast to those for casualty non-proportional reinsurance. Overall, the results for U.S. property and liability business excluding non-proportional reinsurance are more stable. The property non-proportional loss ratios for 1989, 1992, and

Table 1. Accident Year Loss Ratio Trends.

Accident Year	Property Non-proportional Reinsurance	Casualty Non-proportional Reinsurance
1988	59.8	62.7
1989	114.1	77.1
1990	87.3	78.3
1991	77.4	78.8
1992	132.7	84.4
1993	59.1	74.2
1994	133.6	75.8
1995	54.7	77.3

Note: Loss ratios are accident year losses divided by premiums earned multiplied by 100.
Source: A. M. Best Co, *Best's Aggregates and Averages*, 1996.

Table 2.   The Ten Most Costly Insured Catastrophes.

Month/Year	Catastrophe	Estimated Insured Loss
August 1992	Hurricane Andrew	$16.5
January 1994	Northridge Earthquake	$12.5
September 1989	Hurricane Hugo	$4.2
October 1995	Hurricane Opal	$2.1
March 1993	Blizzard of 1993	$1.7
October 1991	Oakland Fire	$1.7
September 1992	Hurricane Iniki	$1.6
May 1995	Texas Hailstorm	$1.1
October 1989	Loma Prieta Earthquake	$1.0
Oct/Nov. 1993	California Brush Fires	$1.0

Note: Dollars in billions.
Source: Insurance Information Institute, *Property/Casualty Insurance Facts*, 1996.

Table 3.   Total Insured Catastrophic Losses by Year.

Year	Losses
1985	$2,816
1986	$872
1987	$905
1988	$1,409
1989	$7,642
1990	$2,825
1991	$4,723
1992	$22,970
1993	$5,705
1994	$17,010
1995	$8,310
1996	$7,375
1997	$2,600

Note: Dollars in billions.
Source: Insurance Information Institute, *Property/Casualty Insurance Facts*, 1999.

1994 reflect catastrophic losses from Hurricane Hugo, Hurricane Andrew and the Northridge earthquake, respectively. Tables 2 and 3 show the ten most costly insured catastrophes and total insured catastrophic losses by year. Most of the catastrophic losses occurred over the period 1990 to 1995.

The degree of market concentration can be assessed with a Herfindahl index calculated using property non-proportional reinsurance premiums assumed. This index increased from 0.039 to 0.053 from 1992 to 1993. By 1995 the Herfindahl index had increased further to 0.07 (probably due to the Northridge earthquake).[3]

Meanwhile, casualty non-proportional reinsurers were suffering from the same ills as general liability insurers, especially with respect to asbestos and environmental liability. Since the 1980s, many reinsurers were found to be under-reserved for these claims. The insolvency of some reinsurers during the 1980s added to the problems of primary insurers providing general liability insurance, because some of the primary insurers were left with uncollectible reinsurance recoverables. Pressured by capital markets and rating agencies, some reinsurers and insurers have increased reserves in recent years. For example, American Re, one of the largest reinsurers in the U.S., increased reserves for asbestos and environmental liability by $231 million, reducing its surplus from $1,341 million to $1,110 million (or 20%) (American Re Annual Report, 1995). Retroactive loss shocks may continue to plague these insurers for years to come.

Capacity shortages for property catastrophe reinsurance and uncollectible reinsurance recoverables purportedly led to a "flight to quality" by the mid 1980s. In the late 1970s and early 1980s, insurers frequently ceded small amounts of business to many reinsurers to reduce credit risk (Kellogg & Watson, 1996). This practice changed in the 1980s, and primary companies began buying reinsurance from fewer, better capitalized reinsurers with long-term commitments to the insurance industry.[4] The adoption of Risk-Based Capital Standards during the period probably contributed to the trend.[5]

During the period 1990 to 1995, non-proportional reinsurance premiums increased by 64.3% while total U.S. insurance industry premiums rose by 19.2% (*Best's Aggregates and Averages*, 1996). Between 1985 and 1995, the number of U.S. reinsurers with policyholders' surplus in excess of $500 million increased from two to ten, while the number of reinsurers writing non-proportional reinsurance decreased from 93 to 83 (*Best's Aggregates & Averages*, 1986 and 1996). Bankruptcies associated with the U.S. liability crisis and a streak of natural catastrophes in the early 1990s account for some of the decline. (For example, some reinsurer insolvencies were related directly to Hurricane Andrew (Swiss Re, 1998)). Consolidation through acquisitions also has occurred, as it appears that policyholders are gravitating to large professional reinsurers. The consolidation among professional reinsurers world-wide still continues.[6]

2.2. Alien Reinsurance Market

From its beginning, reinsurance has been an international business. While U.S. reinsurers may assume reinsurance premiums from abroad, in fact, overall, alien reinsurers assume a substantial portion of U.S. reinsurance premiums.[7] Over the period 1991 to 1995, approximately 42% of all U.S. reinsurance premiums ceded were placed with alien reinsurers (Reinsurance Association of America, 1997). The latter estimate pertains to proportional and non-proportional reinsurance combined. In the case of non-proportional reinsurance, the figure is probably larger than 42% due to the relatively larger capacity demands for this business. In the remainder of this section, the capacity and financial performance of large alien reinsurers are reviewed, including Lloyd's of London and Bermuda-based property catastrophe reinsurers.

2.2.1. The London Market

The unique feature of the London market is the presence of Lloyd's of London. It is an organization of underwriters (mostly individuals) who can trace their history back to the merchant underwriters of the 17th century. It is supervised by the Corporation of Lloyd's under the Lloyd's Acts. Until 1994, all business was accepted for the accounts of individual members who provided capital. Saddled with financial troubles, which primarily stemmed from past U.S. insurance and reinsurance business, Lloyd's has opened its door to corporate members. While individual members have unlimited liability for risks written for their account, corporate members' liability is limited to the funds they have deposited at Lloyd's. Corporate capital has grown significantly. In 1997, capacity provided by corporate members was £4,500 million which accounted for 43.6% of Lloyd's total capacity of £10,323 million as shown in Table 4.[8] At Lloyd's, non-marine syndicates are a main vehicle to write U.S. property-liability insurance and reinsurance business. Table 4 also shows how non-marine syndicates' capacity changed over time.

Table 5 shows how Lloyd's U.S. situs direct and reinsurance premiums changed over the period from 1987 to 1996. Lloyd's U.S. situs direct and reinsurance premiums are defined as business in which the broker, assured, or risk is in the U.S. Lloyd's U.S. situs reinsurance premiums continued to decrease after 1992, which reflected a decrease in Lloyd's capacity. Insurance and reinsurance companies operating in the London market constitute the London company market. The core of the London company market is the companies that are members of the Institute of London Underwriters (ILU) and/or the London International Insurance and Reinsurance Market Association

Table 4. Lloyd's Capacity.

Year of Account	Capacity from Individual Members	Capacity from Corporate Members	Non-Marine Total Capacity	Syndicates Capacity
1988	10,740		10,740	4,206
1989	10,622		10,622	4,267
1990	10,742		10,742	4,577
1991	11,063		11,063	4,952
1992	9,833		9,833	4,235
1993	8,784		8,784	3,502
1994	9,303	1,595	10,898	4,499
1995	7,835	2,360	10,195	4,351
1996	6,950	3,044	9,994	4,301
1997	5,823	4,500	10,323	4,973

Note: Figures in millions of British pounds. Capacity is defined as the maximum premium writing allowed.
Source: Commercial Policy Unit of Lloyd's, *Statistics Relating to Lloyd's 1997*.

Table 5. Lloyd's U.S. Situs Direct and Reinsurance Premiums.

Year	U.S. Situs Direct Premiums	U.S. Situs Reinsurance Premiums	Total U.S. Situs Premiums
1987	$2,011	$1,719	$3,730
1988	$1,841	$1,643	$3,483
1989	$1,759	$1,699	$3,458
1990	$2,128	$2,021	$4,149
1991	$2,603	$2,255	$4,858
1992	$2,709	$2,377	$5,086
1993	$2,910	$2,051	$4,961
1994	$2,542	$1,911	$4,453
1995	$2,496	$1,876	$4,372
1996	$2,295	$1,667	$3,962

Note: Dollars in million.
Source: Commercial Policy Unit of Lloyd's, *Statistics Relating to Lloyd's 1997*.

(LIRMA).[9] ILU members write marine, aviation, and transport insurance and reinsurance business, including energy and marine liability. LIRMA members write primarily non-marine insurance and reinsurance business. Most of the

LIRMA members are U.K. subsidiaries or branches of major international insurers and reinsurers worldwide. On the basis of gross premiums written in 1994, LIRMA members wrote 63.2% of the non-marine treaty reinsurance business placed in the London market with the remainder written by Lloyd's (LIRMA, 1997).

2.2.2. The Bermuda Market

A string of catastrophes worldwide, including Hurricane Andrew in 1992 forced many reinsurers to exit or retract from the property catastrophe reinsurance market; at the same time Lloyd's experienced poor underwriting results (*Statistics Relating to Lloyd's*, 1997). In late 1992 and in 1993, eight strongly capitalized property catastrophe reinsurers with a combined capital of about $4 billion were established in Bermuda to fill the void.[10] Bermuda has become one of the prominent reinsurance markets in the world with a significant share in property catastrophe reinsurance. In 1997, these property catastrophe reinsurers accounted for $1.1 billion in premiums and $4.8 billion in capitalization (Swiss Re, 1998).

As newly established reinsurers specializing in property catastrophe reinsurance business, Bermuda reinsurers are not encumbered by long tail liabilities such as asbestos and environmental liabilities. In this respect, they may have a competitive advantage over other reinsurers including Lloyd's of London. According to Ketchum and Wynn (1997), Bermuda-based property catastrophe reinsurers are estimated to account for 25 to 30% of the worldwide property catastrophe reinsurance business.

2.2.3. The European Reinsurance Market

In Europe, there has been little trade restriction in reinsurance. The 1964 EC Reinsurance Directive provided for both freedom of establishment and freedom of services for all reinsurers within the European Union (EU).[11] It gave reinsurers established within an EU member state the right to supply reinsurance (or retrocession) to insurers established in any other member state. For direct non-life insurance, freedom of establishment was achieved in 1973 but freedom of services was not achieved until 1994.

The largest three reinsurance markets in Europe (in order of size) are Germany, Switzerland, and France. The reinsurance markets in these countries are dominated by professional reinsurers. Swiss reinsurers benefit from a liberal regulatory climate with practically no exchange restrictions on the transfer of funds.

There are also professional reinsurers in other countries including Ireland and Italy. These reinsurers may also assume reinsurance premiums from U.S. insurers.

2.2.4. Other International Reinsurance Markets

Many professional reinsurers exist in Asia, Australasia, the Middle East, Africa, North America and Latin America.[12]

SUMMARY

Table 6 contains a breakdown of the 100 largest reinsurers in the world in 1995, ranked by net reinsurance premiums written. Note that Lloyd's of London is not included in the survey. Lloyd's, based on its combined facultative and treaty reinsurance net premium income, would rank third among the world's largest reinsurance groups (Carter & Falush, 1996).

Table 6.   1995 Breakdown of World's 100 Largest Reinsurers by Country.

Country	Number of Reinsures	Net Premiums Written	Percent
U.K. (London Company Market)	7	$3,078	4.1%
Bermuda (Property Cat Reinsurers)	5	$1,332	1.8%
Bermuda (Other Reinsurers)	2	$1,217	1.6%
Germany	15	$24,829	32.9%
Switzerland	8	$8,453	11.2%
France	9	$5,352	7.1%
Other European Countries	8	$5,152	6.8%
Japan	14	$6,608	8.8%
U.S.	25	$16,653	22.1%
All Other	7	$2,787	3.7%
Total	100	$75,461	100.0%

Notes: Dollars in millions.
Reinsurers ranked by net reinsurance premiums written.
Source: Reactions Publishing Group, Ltd, "Standard & Poor's Top 100 Reinsurers," *reaction*, (London, U.K.), March 1997.

3. UNDERWRITING CYCLE THEORIES AND EVIDENCE

This research focuses on the two principal economic theories of underwriting cycles: (1) the capacity constraint hypothesis (Winter, 1994; Gron 1989, 1994); and (2) the risky debt hypothesis (Cummins & Danzon, 1997). Under the capacity constraint hypothesis, insurance prices are related to capacity (or equity) of the insurer with low capacity associated with high prices. Alternatively, the risky debt hypothesis posits that policyholders are sensitive to the financial quality of an insurer so that "safer" (better capitalized) insurers command higher prices (premiums). These two theories are summarized briefly below.

3.1. Capacity Constraint Hypothesis

The capacity constraint hypothesis rests upon two key assumptions: (1) Uncertainty exists about average claims; and average claims are correlated across policies. For example, changes in the interpretation of tort law by the courts affect liability claims across lines and insurers. In this theory, insurers are assumed to be free of default risk. Because insurers have limited liability, insurers' equity determines capacity; and (2) Capital market imperfections exist so that the cost of external equity exceeds that of internal equity (e.g. retained earnings). The cost disparity might be induced, for example, by tax restrictions (the trapped equity effect) or some other impediment (e.g. asymmetric information about the firm among insurer managers and external equity holders (Winter, 1994). Thus, in soft markets insurers hold on to seemingly excess capital in anticipation of tight markets in which equity will be relatively scarce.[13] The remainder of this section discusses the Winter model in more detail.

Winter develops a one period model in which demand for insurance is downward sloping, an identical probability of loss exists among policyholders, and policyholders are risk averse. The supply of insurance is assumed to be provided by an aggregate price-taking firm. The following equation specifies the equity path

$$X_{t+1} = [S_t + (P_t - p_t)Q_t](1 + r - c), \tag{1}$$

where

$$S_t = X_t + e_t - d_t,$$

X_{t+1} is surplus or net worth, p_t is the actual probability of loss realized, P_t is the loss probability reflected in the premium, e_t is contributions to equity, d_t is dividends paid to stockholders and the subscript t is year. More specifically, $P_t * Q_t$ is the premium, where Q_t is the amount of coverage. The interest rate r is the riskless rate (net of personal taxes), and c is the cost of maintaining equity.

The company is assumed to maximize the present value of net cash flows to shareholders. Specifically, the following is maximized

$$\underset{Q}{\text{MAX}} \quad E[q_{t+1}(1 - r - c)(S_t + (P_t - p_t)Q_t)]/1 + r, \tag{2}$$

subject to the no insolvency constraint. The factor q_{t+1} is Tobin's q.[14] With competition, economic profit is zero at

$$P'_t = \tilde{p} + [\text{Cov}(\tilde{q}_{t+1}, p_t)/E(\tilde{q}_{t+1})] \tag{3}$$

So the premium charged is

$$\text{Max } [P'_t, P_H - (S_t/Q)], \tag{4}$$

where P_H is the maximum possible value for p_t. When the capacity constraint is not binding, the price is indicated by the flat horizontal line in Fig. 1; otherwise price is determined by the positive concave section of the curve in the graph. Winter further develops the model to explain the nonlinear pricing evident in the figure and why some lines are affected more than others.

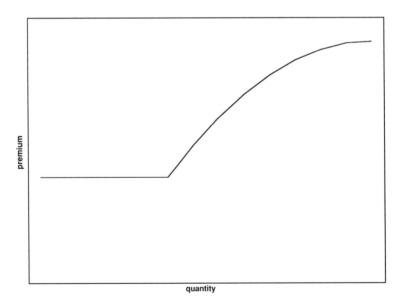

Fig. 1. Supply Curve.

To test the theory, Winter regresses the estimated economic loss ratio on the "cyclical component of the real surplus" (p. 401). The economic loss ratio is defined as the present value of losses divided by the premium. The cyclical component of real surplus is defined as current surplus divided by its average value. Specifically, the following regression equation is estimated:

$$\text{(Economic Loss Ratio)}_t = \text{(Surplus}_t/\text{Average Surplus)}^\alpha \exp(\varepsilon_{it}), \qquad (5)$$

where average surplus is a five year average over the period $t - 6$ to $t - 1$, and ε_{it} is a random error term. Annual industry-wide data for the period 1948 to 1988 are used.[15] The results support the capacity constraint hypothesis for part of the sample period only, the period from 1948 to 1980. Thus the results do not explain the liability insurance crisis of 1984–1985.

Gron (1994) also developed a model for testing the capacity constraint hypothesis, which focused on the underwriting margin defined as the difference between premiums and (undiscounted) losses and expenses.[16] Under the capacity constraint hypothesis, the underwriting margin should be higher (lower) when relative capacity is lower (higher). Gron (1994) estimates a regression model that includes relative capacity and other control variables for interest rate and inflation as independent variables. Relative capacity is measured as the residual from a regression of relative net worth, defined as aggregate stock insurers' policyholders surplus divided by GNP, on a time trend and constant. Four lines of business are analyzed (i.e. auto physical damage, homeowners multiple peril, auto liability, and general liability) over the period 1952 to 1986. The capacity constraint theory was supported for all of the lines tested except for general liability. Notably, this research also failed to explain the liability crisis.

In conclusion, the evidence in support of the capacity constraint hypothesis is mixed, especially with respect to the 1984–85 liability crisis. One possible explanation for this is that important factors were omitted in the analyses (e.g. due to data availability). The usual suspects include omission of a reinsurance supply variable, the captive formation movement, and unexpected losses over the period (so that ex ante and ex post measured losses diverged). Another explanation is that the underlying assumptions of no insolvency risk and capital market imperfections are not met.

In view of this, Cagle and Harrington (1995) developed a pricing model that incorporates endogenous insolvency risk. According to this theory, insolvency risk is endogenously determined by the firm's choice of output and capital. If market demand is inelastic with respect to price and capital, the model predicts that price will increase following a negative shock to capital, but by less than the amount needed to offset the shock. If market demand is elastic with respect to price and capital, the model suggests that the effect of the shock on price will be smaller. This theory is not tested empirically.

3.2. Risky Debt Hypothesis

As an alternative to the capacity constraint hypothesis, Cummins and Danzon (1997) use an option pricing model to explain insurer pricing behavior and the liability crisis. It is assumed in their risky debt model that buyer demand for insurance is inversely related to price and directly related to safety levels. The result is that insurers have an optimal capital structure.

The option model can be expressed most simply as

$$C(A, L, r, \sigma^2, \tau) = A - [L\, e^{r\tau} - B(A, L, \tau)], \tag{6}$$

where

C = Call option for firm's equity,
r = riskless rate of interest,
L = market value of liabilities,
A = market value of assets,
τ = time until liabilities expire,
σ^2 = firm risk parameter, and
B = insolvency put option.

The value of risky debt is $Le^{r\tau}$ (i.e. the present value of losses discounted at the riskless rate) minus the insolvency put $B(A, L, \tau)$.

It is assumed initially that policies issued at time 0 mature two periods later, and that the firm has an opportunity to issue policies with price P_2 and liabilities of L_2 at time period 1. The insurer also has the opportunity to issue new equity or pay a dividend. The call option model of the firm's equity at time 1 then becomes

$$C(A_1 + A_2, L_1 + L_2, \tau) = A_1 + A_2 - (L_1 + L_2)e^{r\tau} + (L_1 + L_2)\, b(x), \tag{7}$$

where $b(x)$ is the insolvency put per \$1 of liabilities and x is assets divided by liabilities. An equal priority rule regarding payment of L_1 and L_2 in the case of bankruptcy is assumed to apply.[17] Capital markets are assumed to be efficient so that the insurer will not dilute old equity or impose a capital loss on new equity.

If the price charged P_2 is the efficient, competitive price then Cummins and Danzon (1997) show that the insolvency put must remain unchanged or increase. (It cannot decrease because it would penalize equity.) Thus, the old policyholders lose economic value if the put value increases. If the price charged is not the efficient price but a markup price $[(1+m) P_2]$ then realization of retained earnings could permit the company to improve its safety level.

Next a retroactive loss shock is introduced into the model. While the capacity constraint hypothesis predicts a price increase following a retroactive loss shock, the risky debt model does not unambiguously indicate what will happen to price. Price may decrease as insolvency risk increases since the value of private information the insurer and the buyer have on each other declines.[18] If a positive markup price over cost is charged by the insurer however, the positive markup might be used to restore safety levels from their post shock level.

New external capital inflows would be expected after a loss shock only after a price increase occurs to avoid a transfer of value from the new equity holders to old and new policyholders and only if quality increases. Thus, the latter suggests that price may respond differently to different sources of equity shocks (e.g. retroactive loss shock vs. other shocks).

Cummins and Danzon (1997) test the risky debt model using A. M. Best data on 45 firms which wrote general liability insurance between 1980 and 1988. As a measure of price, the ratio of company-wide premiums written (net of underwriting expenses and dividends) to the present value of company-wide accident year losses incurred is used. The empirical analysis confirms a strong positive cross-sectional relationship between price and financial quality, supporting the hypothesis. Also, consistent with the hypothesis, the results suggest that new internal and external capital flows are positively related to price and that a retroactive loss shock is negatively related to price.

The Anomaly
The capacity constraint and risky debt theories are interesting in many respects. Perhaps the most notable is that the posited relationship between capacity and prices are the opposite of each other. Yet evidence in support of each exist. How can this be?

The capacity constraint related variables used in previous studies focus on (aggregate) time series data for surplus. However, the testing of the risky debt hypothesis is based on cross-sectional (company specific) data. Thus the results of tests of both of these hypotheses are consistent with the notion that overall supply does affect pricing, but these effects vary by firm such that relatively better capitalized insurers (i.e. having higher relative surplus) benefit from their position by garnering higher prices. The latter firms also seem better able to raise new capital.

But why does the capacity constraint hypothesis fail during particular time periods? The period and line of business studied in Cummins and Danzon

(1997) coincide with a confluence of (unanticipated) factors working against insurers, especially those writing general liability insurance. The main culprits usually recognized for disruptions in the general liability line are exogenous shifts in loss distributions and development of adverse tort liability case law. Is worldwide reinsurance capital supply also important, as suggested by Winters (1994)?

The reinsurance market is particularly well suited to test both the capacity constraint and risky debt hypotheses as explained earlier. Study of reinsurance may shed some light also on the role of reinsurance on insurer pricing in general by providing evidence as to whether the reinsurance marketplace is governed by the same pricing principles as the primary market.

4. MODEL SPECIFICATION

The model used is designed to test the capacity constraint and risky debt hypotheses in the reinsurance market. The model can be expressed in its simplest form as follows:

$$p = f(q, c, z),$$

where p is price of property (casualty) non-proportional reinsurance, q is a vector of financial quality related variables, c is a vector of capacity constraint related variables and z is a vector of other independent variables. Given that reinsurance transactions are international in nature, the capacity constraint related variables take into account the capacity of each of the major international reinsurance markets as well as the capacity of the U.S. reinsurance industry. This section describes the model variables and sample selection procedures in more detail.

4.1. Sample Selection

The empirical analysis focuses on the U.S. reinsurance market over the period 1991 to 1995. The sample consists of large, U.S. professional reinsurers writing non-proportional property and liability reinsurance. Note that this sample period encompasses turmoil and rejuvenation at Lloyd's of London, several insured catastrophes, the birth of the Bermuda CAT reinsurance market, and a "flight to quality" in reinsurance. Thus this time period should be adequate to test the capacity constraint and risky debt hypotheses.

Separate samples of U.S. non-proportional property and non-proportional casualty reinsurers are constructed so as to test the risky debt and capacity constraint hypotheses separately for the two lines. In order to identify important players in non-proportional reinsurance in the U.S., the following criteria are used to select the reinsurers in each sample: (1) The reinsurer must be operating in the U.S and file an annual statement with the NAIC.[19] (2) The market share of the property (casualty) reinsurer must exceed 0.1% of the total property (casualty) non-proportional reinsurance premiums in the U.S. The latter ensures that the sample reinsurers write a significant market share in property (casualty) non-proportional reinsurance. (3) At least 5% of total premiums written by the reinsurer must be property (casualty) non-proportional reinsurance. (4) The proportion of property (casualty) non-proportional reinsurance premiums assumed from non-affiliates must exceed 70%. This criterion is used to exclude reinsurers that rely excessively on intra-group transactions. (5) For continuity purposes, only reinsurers with data available for the entire five year period are included. Initially, 30 companies were identified for the property sample and 25 for casualty. The lists of reinsurers in each sample are in Appendix 1.

4.2. Dependent Variable

The dependent variable in each regression is price in property (casualty) non-proportional reinsurance in the U.S. reinsurance market. Price is defined as premiums earned divided by the present value of accident year losses incurred. To calculate price, Schedule P industry-wide payout tails for property and for casualty non-proportional reinsurance are used to determine payout proportions in each line.[20] U.S. Treasury yields were then applied to discount losses (see, e.g. Winter, 1994; Cummins & Danzon, 1997).

4.3 Independent Variables

Financial quality variables
Relative policyholders surplus is used to gauge the insurer's financial quality. Following Cummins and Danzon (1997) policyholders surplus (PHS) at time $t - 1$ is decomposed as follows:

$$PHS_{t-1} = PHS_{t-2} + (\text{New Internal Capital})_{t-1} + (\text{New External Capital})_{t-1}$$
$$- (\text{Retroactive Loss Shock})_{t-1} \qquad (8)$$

New internal capital in year $t - 1$ is the sum of underwriting income (net of the retroactive loss shock), investment income, other income and other gains in surplus in year $t - 1$. New external capital in year $t - 1$ is capital paid in minus dividends in year $t - 1$.

The retroactive loss shock used in this study is the change in loss reserves resulting from past reserving errors. More specifically, the change in accident year losses (reserving errors) from time $t - 2$ to $t - 1$ is used to measure the retroactive loss shock. Both company-wide and line specific retroactive loss shock variables are tested. That is, reserving errors between time $t - 1$ to $t - 2$ are calculated for: (1) non-proportional property reinsurance only (from Schedule P, Part 2N, Reinsurance A); (2) non-proportional liability reinsurance only (from Schedule P, Part 2O, Reinsurance B); and (3) company-wide losses (Schedule P, Part 2, Summary).

The company-wide retroactive loss shock can be justified on the grounds that it affects the overall risk of the reinsurer by reducing surplus (in the case of an adverse deviation).[21] However, if a retroactive loss shock in a line of business causes the reinsurer to re-evaluate risk in that line and adjust price accordingly, the line specific retroactive loss shock may be more important. The latter effect would be consistent with news stories after Hurricane Andrew that reported that insurers raised prices and/or curtailed coverage in homeowners multiple peril in Florida.

The right hand side variables in Eq. (8) are included as independent variables in the model after normalization. Each component is normalized by dividing it by total liabilities at the end of $t - 2$ except for PHS_{t-2} which is normalized to total liabilities at the end of year $t - 3$. (Cummins and Danzon (1997) normalized their variables in the same way.) The expected sign of the normalized variables are hypothesized to be positive according to the risky debt theory, except for the retroactive loss shock. As explained earlier, the sign of the retroactive loss shock variable is uncertain, although Cummins and Danzon (1997) found it to be negative in their sample of general liability insurers.

In non-proportional reinsurance, especially property catastrophe reinsurance, the size of policyholders surplus may be an important criterion for a cedent in selecting reinsurers. Insurers with larger surplus are capable of paying higher losses, signaling financial strength to cedents. Better diversification of risk may accrue to larger reinsurers, affecting price for their business. This variable captures any purported "flight to quality" in reinsurance and a positive relationship between price and size is expected. To control for size, sample reinsurers are ranked by size of policyholders surplus into quartiles, and the reinsurer's size category is used as an independent variable. Alternatively, policyholders' surplus and the log of policyholders' surplus are tested also.

The A. M. Best's rating for each reinsurer is used as another indicator of financial quality. Two specifications are tested. One specification is that used in Cummins and Danzon (1997): reinsurers with an A or better Best's rating are assigned a value of one, while all other reinsurers are assigned a value of zero. The alternative specification assigns a value of one if the reinsurer has an A +

or better rating, and zero otherwise. The alternative specification is more relevant if most of the reinsurers in the study have a high Best's rating already, or if Best's ratings fail to discriminate accurately among A or better rated reinsurers.

Capacity Constraint Variables
Winter (1994) and Cummins and Danzon (1997) use the ratio of surplus to its prior five year historical average to test the capacity constraint hypothesis. The capacity constraint variables used in this study are defined in the same way. However, in the present paper a "worldwide" relative capacity variable is constructed using data from reinsurers on Standard & Poor's (S&P's) top 100 world reinsurers list and the property CAT reinsurers in Bermuda (discussed earlier).[22] More specifically, surplus of the world's top 100 reinsurers and Bermuda CAT reinsurers in each year is divided by its 5 year prior average value to measure worldwide relative capacity.[23] Regional relative capacity variables are constructed as well. That is, separate relative capacity variables are estimated for the U.S., for Bermuda property CAT reinsurers, and the remaining reinsurers in S&P's top 100 reinsurer list, using surplus data for the reinsurers in each region.[24]

The effect on price of regional relative capacity levels may differ if reported capacity is not consistent with perceived capacity (e.g. due to underreserving of liability losses) and if regulation imposes different costs on U.S. reinsurers compared to alien reinsurers. For example, when assuming U.S. business, a 1% excise tax on premiums is imposed on the alien reinsurer, and the alien reinsurer should post a letter of credit for the sum of unearned premiums and outstanding losses, including incurred but not reported (IBNR) losses. The latter costs must be gauged relative to the tax and regulatory cost of maintaining a license as a U.S. reinsurer.

Capacity of Lloyd's is stated in terms of the maximum premiums the underwriters at Lloyd's can write.[25] Relative capacity at Lloyd's then is measured in this study based on the relative values of premiums actually written to the maximum allowed. More specifically, Lloyd's relative capacity for $t-1$ is measured using the ratio of the non-marine syndicates' average utilized capacity in year $t-1$ to the non-marine syndicates' average utilized capacity over the period $t-6$ to $t-2$. This ratio is included as an independent variable. Under the capacity constraint hypothesis, the coefficient for this variable is expected to be positive. That is, as capacity utilization increases, excess capacity declines. Declines in capacity are associated with price increases according to the capacity constraint hypothesis.

Other Independent Variables

Berger, Cummins and Tennyson (1992) suggest that an insurer's profitability is positively related to the proportion of premiums ceded to a reinsurer because it reduces leverage and enhances diversification. Similarly, reinsurers may use retrocession to increase profitability. The ratio of property (casualty) non-proportional reinsurance premiums ceded to property (casualty) reinsurance premiums assumed for each reinsurer is used as a control variable, and its expected sign is positive.[26] Finally, three company-specific dummy variables are used to control for foreign-owned insurers, group membership, and distribution system. It is possible that U.S.-owned reinsurers may have an advantage over foreign owned reinsurers in the U.S. market because they are domestic. A dummy variable equal to one if the reinsurer is U.S. owned, and zero otherwise is included in the models. Barrese and Nelson (1997) found that direct reinsurers operate with higher costs than non-direct reinsurers, and therefore might be expected to charge higher prices. A dummy variable assigned the value one is used to identify direct reinsurers; this dummy variable is equal to zero otherwise. Insurers that are members of a group are identified by a dummy variable equal to one for group members and zero otherwise. Group members may be considered more financially viable if policyholders believe that the parent company would contribute additional resources if the reinsurer developed financial problems.

4.4. Regression Model

The following pooled, cross-sectional, time series model is estimated:

$$P_{it} = \alpha + \sum_{j=1}^{n} \beta_j \, x_{ij,t-t} + \beta_p PHS_{i,t-2} + \varepsilon_{it}, \tag{9}$$

where P_{it} is price for non-proportional property reinsurance, $x_{ij,t-1}$ and $PHS_{i,t-2}$ are independent variables (with PHS representing policyholders surplus), ε_{it} is the error term, and the subscripts i and t represent reinsurer i and year t, respectively. The same general model was estimated again with casualty non-proportional reinsurance price as the dependent variable. Use of a pooled model allows for testing time effects posited by the capacity constraint hypothesis and cross sectional differences expected under the risky debt hypothesis.

Analysis of OLS residuals from both price regressions indicated that heteroscedasticity was present.[27] Therefore, weighted least squares were used. The heteroscedasticity tests indicated that the retrocession percent was significantly related to the variance from the price equations, perhaps indicating that reinsurers price business with availability of retrocessions (e.g. through treaties) in mind. Therefore, weights in both the property and casualty non-proportional price regressions were based on the retrocession percent variable.[28]

Initial regression analysis of both equations indicated the presence of two outliers in the casualty sample and two in the property sample.[29] The two reinsurers classified as outliers are National Indemnity and Underwriters Reinsurance Group. Both reinsurers were eliminated from the samples.

4. DATA

Data for the sample reinsurers were obtained primarily from the individual reinsurers' Annual Statements that are filed with the NAIC. Additional information was gathered from *Best's Insurance Reports Property/Casualty Edition* (various years). Data for 1990 to 1995 were used (as these data were available to the authors).[30] To estimate the capacity and leverage variables worldwide and by region, additional data were needed. *Statistics Relating to Lloyd's 1997* was used to obtain information about Lloyd's of London. The data on Bermuda based property catastrophe reinsurers were obtained from *Standard & Poor's Classic Database*. The data on other alien reinsurers worldwide were obtained from *reactions*, published by Reactions Publishing Group, Ltd. Each year a listing of the world's 100 largest reinsurers is published in this journal.

5. RESULTS

Summary statistics for the regression model variables are found in Table 7. Means tests were performed on the variables reported in Table 7. The results indicate that reinsurers in the casualty sample rely less on retrocessions, are less likely to be U.S.-owned, and are less prone to direct writing than reinsurers in the property sample; and these differences are significant. The coefficient for normalized policyholders surplus is significantly lower for the casualty sample. The retroactive loss shocks in both samples are negative and the casualty reinsurers' average retrospective loss shock is larger (in absolute value). Neither policyholders' surplus nor group membership is significantly different between the two samples.

Regression results are presented in Tables 8 and 9. The coefficients for all of the financial quality variables except size in Table 8 are significant in at least some regressions, with the expected signs. The coefficients for policyholders surplus, new internal capital, new external capital, and Best's rating are positive and significant with the expected signs in all models, consistent with the risky debt hypothesis.[31] The retroactive loss shock variable in the casualty equations are negative and significant in the models using the line-specific retroactive loss shock (models 4 through 6). Cummins and Danzon (1997) found a negative coefficient for their retroactive loss shock variable as well.

The coefficients for new internal capital are higher than for external capital in the casualty model, just as Cummins and Danzon (1997) found. Thus, the coefficients do not support the hypothesis that external equity is more costly than internal equity. However this statement should be tempered; new external

Table 7.   Summary Statistics.

Variable	Property		Casualty	
	Mean	Standard Deviation	Mean	Standard Deviation
Price	$1.6124	$1.0876	$1.6592	$0.4193
Financial Quality Related				
Policyholders surplus$_{t-2}$	0.8762	0.7903	0.7174	0.7826*
New internal capital$_{t-1}$	0.0425	0.1408	0.0295	0.1363
New external capital$_{t-1}$	0.0879	0.5448	0.0848	0.5757
Retroactive loss shock$_{t-1}$	−0.00232	0.0291	−0.00896	0.0579
Policyholders Surplus$_{t-1}$	$365	$682	$445	$731
Best's rating (equals 1 if A+)	0.3000	0.4600	0.3220	0.4690
Capacity Related Variables				
U.S. relative capacity$_{t-1}$	1.1508	0.0400	1.1508	0.0400
Lloyd's capacity utilization$_{t-1}$	0.9739	0.1300	0.9739	0.1300
Relative capacity, rest of world$_{t-1}$	1.3803	0.0538	1.3803	0.0538
Relative world capacity$_{t-1}$	1.3934	0.0886	1.3934	0.0886
U.S. leverage$_{t-1}$	1.1879	0.0996	1.1879	0.0996
Bermuda leverage$_{t-1}$	0.2541	0.3630	0.2541	0.3630
Leverage, rest of world$_{t-1}$	1.5544	0.1111	1.5544	0.1111
World leverage$_{t-1}$	1.2971	0.1007	1.2971	0.1007
Other Variables				
Retrocession percent$_{t-1}$	0.3799	0.2026	0.3321	0.2071**
U.S. (vs. foreign) owned	0.6429	0.4809	0.5217	0.5017**
Direct writer dummy	0.7143	0.4534	0.4348	0.4979***
Group membership dummy	0.7357	0.4425	0.7652	0.4979
Number of observations	140		115	

Note: Means tests conducted on all variables.
*** Significant at 1% level; ** Significant at 5% level; * Significant at 1% level.

Table 8. Non-proportional Casualty Reinsurance
Dependent Variable: Price of Casualty Non-proportional Reinsurance.

	Company-wide Retroactive Loss Shock						Line-Specific Retroactive Loss Shock					
	Model 1		Model 2		Model 3		Model 4		Model 5		Model 6	
Independent Variables	Coeff.	t-ratio	Coeff.	t-ratio	Coeff.	t-ratio	Coeff.	t-ratio	Coeff.	t-ratio	Coeff.	t-ratio
Intercept	1.7548	15.81***	1.5647	3.47***	1.7311	4.25***	1.5866	16.54***	2.3850	5.60***	2.8129	7.77***
Financial Quality Related												
Policyholders surplus$_{t-2}$	0.0486	4.15***	0.0339	2.13**	0.0317	1.93*	0.1141	8.04***	0.0781	5.04***	0.0950	5.94***
New Internal Capital$_{t-1}$	1.2013	5.98***	1.2899	6.81***	1.4257	6.33***	1.0369	6.39***	0.9129	5.36***	1.3191	7.45***
New External Capital$_{t-1}$	0.1358	3.98***	0.1508	4.90***	0.1585	4.96***	0.1369	4.82***	0.1281	4.75***	0.1559	6.07***
Retroactive Loss Shock$_{t-1}$	0.0794	0.52	0.2204	1.58	0.1995	1.47	-0.9909	-6.40***	-0.9315	-5.63***	-1.1460	-7.23***
Best's Rating$_{t-1}$	0.2409	2.69***	0.2533	3.14***	0.2298	2.84***	0.2124	2.80***	0.1862	2.57**	0.1249	1.84*
Size 2	-0.0184	-0.53	-0.0898	-2.09**	-0.1284	-2.79***	0.0122	0.44	-0.0776	-2.22**	-0.1624	-4.38***
Size 3	0.1391	1.60	0.0551	0.71	0.0516	0.67	0.1696	2.31**	0.1139	1.66	0.1172	1.86*
Size 4	-0.0182	-0.42	-0.0289	-0.74	-0.0263	-0.64	0.0248	0.67	0.0279	0.80	0.0332	0.98
Capacity Related Variables												
U.S. Relative Capacity$_{t-1}$					-0.0654	-0.19					-0.3290	-1.14
Lloyd's Capacity Utilization$_{t-1}$			0.4320	2.61**	0.7681	4.35***			-0.0335	-0.20	0.7508	5.22***
Relative Capacity Rest of World$_{t-1}$					-0.4884	-1.62					-1.1447	-4.36***
Relative World Capacity$_{t-1}$			-0.1935	-0.92					-0.5365	-2.73***		

Table 8. Continued.

Independent Variables	Company-wide Retroactive Loss Shock						Line-Specific Retroactive Loss Shock					
	Model 1		Model 2		Model 3		Model 4		Model 5		Model 6	
	Coeff.	t-ratio	Coeff.	t-ratio	Coeff.	t-ratio	Coeff.	t-ratio	Coeff.	t-ratio	Coeff.	t-ratio
Other Variables												
Retrocession percent$_{t-1}$	-2.0716	-4.05***	-2.1410	-4.75***	-2.1382	-4.79***	-1.0075	-2.19**	-1.0849	-2.51**	-0.8585	-2.15**
U.S.-owned	-0.0839	-0.81	-0.0782	-0.86	-0.0950	-1.05	-0.0345	-0.39	-0.0542	-0.67	-0.0807	-1.09
Direct writer	-0.0574	-0.56	-0.0266	-0.29	-0.0186	-0.21	-0.0903	-1.03	-0.0571	-0.71	-0.0440	-0.60
Group membership	-0.0495	-1.17	0.0198	0.50	0.0056	0.14	-0.0045	-0.16	0.0008	0.03	-0.0105	-0.41
Adjusted R^2	0.768		0.82		0.824		0.834		0.8601		0.8821	

Note: New Internal Capital is sum of underwriting income (net of retroactive loss shock) investment income, other income and other gains in surplus; New external capital is new capital paid in minus dividends; Retroactive Loss Shock is change in prior years' incurred losses; Relative Capacity is average surplus for the year divided by its prior year five year average value; Lloyd's capacity utilization is the ratio of premiums written to maximum premium writings allowed; Retrocession Percent is ratio of property non-proportional reinsurance premiums ceded to property reinsurance premiums assumed; U.S.-owned is equal to one if U.S. owned insurer and zero otherwise; Direct writer equals one if direct writer and zero otherwise; Group membership is equal to one if member of a group and zero otherwise; and t is year. Financial quality variables normalized by dividing by liabilities at time t − 1, except for policyholders surplus which is divided by liabilities at t − 2. Best's rating is equal to 1 if rating is A + or above and zero otherwise. Firms ranked by policyholders surplus. Size 1 is smallest sized group.
*** significant at 1% level ** significant at 5% level * significant at 1% level.

Table 9. Non-proportional Property Reinsurance
Dependent Variable: Price of Property Non-proportional Reinsurance.

Independent Variables	Company-wide Retroactive Loss Shock						Line-Specific Retroactive Loss Shock					
	Model 1		Model 2		Model 3		Model 4		Model 5		Model 6	
	Coeff.	t-ratio	Coeff.	t-ratio	Coeff.	t-ratio	Coeff.	t-ratio	Coeff.	t-ratio	Coeff.	t-ratio
Intercept	0.9013	3.13***	2.6153	1.70	5.1430	3.39***	0.9498	3.30***	4.1393	2.51**	7.1984	4.07**
Financial Quality Related												
Policyholders surplus$_{t-2}$	0.1210	2.51**	0.1050	2.09**	0.1319	2.89***	0.1333	2.70***	0.1089	2.16**	0.1269	2.72**
New Internal Capital$_{t-1}$	-0.0033	-0.02	0.0041	0.02	0.3392	1.95	0.0626	0.28	0.1455	0.63	0.5038	2.24*
New External Capital$_{t-1}$	0.0983	1.10	0.1214	1.35	0.1228	1.52	0.0877	0.98	0.1184	1.31	0.1151	1.39
Retroactive Loss Shock$_{t-1}$	1.3612	3.54***	1.3551	3.46***	1.7708	4.84***	2.3548	3.25***	2.8869	3.40***	3.5735	4.15**
Best's Rating$_{t-1}$	-0.2044	-1.23	-0.1941	-1.16	-0.0740	-0.49	-0.2335	-1.39	-0.1977	-1.18	-0.0943	-0.61
Size 2	-0.1792	-1.46	-1.6050	-1.30	-0.2578	-2.30**	-0.3772	-2.68***	-0.3945	-2.75***	-0.5338	-3.92**
Size 3	0.1989	1.29	0.1632	1.03	0.1330	0.94	0.0827	0.53	-0.0161	-0.10	-0.0864	-0.56
Size 4	-0.1499	-0.69	-0.1750	-0.80	-0.2302	-1.17	-0.2270	-1.03	-0.2985	-1.34	-0.3508	-1.71*
Capacity Related Variables												
U.S. Relative Capacity$_{t-1}$			-0.2059	-0.46	-5.4532	-5.56****			-0.8091	-1.59	-5.3437	-5.31****
Lloyd's Capacity Utilization$_{t-1}$					-0.5311	-1.54					-0.6244	-1.75***
Relative Capacity Rest of World$_{t-1}$					1.8529	2.07***					0.4917	0.49
Relative World Capacity$_{t-1}$			-1.0319	-1.35					-1.6017	-2.01***		

Table 9. Continued.

Independent Variables	Company-wide Retroactive Loss Shock						Line-Specific Retroactive Loss Shock					
	Model 1		Model 2		Model 3		Model 4		Model 5		Model 6	
	Coeff.	t-ratio	Coeff.	t-ratio	Coeff.	t-ratio	Coeff.	t-ratio	Coeff.	t-ratio	Coeff.	t-ratio
Other Variables												
Retrocession percent$_{t-1}$	0.8241	2.49**	0.8053	2.38**	0.6480	2.10**	0.9846	2.84***	0.9310	2.70***	0.7746	2.42***
U.S.-owned	0.5226	3.63***	0.5260	3.58***	0.4246	3.16***	0.5061	3.50***	0.4856	3.36***	0.3597	2.65****
Direct writer	-0.2608	-1.20	-0.2876	-1.32	-0.2127	-1.09	-0.2592	-1.19	-0.3037	-1.40	-0.2345	-1.18
Group membership	0.2815	2.82***	0.2412	2.28**	0.3532	3.70***	0.3296	3.28***	0.2615	2.48**	0.3658	3.76****
Adjusted R²	0.23		0.24		0.38		0.22		0.24		0.35	

Note: New Internal Capital is sum of underwriting income (net of retroactive loss shock) investment income, other income and other gains in surplus; New external capital is new capital paid in minus dividends; Retroactive Loss Shock is change in prior years' incurred losses;Relative Capacity is average surplus for the year divided by its prior year five year average value; Lloyd's capacity utilization is the ratio of premiums written to maximum premium writings allowed; Retrocession Percent is ratio of property non-proportional reinsurance premiums ceded to property reinsurance premiums assumed; U.S.-owned is equal to one if U.S. owned insurer and zero otherwise; Direct writer equals one if direct writer and zero otherwise; Group membership is equal to one if member of a group and zero otherwise; and t is year. Financial quality variables normalized by dividing by liabilities at time t − 1, except for policyholders surplus which is divided by liabilities at t − 2. Best's rating is equal to 1 if rating is A+ or above and zero otherwise. Firms are ranked by total policyholders surplus. Size 1 is the smallest size group.
*** significant at 1% level ** significant at 5% level * significant at 1% level.

capital is, in general, much easier to observe than yearly net income because of loss reserving errors.

Some evidence in support of the capacity constraint hypothesis can be found in the Table 8 results. The discussion will focus on models 3 and 6 since these models break down capacity by region of the world. In both models, the coefficient for the Lloyd's capacity utilization variable is significant at the 1% level. Prices are negatively related, too, to relative world capacity net of U.S. capacity, and the coefficient is significant in model 6. U.S. relative capacity is not significantly related to price, consistent with the findings of Winter (1994) for the period after 1980 for general liability insurance. Evidence concerning the capacity constraint variables tested in Cummins and Danzon (1997) is mixed. That is, in the latter research, the coefficients of the capacity constraint variables are insignificant in some regressions while in others they are not, and their signs fluctuate.

Size is controlled for in the regressions through the dummy variables Size 2, Size 3, and Size 4, which are determined by ranking sample insurers by their policyholders surplus into quartiles. For example, if a reinsurer's policyholders surplus falls in the second quartile of the sample, then the variable Size $2 = 1$, and is zero otherwise. Size 1 is the smallest size category.[32] The regression results in Table 8 indicate that reinsurers in quartile 3 charge higher prices than reinsurers in size category 1, and the coefficient is significant in models 4 and 6. Results for the other size categories are mixed. Overall, the results do not support a widespread "flight to quality " when quality is measured merely in terms of size of policyholders surplus.

In Table 8, the retrocession variable is negative and significant in all models. The reason is not clear, but may be related to concerns of the policyholders about the financial quality (credit risk) of the retrocessionaires (e.g. reserving errors). Recall that capacity in this line is significantly related to capacity at Lloyd's of London, and Lloyd's has made several reserve adjustments over the years. The control variables for direct writers, members of groups, and U.S.-owned companies do not appear to be significantly related to price in the casualty model.

The non-proportional property price regression results are reported in Table 9. Some support for the risky debt hypothesis is found. The relative normalized policyholders surplus variable (at time $t - 2$) has a coefficient of greater than zero in all models and is significant at the 5% or better level. The coefficients for the retroactive loss shock variable are significant across all models at the 1% level. Recall that the sign of this variable can be positive or negative according to the risky debt hypothesis. No significant relationships between new internal or new external capital and price are found. The coefficients for the Best's rating variable are never significant in the models in Table 9.

The coefficients for the capacity constraint related variables in Table 9 provide some support for the capacity constraint hypothesis. In model 5, price is negatively related to world capacity as hypothesized and is significant at the 5% level. When world capacity is broken down by region of the world (U.S. vs. non-U.S.) in model 6, only U.S. relative capacity is significant at the 1% level. The Lloyd's capacity utilization level is not significant at the 5% level. A separate relative capacity variable for Bermuda is omitted from the models, as it was highly correlated with the other capacity variables. Therefore, the capacity (surplus) of the Bermuda CAT reinsurers were included in the relative capacity variable for the rest of the world in the Table 9 equations.

The regressions results in Table 9 with respect to size categories are similar to the casualty model results and do not support the hypothesis that reinsurers with higher absolute policyholders surplus are associated with higher prices. The coefficient for the retrocession variable is positive and statistically significant at the 5% or better level in all models in Table 9. Thus reinsurers in the sample relying relatively more on retrocession experienced higher prices and perhaps higher profitability. For example, it may suggest that reinsurers which are aggressive in risk spreading activity through ceding property non-proportional reinsurance enjoy high profitability in assumed non-proportional reinsurance. Alternatively it may indicate that prices are higher on retroceded business to provide for an adequate profit to both the reinsurer and the retrocessionaire.

The results show that reinsurers in the property sample that are members of a group are associated with higher prices, as expected. Also, in the property non-proportional price regression, U.S. reinsurers (vs. foreign-owned) are associated with higher prices. The coefficient for the direct writer variable is never significant in the models in Table 9.

Overall, the results for the non-proportional reinsurance property and casualty price models in Tables 8 and 9 provide support for both the risky debt hypothesis and the capacity constraint hypothesis. In both price models, price is significantly and positively related to the financial quality variable normalized policyholders surplus (in time $t-2$). The line-specific retroactive loss shock variable is significant in all models. In the models with the most detailed region variables (models 3 and 6), at least one capacity constraint related variable is significant with the expected sign. This is the first study to show support in favor of both theories in the same sample.

Some important and interesting differences exist too between the results in Tables 8 and 9. Lloyd's capacity utilization and rest of the world (non-U.S.)

capacity are significantly related to prices for casualty reinsurance but for property reinsurance U.S. relative capacity is the only significant capacity variable. Also, the Best's rating is significant in the casualty equation models but not for property reinsurance, perhaps suggesting less transparency in the casualty reinsurers and therefore more reliance on outside evaluations. The results for the control variables differ also across the property and casualty models.

6. CONCLUSION

The puzzle of underwriting cycles and insurance crises have led to numerous economic hypotheses and empirical analyses, yet no single theory seems capable of explaining all of its aspects. The capacity constraint hypothesis is by now a well known theory for explaining this phenomenon, but the evidence to date (all U.S.) indicates that it cannot explain results in all lines after 1980 (and in particular general liability), at least with readily available data. This study innovates by studying non-proportional reinsurance with relative capacity variables broken down by region of the world. The results indicate that U.S. prices for non-proportional reinsurance are significantly related to capacity elsewhere in the world, as the capacity constraint hypothesis predicts.

The risky debt hypothesis is a relative newcomer to the underwriting cycle arena; this theory stresses the role of capital as a buffer for the insurer in financially trying times. The results of this study suggest that the risky debt hypothesis is very important in explaining casualty non-proportional reinsurance prices, but it does not seem to be as important for property reinsurance. Retroactive loss shocks are important for both types of coverage, supporting the risky debt hypothesis.

Factors in the reinsurance market such as relative capacity or risk, might play a role in primary market pricing, if the primary market relies on reinsurance for capacity. Thus, developments for reinsurance outside of the U.S. may exert pressure on U.S. primary insurance prices, too. Fortunately, data of the type used here are becoming more available than in the past. The role of reinsurance on pricing in the primary market should be a fruitful area for research in the future, especially given the competitive potential of the capital markets to provide a "reinsurance-like" product for large losses.

NOTES

1. These figures are for non-proportional reinsurance only, and do not include proportional reinsurance that is mainly used for intra-group business or involuntary

market business. Unlike proportional reinsurance, non-proportional reinsurance pays losses not from the ground up but only in excess of an attachment point. In 1995, 86% of proportional reinsurance premiums was assumed from affiliates. In contrast, only 10.9% of non-proportional reinsurance premiums was assumed from affiliates, with the remainder assumed from non-affiliates.

2. The accident year is the calendar year in which the accident occurred. The accident year loss ratio is defined as the ratio of accident year losses incurred to premiums earned.

3. The Herfindahl index is defined as the sum of each firm's market share squared. Higher values for the index are associated with higher concentration. The Herfindahl index is calculated using industry-wide company data from insurers' Annual Statements which are filed with the NAIC. The Herfindahl indexes of reinsurance premiums assumed from 1991 to 1995 are 0.047, 0.039, 0.053, 0.056, and 0.07, respectively.

4. The NAIC also has tightened regulatory control over reinsurance recoverables through a series of reporting rule changes since 1989.

5. Risk-Based Capital (RBC) requirements for property/liability insurers were adopted by the NAIC in 1993 to monitor an insurer's capital relative to its risk. An insurer's risk-based capital is calculated based on a formula that takes into account underwriting risk, investment risk, credit risk and off balance sheet risk. Then the insurer's risk-based capital is compared with its surplus (net worth) to determine capital adequacy.

6. For example, in 1998 acquisitions by the following reinsurers took place: EXEL, Berkshire Hathaway, Gerling Globale Swiss Re, GE Capital, and Munich Re (Swiss Re, 1998).

7. An alien reinsurer is a reinsurer organized outside of the U.S.

8. At Lloyd's, capacity refers to a premium income limit, which is calculated by applying specific ratios to the Lloyd's Deposits and qualifying means (or financial assets) of individual and corporate members.

9. Subsequent to the sample period, these organizations merged.

10. These reinsurers are CAT Ltd., Global Capital Re, International Property Cat Re, Lasalle Re, Mid Ocean Re, Partner Re, Renaissance Re, and Tempest Re. Mid Ocean Re was formed in 1992, while the other reinsurers mentioned were formed in 1993.

11. Freedom of establishment allows a foreign company (or individual) to set up a new business in another member state or open a branch office of an existing company in that member state. Freedom of services allows a company (or individual) in one member state to conduct business in other member states without first establishing a presence in that state.

12. Australasia refers to Australia, New Zealand and neighboring islands in the Pacific Ocean.

13. Adjustment costs for equity are incurred also such as agency costs induced by conflicting goals of managers, shareholders, and policyholders.

14. Tobin's q is defined as the market value of the firm's debt and equity divided by the replacement value of the firm's assets.

15. Additionally, an interest rate variable is included in the regression.

16. Gron's model was used also to test the arbitrage or rational expectations/ institutional intervention hypothesis. Under the latter, underwriting cycles are hypothesized to be caused by external events and market features not under the control of the insurer. It is reactions to these phenomena which make it appear that insurers

behave irrationally under this hypothesis (Cummins & Outreville, 1987; Lamm-Tennant & Weiss, 1997).

17. This seems reasonable, given the treatment of insurer bankruptcies by the NAIC (NAIC, 1993).

18. For example, the policyholder would need to start over "fresh" with another insurer that does not know the risk history of the policyholder.

19. Data for alien reinsurers were used to construct some relative capacity variables; that is, data on alien reinsurers were used to specify some independent variables.

20. Specifically, net premiums earned data for property and casualty non-proportional reinsurance premiums earned are obtained from Schedule P, Parts 1N and 1O, respectively. Loss payout patterns are based on industry-wide data in Schedule P, Parts 3N and 3O, as reported in *Best's Aggregates and Averages*.

21. In Cummins and Danzon (1997), the total company-wide retroactive loss shock was used since the dependent variable was company-wide price.

22. In the casualty models, surplus of the Bermuda property CAT reinsurers that are not included in S&P's top 100 reinsurer list are not included, as they provide no capacity for casualty non-proportional reinsurance.

23. Surplus is deflated in each year to produce comparable values.

24. For example, Bermuda capacity is estimated using surplus for the Bermuda CAT reinsurers only. The S&P's top 100 reinsurers list is used to identify alien reinsurers. The Japanese insurers in the list (except for Toa Re) can better be described as some of the world's largest primary insurers rather than reinsurers. It is unlikely that they actually write U.S. property or casualty non-proportional reinsurance. Further, they did not report the policyholders surplus data needed for this study. Hence they are excluded. Winterthur Group is excluded also because of missing data. After these deletions, approximately sixty alien reinsurers are used to determine relative capacity each year.

25. Data for Lloyd's of London are not included in the capacity variables just discussed because a measure of surplus is not available. (Neither are they included in S&P's top 100 reinsurers list during the sample period.) Another potential capacity measure is the ratio of premiums written divided by the maximum premiums allowed. But the latter variable does not provide any information about whether capacity utilization is larger or smaller compared to other years. That is, it doesn't provide a measure of *relative* capacity utilization as do the other measures of relative regional capacity used in this study.

26. The property (casualty) non-proportional reinsurance premiums ceded may include premiums that are not part of the property (casualty) non-proportional reinsurance premiums assumed. In other words, a reinsurer may cede part of its property (casualty) proportional reinsurance premiums assumed or direct premiums in the form of non-proportional reinsurance. In this case, the above measure could also be interpreted as a measure of a reinsurer's risk spreading activity.

27. The test for heteroscedasticity used is described in Breusch and Pagan (1979). The value of the Chi-squared variables from the heteroscedasticity tests were 32.35 and 77.47 with 1 and 3 degrees of freedom, respectively, for property and casualty. The results are significant at better than the 1% level.

28. More specifically, regressions of price of property (casualty) non-proportional reinsurance were run and the error term saved. The normalized squared residuals from this equation were regressed on each independent variable and their squared values along with premiums earned. Subsets of the independent variables and premiums

earned (and their squared values) and interactions were tested also in some error regressions. The results for both property and casualty indicated that heteroscedasticity was related to the retrocession percent variable. In the case of non-proportional property reinsurance price, ownership (U.S. vs. foreign owned) and the interaction between ownership and retrocessions were significantly related to heteroscedasticity as well. To conclude, the weight in the casualty price equation uses the retrocession percent. The weight in the property equation uses the predicted values from the regression of the normalized error term on ownership, retrocession percent and the interaction among the latter two variables. These are the recommended procedures for dealing with heteroscedasticity as outlined in Pindyck and Rubinfeld (1997). The limited time series prevented any adjustment for autocorrelation.

29. Studentized residuals were used to identify outliers. National Indemnity is a member of the Berkshire Hathaway Insurance Group, and its leverage ratio was an extraordinarily low 0.1 throughout the sample period. This reinsurer is classed as a "super cat" reinsurer because of its extraordinary capitalization. As a super cat reinsurer, it is not comparable with other reinsurers included in the sample. Underwriters Reinsurance Company is a member of the Underwriters Reinsurance Group. This reinsurer underwent a management buyout in the middle of the sample period. Unusual transactions associated with the sale of the company probably led to its outlier status. The studentized residuals exceeded 11 and 5, respectively, for National Indemnity and Underwriters Re.

30. Six years of data are required to estimate some of the variables described earlier.

31. An alternative specification of Best's rating was tested in which the Best rating variable was assigned a value of one if the Best rating was A or better, and zero otherwise. This variable was never significant in the property non-proportional reinsurance price equation, but was significant in models 3 through 6 in the casualty non-proportional reinsurance price equation.

32. Other size variables were tested, specifically the (absolute level) of the reinsurer's policyholders surplus and the log of policyholders surplus. Neither variable was found to be significant in any of the models.

REFERENCES

Barrese, J., & Nelson, J. M. (1997). Relative Efficiencies of Non-Life Reinsurance Marketing Methods. *Risk Management and Insurance Review, 1*, 51–64.

Berger, L. A., Cummins, J. D., & Tennyson, S. (1992). Reinsurance and the Liability Insurance Crisis. *Journal of Risk and Uncertainty, 5*, 253–272.

Berger, L. A. (1988). A Model of the Underwriting Cycle in the Property/Liability Insurance Industry. *Journal of Risk and Insurance, 50*, 298–306.

Breusch, T. S., & Pagan, A. R. (1979). A Simple Test for Heteroscedasticity and Random Coefficient Variation. *Econometrica, 47*, 1287–1294.

Cagle, J. A. B., & Harrington, S. (1995). Insurance Supply with Capacity Constraints and Endogenous Insolvency Risk. *Journal of Risk and Uncertainty, 11*, 219–232.

Carter, R. L., & Falush, P. (1996). *The London Insurance Market*. Rochester, Kent, Great Britain: Delco Creative Services Limited.

The "Flight to Quality"   203

Cummins, J. D., & Danzon, P. M. (1997). Price, Financial Quality, and Capital Flows in Insurance Markets. *Journal of Financial Intermediation*, *6*, 3–38.
Cummins, J. D., Harrington, S. E., & Klein, R. W. (Eds) (1991). *Cycles and Crises in Property/ Casualty Insurance: Causes and Implications for Public Policy.* Kansas City, MO: National Association of Insurance Commissioners.
Cummins, J. D., & Outreville, J. F. (1987). An International Analysis of Underwriting Cycles in Property-Liability Insurance. *Journal of Risk and Insurance*, *54*, 246–262.
Ettlinger, K. H., Hamilton, K., & Krohm, G. (1995). Solvency Regulation. In: *State Insurance Regulation* (pp. 129–164). Malvern, PA: Insurance Institute of America.
Gron, A. (1994). Capacity Constraints and Cycles in Property-Casualty Insurance Markets. *RAND Journal of Economics*, *25*, 110–127.
Gron, A. (1989). Property-Casualty Insurance Cycles, Capacity Constraints, and Empirical Results. Ph.D. Dissertation Department of Economics. Cambridge, MA: Massachusetts Institute of Technology.
Carpenter, G. (1997). *Global Reinsurance Analysis*. New York.
Kellog, P. B., & Watson, T. (1996). Performance Gap to Widen in Domestic Reinsurance. *Best's Review – P/C*, March, 36–42.
Ketchum, G. L., & Wynn, J. B. (1997). A Growing Global Powerhouse. *Best's Review-P/C*, June, 52–53.
Lamm-Tennant, J., & Weiss, M. A. (1997). International Insurance Cycles: Rational Expectations/ Institutional Intervention. *Journal of Risk and Insurance*, *64*, 415–439.
LIRMA (1997). *Reinsurance Statistics 1982–1996.* London, Great Britain, Vernon Oakley Limited.
Lloyd's (1997). *Corporate Participation at Lloyd's* (2nd ed.). London, Great Britain.
National Association of Insurance Commissioners (1993). Model Laws, Regulations, and Guidelines. Kansas City, MO.
Pindyck, R. S., & Rubinfeld, D. L. (1997). *Econometric Models and Economic Forecasts* (4th ed.). New York, NY, Irwin McGraw-Hill.
Raphael, A. (1995). *Ultimate Risk: The Inside Story of the Lloyd's Catastrophe.* New York: Four Walls Eight Windows.
Reinsurance Association of America (1997). *Alien Reinsurance in the U.S. Market, 1995 Data.* Washington, D.C.
Standard & Poor's *Global Reinsurance Highlights* (1997 edition), London.
Stewart, B. (1981). Profit Cycles in Property-Liability Insurance. In: J. D. Long (Ed.), *Issues in Insurance*. Malvern, PA: American Institute for Property-Liability Underwriters.
Swiss Re (1994). Reinsurance 1992: A Stocktaking of Ten Countries. *Sigma*, *5*. Zurich, Switzerland.
Swiss Re (1995). Nonproportional Reinsurance of Losses Due to Disasters in 1995: Prices Down Despite Insufficient Cover. *Sigma*, *6*. Zurich, Switzerland.
Swiss Re (1998). The Global Reinsurance Market in the Midst of Consolidation. *Sigma*, *9*. Zurich, Switzerland.
Winter, R. A. (1994). The Dynamics of Competitive Insurance Markets. *Journal of Financial Intermediation*, *3*, 379–415.

APPENDIX

List of Sample Reinsurers

Property Reinsurer Sample

American Agricultural Insurance Co.
American Re-Insurance Co.
AXA Reinsurance Co.
Cologne Reinsurance Co. of America
Employers Reinsurance Corp.
Everest Reinsurance Company
Excess Reinsurance Co.
Farmers Mutual Hail Insurance Co. of IA
First Excess & Reinsurance Corp.
Folksamerica Reinsurance Co.
General Reinsurance Corp.
Grinnell Mutual Reinsurance Co.
Kemper Reinsurance Co.
Munich American Reinsurance Co.
NAC Reinsurance Corp.
National Reinsurance Corp.
PMA Reinsurance Corp.
PXRE Reinsurance Company
San Francisco Reinsurance Co.
SOREMA North America Reinsurance Co.
Swiss Reinsurance America Corp.
Sydney Reinsurance Corp.
Trenwick America Reinsurance Corp.
United Fire & Casualty Co.
U.S.F Re Insurance Co.
Winterthur Reinsurance Corp. of America
Wisconsin Reinsurance Corp.
Zurich Reinsurance Centre Inc.

Casualty Reinsurer Sample

American Agricultural Insurance Co.
American Re-Insurance Company
AXA Reinsurance Co.
Chartwell Reinsurance Co.
Christiania General Ins. Corp. of NY
Employers Reinsurance Corp.
Everest Reinsurance Company
First Excess & Reinsurance Corp.
Folksamerica Reinsurance Co.
General Reinsurance Corp.
Kemper Reinsurance Co.
Mercantile & Gen Reins. Co. of America
Munich American Reinsurance Co.
NAC Reinsurance Corp.
National Reinsurance Corp.
Skandia America Reinsurance Corp.
SOREMA North America Reinsurance Co.
Swiss Reinsurance America Corp.
Sydney Reinsurance Corp.
Transatlantic Reinsurance Co.
Trenwick America Reinsurance Corp.
Winterthur Reinsurance Corp. of America
Zurich Reinsurance Centre Inc.

ABOUT THE EDITORS

J. Jay Choi

Dr. J. (Jongmoo) Jay Choi is Laura H. Carnell Professor of Finance and International Business at Temple University. Professor Choi received his BBA at Seoul National University, and his MBA and Ph.D. at New York University. He is a former Chair of the Department of Finance, and a doctoral advisor of International Business at Temple. His research focuses on international financial management, exchange exposure, corporate finance and risk management, global capital markets, and international investments. He is a recipient of the Musser Award for Excellence in Leadership for Research, a former president of the Korea-America Finance Association, and a trustee of the Multinational Finance Society. Formerly, he taught at Columbia University, was an international financial economist at Chase Manhattan Bank, and has served as a visiting faculty at numerous institutions around the globe. He is the editor of this Elsevier series, *International Finance Review*, a section editor of the *Journal of Economics and Business*, and is on editorial boards of several journals.

Michael R. Powers

Dr. Michael R. Powers is Professor of Risk Management and Insurance and Director of the Advanta Center for Financial Services Studies at Temple University. He also serves as Editor of the *Risk Management and Insurance Review*. A former Chairman of the Department of Risk, Insurance, and Healthcare Management, his research covers a wide range of regulatory and public policy issues including insurer profitability and solvency, the tax treatment of hedging instruments and other risk transfers, and no-fault automobile insurance legislation. Dr. Powers has contributed to many scholarly journals and proceedings, and has received awards for outstanding research from *The Journal of Risk and Insurance*, the Risk and Insurance Management

207

Society, and the International Insurance Society. His current research interests include applications of strategic games and stochastic control theory to the analysis of market equilibrium. Prior to joining Temple, Dr. Powers was Deputy Insurance Commissioner for the Commonwealth of Pennsylvania. He received his B.S. in Applied Mathematics from Yale University, and his Ph.D. in Statistics from Harvard University.